Communications in Computer and Information Science 1707

More information about this series at https://link.springer.com/bookseries/7899

Vanessa Agredo-Delgado · Pablo H. Ruiz ·
Omar Correa-Madrigal (Eds.)

Human-Computer Interaction

8th Iberoamerican Workshop, HCI-COLLAB 2022
Havana, Cuba, October 13–15, 2022
Revised Selected Papers

 Springer

Editors
Vanessa Agredo-Delgado ⓘ
Corporación Universitaria Comfacauca
Unicomfacauca
Popayán, Colombia

Universidad del Cauca
Popayán, Colombia

Omar Correa-Madrigal ⓘ
Universidad de las Ciencias Informáticas
La Habana, Cuba

Pablo H. Ruiz ⓘ
Corporación Universitaria Comfacauca
Unicomfacauca
Popayán, Colombia

Universidad del Cauca
Popayán, Colombia

ISSN 1865-0929   ISSN 1865-0937 (electronic)
Communications in Computer and Information Science
ISBN 978-3-031-24708-8   ISBN 978-3-031-24709-5 (eBook)
https://doi.org/10.1007/978-3-031-24709-5

This Springer imprint is published by the registered company Springer Nature Switzerland AG
The registered company address is: Gewerbestrasse 11, 6330 Cham, Switzerland

Preface

The eighth edition of the Ibero-American Workshop on Human-Computer Interaction (HCI-COLLAB 2022) was held in Havana, Cuba, and organized by the Universidad de las Ciencias Informáticas and the HCI-COLLAB network. This workshop has had increasing support and participation of researchers from different parts of the world and has been increasing its thematic lines. The eighth edition was held in person, with some virtual presentations of papers, which allowed participation in the paper discussions, attendance at the keynote lectures, workshops, and the various presentations that were made.

This book gathers a set of papers that were presented at HCI-COLLAB 2022, with topics related to human-computer interaction (HCI) in specialized areas such as emotional interfaces, usability, video games and their use in education, computational thinking, collaborative systems, IoT, software engineering, ICT in education, augmented and mixed virtual reality for education, gamification, adaptive instructional systems, accessibility, artificial intelligence in HCI, and infotainment, among others.

Human-computer interaction (HCI) is a multidisciplinary field of study that focuses on the design of information technology and the interaction between computers and people, thus covering all forms of information technology design. As such, HCI is a field where its researchers try to observe the way in which humans interact with computers in order to design technologies that allow them to interact in a more human and novel way.

The call for papers for the 8th Ibero-American Workshop on HCI (HCI-COLLAB 2022) resulted in 53 submissions, of which 15 were accepted for publication in this book. Each submission was reviewed by at least three national or international Program Committee members in a double blind process.

We thank the members of our Program Committee for their work and contribution to the success of our workshop, the authors for their submissions, the organizers, and Springer, which over the past years has allowed us to gather the best papers for publication in the Communications in Computer and Information Science (CCIS) series.

November 2022

Vanessa Agredo-Delgado
Pablo H. Ruiz
Omar Correa-Madrigal

Organization

Academic Committee President

Omar Correa-Madrigal   Universidad de las Ciencias Informáticas, Cuba

Program Committee President

César Alberto Collazos   Universidad del Cauca, Colombia

Editorial Committee

Vanessa Agredo-Delgado	Corporación Universitaria Comfacauca and Universidad del Cauca, Colombia
Pablo H. Ruiz	Corporación Universitaria Comfacauca and Universidad del Cauca, Colombia
Omar Correa-Madrigal	Universidad de las Ciencias Informáticas, Cuba

Program Committee

Alejandro Fernández	Universidad Nacional de la Plata, Argentina
Alfredo Garcia	Benemérita Universidad Autónoma de Puebla, Mexico
Alicia Mon	Universidad Nacional de La Matanza, Argentina
Ana Isabel Molina Díaz	Universidad Castilla-La Mancha, Spain
Anas Abulfaraj	King Abdulaziz University, Saudi Arabia
Antonio Silva Sprock	Universidad Central de Venezuela, Venezuela
Arturo Moquillaza	Pontificia Universidad Católica del Perú, Peru
Beatriz Eugenia Grass Ramírez	Universidad de San Buenaventura, Colombia
Carina Gonzalez-González	Universidad de La Laguna, Spain
Carlos Eric Galván Tejada	Instituto Tecnológico y de Estudios Superiores de Monterrey, Mexico
Cesar A. Collazos	Universidad del Cauca, Colombia
Claudia González Calleros	Benemérita Universidad Autónoma de Puebla, Mexico
Cristina Manresa-Yee	Universitat de les Illes Balears, Spain
Daniela Quiñones Otey	Pontificia Universidad Católica de Valparaíso, Chile
Erika Martínez	Benemérita Universidad Autónoma de Puebla, Mexico

Francisco Luis Gutiérrez Vela	Universidad de Granada, Spain
Germán Ezequiel Lescano	Universidad Nacional de Santiago del Estero, Argentina
Guillermina Sánchez Román	Benemérita Universidad Autónoma de Puebla, Mexico
Gustavo Rossi	Universidad Nacional de la Plata, Argentina
Gustavo Eduardo Constain Moreno	Universidad Nacional Abierta y a Distancia, Colombia
Habib Fardoun	King Abdulaziz University, Saudi Arabia
Héctor Cardona Reyes	Centro de Investigación en Matemáticas A.C, Mexico
Horacio Del Giorgio	Universidad Nacional de La Matanza, Argentina
Huizilopoztli Luna-García	Universidad Autonoma de Zacatecas, Mexico
Jaime Muñoz-Arteaga	Universidad Autónoma de Aguascalientes, Mexico
Javier Alejandro Jiménez Toledo	Universidad CESMAG, Colombia
Jesús Gallardo Casero	Universidad de Zaragoza, Spain
Jorge Hochstetter	Universidad de La Frontera, Chile
Jose García-Alonso	Universidad de Extremadura, Spain
José Antonio Macías Iglesias	Universidad Autónoma de Madrid, Spain
José Guadalupe Arceo Olague	Universidad Autónoma de Zacatecas, Mexico
Jose Maria Celaya Padilla	Universidad Autónoma de Zacatecas, Mexico
Juan Manuel Murillo Rodríguez	Universidad de Extremadura, Spain
Juan Ruben Delgado Contreras	Tecnologico de Monterrey, Mexico
Klinge Orlando Villalba-Condori	Universidad Nacional de San Agustín de Arequipa, Peru
Laura Cortés-Rico	Universidad Militar Nueva Granada, Colombia
Lourdes Moreno	Universidad Carlos III de Madrid, Spain
Manuel Ortega Cantero	Universidad Castilla-La Mancha, Spain
Mario Rossainz	Benemérita Universidad Autónoma de Puebla, Mexico
Miguel Redondo	Universidad Castilla-La Mancha, Spain
Nadiela Milan Cristo	Universidad de las Ciencias Informáticas, Cuba
Omar Correa	Universidad de las Ciencias Informáticas, Cuba
Oscar Revelo Sánchez	Universidad de Nariño, Colombia
Oscar David Robles Sanchez	Universidad Rey Juan Carlos, Spain
Pablo Santana Mansilla	Universidad Nacional de Santiago del Estero, Argentina
Pablo Torres-Carrion	Universidad Tecnica Particular de Loja, Ecuador
Pablo H. Ruiz	Unicomfacauca, Colombia
Patricia Paderewski	Universidad de Granada, Spain
Philippe Palanque	University of Toulouse, France
Raúl Antonio Aguilar Vera	Universidad Autónoma de Yucatán, Mexico

Roberto Solis Robles	Universidad Autonoma de Zacatecas, Mexico
Rubén Edel Navarro	Universidad Veracruzana, Mexico
Sandra Baldassarri	Universidad de Zaragoza, Spain
Sergio Zapata	Universidad Nacional de San Juan, Argentina
Soraia Prietch	Universidade Federal de Rondonópolis, Brazil
Valéria Farinazzo Martins	Universidade Presbiteriana Mackenzie, Brazil
Vanessa Agredo-Delgado	Unicomfacauca, Colombia
Victor M. Gonzalez	Instituto Tecnológico Autónomo de México, Mexico
Víctor Manuel Fernández de Para	Universidad de las Ciencias Informáticas, Cuba
Wilson Javier Sarmiento	Universidad Militar Nueva Granada, Colombia

Contents

An Approach to Model Haptic Awareness in Groupware Systems

Andres Rodriguez[1]([✉]) [iD], Luis Mariano Bibbo[1] [iD], Cesar Collazos[2] [iD], and Alejandro Fernandez[1,3] [iD]

[1] LIFIA, Facultad de Informática, UNLP, Calle 50 y 120, La Plata, Argentina
{andres.rodriguez,lmbibbo,
alejandro.fernandez}@lifia.info.unlp.edu.ar
[2] Universidad del Cauca, Popayán, Colombia
ccollazos@unicauca.edu.co
[3] Comisión de Investigaciones Científicas de la Provincia de Buenos Aires, La Plata, Argentina

Abstract. Awareness is of paramount importance to effective collaboration. Groupware systems have traditionally implemented awareness in the form of visual cues. With the advent of alternatives user interface strategies, such as haptic feedback, new ways of implementing awareness are available. The lack of documented experience on the design of effective, haptic awareness mechanisms makes it important to count on flexible prototyping and evaluation tools that can support and shorten an exploratory design process. We argue that design of awareness features should consider modalities from the start. To support the discussion, we present a modeling language and supporting tools to express haptic awareness features, and we show how the language can be used in the context of model driven development of groupware.

Keywords: Haptic interfaces · Awareness · Groupware · Model driven development

1 Introduction

In groupware systems, users are informed regarding the actions that the other users perform and how these actions affect the work environment [1, 2]. This information provided by the system is known as awareness. According to [3], awareness is the perception or knowledge of the group and of the activities performed by others that provides context for your own activities. Awareness information allows users to coordinate their work based on knowledge of what others are doing or have done [4].

Most literature focused on the design of groupware systems assumes that users interact with the system via traditional UI presentation elements displayed on a screen, and that they provide input via traditional devices such as keyboard and mouse (or other equivalent pointing mechanisms). In recent years, there has been an important development of alternative forms of interaction with computers, in particular haptic interfaces, which actively stimulate the sense of touch [5]. In the CSCW and CSCL domains in

V. Agredo-Delgado et al. (Eds.): HCI-COLLAB 2022, CCIS 1707, pp. 1–14, 2022.
https://doi.org/10.1007/978-3-031-24709-5_1

particular, the literature reports case studies, prototypes, and experiments fundamentally based on vibrotactile feedback, either through the creation of new wearable devices or the exploitation of hardware and software available in mass consumer products such as smartphones or smartwatches.

Considering haptic feedback as a means to communicate awareness information, one realizes the existence of at least three complementing interaction modalities namely, the visual modality (the GUI), the audio modality, and the Haptic modality. In practice, this means that groupware designers should be able to express not only the awareness feature they want to attach to an event but also the mode (or combination of modes) in which that feature is to be implemented.

Hapticians (haptics designers) follow an observable process to design haptic interaction. A set of four basic design activities has been identified for the process: browsing, sketching, refining, and sharing [6]. The possibility of establishing a conceptual infrastructure, like haptic design languages, has been mentioned among the main challenges for haptic experience design [7]. Such languages, for example as a formal lexicon of terms, are especially needed in multidisciplinary teams, where experts and novices in haptic design are working together.

Over the last decade, multimodal-multisensory interfaces have become the dominant computer interface worldwide. One of the main reasons is their flexibility as they allow users to select a suitable input mode, or to switch between modalities as needed for different physical contexts. Multimodal interfaces also contribute to improved cognition and performance because they allow users to self-manage and minimize their own cognitive load, based on Gestalt's theory, working memory and activity theories support the conception and design of multimodal interactions [8].

In this article, we argue that the design of awareness features should consider multimodality from the start. To support the discussion, we present a language to express haptic awareness features, and we show how the language can be used in the context of model driven development of groupware.

The rest of the article is organized as follows: Sect. 2 discusses related works on using haptic interfaces and Model Driven Development (MDD) in the development of collaborative systems; Sects. 3 and 4 introduce our language for haptic awareness features based on the haptices and haptemes concepts by Lahtinen [9], and its use in an MDD approach for designing CSCL. Section 5 presents an Evaluation of our proposal with a Demonstration approach, after [10]; finally, Sect. 6 presents Conclusions and further works.

2   Related Work

Literature shows different approaches to the use of tactile mechanisms for awareness in collaborative systems. People (presence, state, location) is the awareness information source [4] most frequently reported.

Comado [11] is a device that aims to explore co-presence between remote users during a video call. To achieve that, Comado adds a blur effect "outside of conversation", as well as a transmission of haptic feedback to the desk of the remote participant.

People emotional state has been explored by Ju et al. [12] and Frey et al. [13]. Ju et al. present an experiment where 28 vibration sample sets for 4 different emotions were recorded and then replayed to test how well they could be recognized. The results support the hypothesis that people can use vibration feedback as a medium for expressing specific subjective feelings. Frey et al. describe the effectiveness of conveying a physiological signal often overlooked for communication: breathing. They present the design and development of digital breathing patterns and their evaluation along three output modalities: visual, audio, and haptic. They found that participants in experiments intentionally modified their own breathing to match the biofeedback. In e-learning scenarios, affective tactile stimulation can be applied to reinvigorate the learner's interest when she or he is bored, frustrated, or angry [14]. Gaffary et al. [15] address the expression of spontaneous emotions. In the context of a game application that involves haptic interaction, a suitable scenario and context were designed to elicit a spontaneous stressed affective state. This study investigated spontaneous haptic behaviors occurring during stressed affective states. Chen et al. [16] used haptic technology for floor control in a conversation. Subjects can express their emotions by changing the ball's color and radius, as well as its speed. With observational experiments, the authors verified the effect that the haptic interaction brings about. Results implied that online negotiation involving haptic interaction can increase the sense of presence and is also helpful for expressing one's emotions.

The paper by Stephanie Wong et al. [17] shows the use of haptics to improve communication and situational awareness among the members of a flight crew. The paper presents a prototype called "Smart Crew"; a smartwatch application that allows flight attendants to maintain an awareness of each other and communicate through messaging with haptic feedback. It is designed with an emphasis on real-time information access and direct communication between flight attendants regardless of their location. Bailenson et al. [18] proposed the concept of Virtual Interpersonal Touch (VIT), people touching one another via force-feedback haptic devices. Participants used a Grounded Force Feedback joystick to express emotions and attempted to recognize the recordings of emotions generated in the previous experiments. Results indicated that humans were above chance when recognizing emotions via VIT but not as accurate as people expressing emotions through non-mediated handshakes.

In the case of modeling collaborative systems, there are some works that propose software engineering resources to model groupware systems [19, 20]. However, initiatives that combine models with transformation to code, as Model Driven Software Development approaches (MDD) [21, 22], that propose to improve the quality and efficiency of the software construction processes are more appropriate. In this paradigm models assume a leading role in the software development process, going from being contemplative entities to becoming productive entities from which implementations are automatically derived. In this context, the inclusion of haptic technologies in the design of awareness applied to collaborative systems must be addressed.

CSSL 2.0 (Collaborative Software System Language) [23] is an extension of UML to support Model Driven Software Development of collaborative applications. Among other design decisions, CSSL lets the designer model awareness features attached to activities, tools, and workspaces. A CSSL model indicates which events trigger the Awareness update. To provide more flexibility and readability to CSSL, different concrete syntaxes are offered, each of them supported by a specific editor. The System Structure Editor allows the designer to create and connect the main components of the system (Activities, Roles, Tools, and Spaces). The System Roles Editor allows the designer to configure the roles involved in the system and which operations are assigned to them. The Process Diagram editor is used to describe collaborative activities that make up each process and in what order they are executed are displayed. Finally, the Activity Diagram Editor allows the designer to specify the states through which a collaborative activity goes. All editors allow the designer to attach awareness behavior. All these concepts can display different types of awareness that are updated by events that occur in the system. The models created with CSSL are then interpreted by transformation tools and as a result, executable applications are obtained. The work described in the present article extends CSSL and the supporting editors to model multimodality in awareness.

3 A Language for Haptic Awareness

Haptic rendering is the modeling and presentation of tactile stimuli to the user. Three approaches are commonly used for rendering: a mathematical and physical model of a real phenomenon [24], the extraction of patterns from a large data set [25] or the design of effects perceptually meaningful for users [26]. The proposal presented in this work is based on the later approach.

The process of providing haptic awareness to a collaborative work environment, such as a hybrid classroom environment [27], involves digitized social and affective touch [28]. In this scenario, it is important for the user to be able to recognize and discriminate the stimulus received and to associate it in a meaningful way with the type of social communication that is to be transmitted. To extend CSSL with haptic awareness, we took inspiration from the notions of haptices and haptemes proposed by Lahtinen [9] for the social touch. She describes how to convey and describe the transmission of messages on the body of a third party by touch. The unique messages shared by touch on the body are called haptices. Together with the other available information (verbal for example) they relate to movements, perception of the environment, and orientation. A haptice consists of touch variables, called hapteme. A hapteme is received through a body channel, it is a grammatical variable related to touch, an element to construct and identify haptices and to separate individual haptices from each other. For example, a vibration hapteme can be recognized by its duration, frequency, amplitude, etc. Haptices include sharing a personal body space, meaningful tactile contact, context, and the use of different communication channels. Social body space includes the areas of the body involved in sending and receiving haptices. Haptices can be used to share multidimensional meanings. A single haptice consists of many layers of messages at the same time (simultaneous multidimensionality). With the training in the use of haptices, the areas of the body used for perception become larger and the perceivable movements become smaller. Haptices are divided into categories, which include confirmation system, rapid social messages, body drawing, contact with people and environment, guiding and sharing artistic experiences through movements [9].

For all of the above, our language proposes the use of a haptices for each type of awareness that the designer proposes through the tactile modality. To design each haptice you have a set of predefined haptemes that you can customize both during design and during implementation. The haptemes are inspired by the proposals of tactons or tactile icons [29]. That is, each one of them corresponds to a specific vibrotactile effect easily differentiated by its envelope and that can be adjusted in one or more parameters. The envelope of a signal is the imaginary curve that delimits it. This envelope contains useful information for the hapticians, as it conveys affective meanings (an ascending ramp is associated with greater urgency or increasing arousal, a peak with confirmation of actions, etc.) [30].

Table 1. Haptemes included in this work

Hapteme	Plateau	DownwardSlope	UpwardSlope	Hill
Envelope	Square	Downward slope	Upward Slope	Symmetric
Parameters	Duration, intensity, repetitions	Format (linear, logarithmic, sinusoidal, exponential), period, amplitude, repetitions	Format (linear, logarithmic, sinusoidal, exponential), period, amplitude, repetitions	Period, amplitude, repetitions
Icon	Plateau	↘	↗	Hill

In this initial version of the language for haptic awareness, our extension to CSSL includes four simple haptemes that can be combined into different haptices to deliver awareness of task, presence, and people (state or location). The haptemes available in this version and their parameters are presented in Table 1: Plateau (constant intensity), Hill (short stimulus with symmetric intensity), Downward/Upward Slope (slope envelope with of decreasing or increasing intensity). For a particular haptic display being designed, a haptice may be run entirely on one actuator or distributed in a manner chosen by the designer among the available actuators. The haptice must also be parameterized to run for a certain time and end or continue to run in a cyclic format until the user deactivates it.

4 Introducing Haptic Awareness in Groupware Models

Undoubtedly, developing groupware is a complex task. Traditional approaches, mostly used in software development processes, which are mainly based on coding, do not facilitate the modeling and development of this kind of system. On the one hand, there is no clear documentation of design decisions taken during the coding phase, making the evolution and maintenance of the systems difficult.

On the other hand, models and diagrams created in the early stages quickly lose their value as coding progresses. To solve these problems, we use the CSSL language that adheres to the MDD paradigm. In this way, graphical models of the system can be created and then used as a source to obtain executable versions. In this case, the models guide the development and future improvements to be made to the system.

Figure 1 depicts a System Structure model in CSSL. Gray squares represent collaborative activities; there is only one activity in the model: Class. Green rhombuses represent groupware collaboration tools. Blue circles represent Roles. Orange circles represent spaces; there is one space in the model: HybridClassroom.

To specify awareness functionality, the designer connects the events of interest to the collaborative element in which the occurrence of those events should be depicted. This is done via the awareness functionality boxes in the model. A box representing an awareness element has two areas. The top of the box provides a name for the awareness functionality. The lower part of the box lists the events of interest. The arrow connecting an awareness functionality box to a tool, space or activity indicates where such awareness should be communicated.

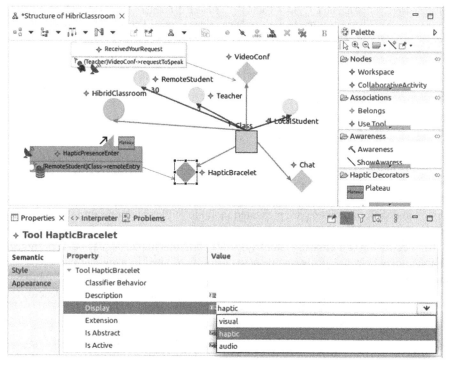

Fig. 1. Structure of a hybrid classroom with a haptic tool

Awareness functionality boxes can be decorated to express additional conditions for the provision of awareness. A satellite dish decorator, for example, indicates that the awareness is online. A datastore decorator indicates that the given awareness functionality should be made persistent. A cloud decorator indicates that the awareness is volatile.

CSSL was extended to model haptic awareness, by following the language proposed in Sect. 3. To introduce haptic awareness in a model, the designer must specify that the target device has support for displaying haptic effects. In the bottom panel of Fig. 1

shows how to configure the haptic display of the tool. The purple rhombus represents a haptic feedback tool, the haptic bracelet, and it is an abstraction of a concrete hardware device. The haptic bracelet in this model can later be implemented as an ad-hoc bracelet or as a smartwatch with haptic feedback functionality.

Besides indicating which events should trigger haptic feedback in a haptic tool, the designer can express the nature of the expected haptic stimuli. The designer can do so via decorators and specific configurations. Currently, the available decorators correspond to the four atomic haptices presented in Sect. 3. In addition, each haptic decorator offers certain configuration possibilities (e.g., the plateau decorator can be configured with duration, intensity, and repetition) which can be set via configuration forms.

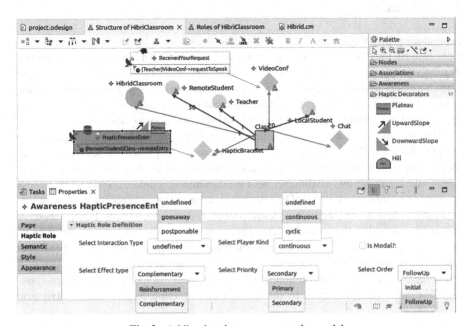

Fig. 2. Adding haptic awareness to the model

Haptic decorators can be combined with other decorators to indicate whether the awareness is synchronous or not and whether it is persistent or transient. Moreover, you can define whether the awareness is modal or not. In addition, you can define the type of interaction of the haptic awareness (undefined or goesaway or postponable) which means describing how the recipient of the awareness notification should react. When awareness is defined as "postponable" it means that the user can postpone the notification. In case the awareness is defined as "goesaway" it means that the user does not have to do anything for the notification to go away. In addition, it is possible to describe characteristics of the awareness reproduction (undefined or continuous or cyclic), if it is "cyclic" it means that the awareness is repeated every certain period, while if it is defined as "continuous" the awareness will be reproduced until the user decides to stop it. All haptic awareness configurations are shown in Fig. 2.

In multimodal interfaces, haptics can play different roles in relation to the other modalities in the device [6]. There are three possible groups of roles for haptics to be included in multimodal interactions: firstly, a haptic signal can work with other senses to provide reinforcing information about the same concept or complementary information about another (effect type); haptics can also be defined as the primary stimulus or secondary to another signal (priority); finally, a haptic signal can present an easy-to-process initial notification with low information density, then the user can continue to refer to a visual modality for more details at a better time, alternatively, the action can be followed by a confirmation (order) (see Properties panel at Fig. 2).

5 Evaluation

Ledo et al. [10] surveyed the evaluation methods employed by researchers for design toolkits in HCI and found that the most reported method is "Demonstrations". A demonstration shows what the toolkit can support and how users can work with it. The goal is to use examples and scenarios to clarify how the toolkit's capabilities facilitate the proposed applications. Demonstrations can use individual examples (new or replicated), collections (case studies, design space explorations), or "how to" scenarios.

The goal of our work is to streamline the inclusion of the haptic modality in the MDD toolbox for CSCL with awareness. Therefore, we approach the validation of our proposal by demonstrating the design space it enables. For the demonstration, we structure the design space by two dimensions. One dimension is the taxonomy of awareness presented by Collazos et al. [4]. They define three basic components for getting awareness information in collaborative systems: people, tasks, and resources. For the scope of this article, we will concentrate on the people component. The other dimension is composed by the different roles that haptics can take in multimodal interaction [6]: Effect type (complement or reinforce), priority (primary or secondary signal), order (initial or follow-up). We base the exploration of the design space on the "hybrid college classroom" scenario strongly driven by the COVID-19 pandemic, as presented by Triyason et al. [27].

5.1 The Hybrid College Classroom Scenario

Imagine a hybrid classroom. Slides are projected onto a screen from a local computer. At the same time, that computer (or another one) allows the teacher to open the videoconference call, give access to remote students and share the presentation with them. A microphone system sends the audio to the videoconferencing system to facilitate listening to the remote students. The remote attendees' camera window is viewed on a second computer monitor or, if available, can be projected onto another screen (see Fig. 3). Consequently, the teacher must be attentive to the activity of the student in the room, to the projection of their slides and, in addition, to the information coming from the video-conference system (images and audios of remote students, their arrivals and departures, as well as requests for participation). In this scenario, several use cases arise that face the teacher with specific needs for awareness, for example:

- UC1 - Remote login: When a student enters the physical classroom, the teacher can see him walking through the door. For remote students, he may enable the waiting room and may need a strong "student-in-waiting" alert to enable him access to the class (for example, for late-coming students).
- UC2 - Remote leaving: Like Remote login, but for the case that a student leaves the virtual session (what can be purposeful or just due to connectivity issues)
- UC3 - Raised hand: When a student in the classroom wishes to speak, it is not difficult for a glance at the teacher to be sufficient to do so. On the other hand, those who are remote can use the "raise hand" functionality but require the teacher to be watching the projection to detect it.
- UC4 - Chat comment: When a remote student sends a chat message, only a constant visualization of the screen allows that message to be detected at that moment.

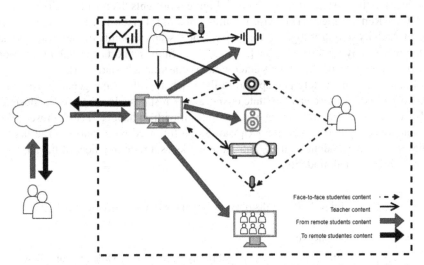

Fig. 3. Hybrid classroom layout, based on [27], including haptic interaction modality for the teacher

Following, we discuss each use case in turn, showing how the proposed approach supports the designer. These four user cases offer adequate coverage of the design space. As depicted in Table 2, they cover the people dimension of awareness. Similarly, as depicted by Table 3 they also offer adequate coverage in terms of the haptic roles they enable.

Table 2. Use cases presented to cover people awareness taxonomy in CSCL [4]

Awareness component		UC1 Remote login	UC2 Remote leaving	UC3 Raised hand	UC4 Chat comment
People	Structure				
	State				
	Location				
	Actions				
	Activity				

5.2 Discussion of the Use Cases

The next paragraphs discuss, for each use case, the modifications that the designer introduces to the System Structure model. Figure 4 presents the resulting model.

UC1 - Remote login: This case requires obtaining Person-Location (remote) and Person-Activity (requires login) information. The disruptive ability of the haptic modality to immediately capture attention [31] can be useful in support of visual information, especially for cases where students enter with the class already started. The use of vibrotactile effects, immediately perceptible to the teacher, without the general distracting effect of an audible alert, can facilitate the necessary response. In this case, the designer adds a class called HapticBracelet and decorates it with an haptice (HapticPresenceEnter) integrated by two haptemes: a UpwardSlope followed by a Plateau. The haptice initiates when the student requests entry and works as a reinforcement of the alert box on the screen (visual modality).

Table 3. Role's distribution for haptics in each use case

Use case	Haptics role		
	Effect: reinforce/complement	Priority: primary/secondary	Order: initial/follow up
Remote login	Reinforce	Primary	Initial
Remote leaving	Reinforce	Secondary	Initial
Raised hand	Complement	Primary	Follow up
Chat comment	Complement	Secondary	Follow up

UC2 - Remote leaving: This second use case is very similar to the previous one, requiring the same awareness information sources. Now, the designer decides to use the same combination of modalities, so he adds a new decorator to the HapticBracelet called HapticPresenceExit, although the haptice will start with a Plateau, ending with a DownwardSlope (usually associated with an event completion [26]). The haptice will be included as a secondary signal of the alert box that stays on the screen until the teacher closes it.

UC3 - Raised hand: It primarily involves Person-location and Person-activity information. Face-to-face students present can be introduced to the dialogue with the teacher in several ways. In some cases, they may raise their hands and wait to be allowed to speak. But in many cases, the teacher's nonverbal language or silence will implicitly enable a quick intervention. This case is not so simple remotely when transmission delay can cause a silence in the classroom to be perceived by remote students when someone has already begun to speak. Therefore, it is common to use the "raise your hand" protocol indicated by a command in the videoconferencing platform. It is often the case that more than one student requests the floor. Then the designer decides to use the haptic modality in conjunction with the visual icon on the screen of the raised hand, but now as a complement to that information. The pattern decided upon can be a chain of Hills, which will not cease unless the teacher deactivates them and whose frequency and/or duration will grow proportionally to the number of students requesting to speak. Therefore, a third decorator for the HapticBracelet, called HapticRaisedHand, is added with the haptice described. In this way, the teacher will have at his disposal the information by visual modality, but the haptic modality will be complementing it with a signal that not only indicates that someone is requesting to speak but, in a way, associated with its intensity or pattern also indicates that others have joined that request.

UC4 - Chat comment: It involves knowledge of People-location (remote), People-action (writing in the chat), and the Task-status (persists). Chat is a form of a conversation held in parallel to the lecture, one-to-one or one-to-all. The use of the haptic modality, in this case, can help facilitate the directed conversation between teacher and learner. The designer then adds a fourth decorator (HapticNewChatMessage) with the haptice used for the previous case, but now it will be issued after the presence of the message in the chat box (secondary signal) complementing the visual modality to follow up on the request.

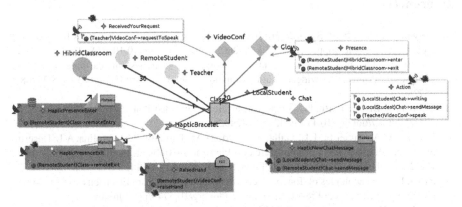

Fig. 4. Model of hybrid classroom with haptic awareness

6 Conclusions

Multimodal interfaces have become the dominant computer interface worldwide. Increasing developments in haptic interfaces, both in available hardware and in the necessary software infrastructure, have facilitated the entry of this modality into new UIs.

To contribute to the incorporation of haptics in this multimodal scenario, in this paper we have presented a tactile event language as an extension of the CSSL language that allows the inclusion of haptic awareness events in Collaborative Systems. Our language is based on the idea of haptices and haptemes [9] and takes advantage of the MDD paradigm to facilitate the conception of awareness events at design time, considering the best contributions of the available modalities as appropriate.

As an extension of CSSL, Sect. 5 presented the demonstration of four use cases for a feasible hybrid classroom scenario that can be satisfied with our extension. Using the presented haptices and haptemes language, the practitioner can manage at design time the flow of modalities according to the convenience of each use case, establishing the characteristics of the appropriate vibrotactile stimulus and the role of this modality in relation to the other intervening ones. As it has been stated among the requirements of haptic experience design [7], the subsequent work at derivation and implementation time will allow adjusting the stimulus parameters to the technology actually available, distributing among multiple actuators, etc.

Future work will include extending the catalog of haptices included in the language, conducting user experiments to fine-tune the parameterization of the included stimuli, and extending the CSSL editing tool to extend the options for integrating modalities into an application.

References

1. Gutwin, C., Greenberg, S.: A descriptive framework of workspace awareness for real-time groupware. Comput. Support. Coop. Work (2002). https://doi.org/10.1023/A:1021271517844
2. Gutwin, C., Greenberg, S., Roseman, M.: Workspace awareness in real-time distributed groupware: framework, widgets, and evaluation (1996). https://doi.org/10.1145/257089.257286
3. Dourish, P., Bly, S.: Portholes: Supporting awareness in a distributed work group. dl.acm.org (1992). https://doi.org/10.1145/142750.142982
4. Collazos, C.A., Gutiérrez, F.L., Gallardo, J., Ortega, M., Fardoun, H.M., Molina, A.I.: Descriptive theory of awareness for groupware development. J. Ambient. Intell. Humaniz. Comput. 10(12), 4789–4818 (2018). https://doi.org/10.1007/s12652-018-1165-9
5. Parisi, D.: Archaeologies of Touch: Interfacing with Haptics from Electricity to Computing. University of Minnesota Press (2018). https://doi.org/10.5749/j.ctt20mvgvz
6. MacLean, K.E., Schneider, O.S., Seifi, H.: Multisensory haptic interactions: understanding the sense and designing for it. In: The Handbook of Multimodal-Multisensor Interfaces: Foundations, User Modeling, and Common Modality Combinations, vol. 1, pp. 97–142. ACM (2017)
7. Schneider, O., MacLean, K., Swindells, C., Booth, K.: Haptic experience design: what hapticians do and where they need help. Int. J. Hum Comput Stud. 107, 5–21 (2017)

8. Oviatt, S.: Theoretical foundations of multimodal interfaces and systems. Association for Computing Machinery and Morgan and Claypool, pp. 19–50 (2017)
9. Lahtinen, R.M.: Haptices and haptemes: a case study of developmental process in social-haptic communication of acquired deafblind people. A1 Management UK (2008)
10. Ledo, D., Houben, S., Vermeulen, J., Marquardt, N., Oehlberg, L., Greenberg, S.: Evaluation strategies for HCI toolkit research. In: Proceedings of the 2018 CHI Conference on Human Factors in Computing Systems, pp. 1–17 (2018)
11. Yamamura, F., Tanichi, T., Pai, Y.S., Minamizawa, K.: Comado: communication system for ambient connection between distance locations. IEEE World Haptics Conference (WHC) **2021**, 588 (2021). https://doi.org/10.1109/WHC49131.2021.9517203
12. Ju, Y., Zheng, D., Hynds, D., Chernyshov, G., Kunze, K., Minamizawa, K.: Haptic Empathy: Conveying Emotional Meaning through Vibrotactile Feedback. In: Extended Abstracts of the 2021 CHI Conference on Human Factors in Computing Systems. Association for Computing Machinery, New York, NY, USA (2021)
13. Frey, J., Grabli, M., Slyper, R., Cauchard, J.R.: Breeze: sharing biofeedback through wearable technologies. In: Proceedings of the 2018 CHI Conference on Human Factors in Computing Systems. Association for Computing Machinery, New York, NY, USA, pp. 1–12 (2018)
14. Huang, K., et al.: Mobile music touch: mobile tactile stimulation for passive learning. In: Proceedings of the SIGCHI Conference on Human Factors in Computing Systems, pp. 791–800 (2010)
15. Gaffary, Y., Martin, J.-C., Ammi, M.: Haptic expressions of stress during an interactive game. In: International Conference on Human Haptic Sensing and Touch Enabled Computer Applications, pp. 266–274 (2014)
16. Chen, M., Katagami, D., Nitta, K.: An experimental investigation of haptic interaction in online negotiation. World Autom. Congr. **2010**, 1–6 (2010)
17. Wong, S., Singhal, S., Neustaedter, C.: Smart crew: a smart watch design for collaboration amongst flight attendants. In: Companion of the 2017 ACM Conference on Computer Supported Cooperative Work and Social Computing, New York, NY, USA, pp. 41–44 (2017). https://doi.org/10.1145/3022198.3023274
18. Bailenson, J.N., Yee, N., Brave, S., Merget, D., Koslow, D.: Virtual interpersonal touch: expressing and recognizing emotions through haptic devices. Hum. Comput. Interact. **22**(3), 325–353 (2007)
19. Gallardo, J., Molina, A.I., Bravo, C., Redondo, M.A., Collazos, C.A.: An ontological conceptualization approach for awareness in domain-independent collaborative modeling systems: application to a model-driven development method. Expert Syst. Appl. **38**(2), 1099–1118 (2011). https://doi.org/10.1016/j.eswa.2010.05.005
20. Kamoun, A., Tazi, S., Drira, K.: FADYRCOS, a semantic interoperability framework for collaborative model-based dynamic reconfiguration of networked services. Comput. Ind. **63**(8), 756–765 (2012). https://doi.org/10.1016/j.compind.2012.08.007
21. Brambilla, M., Cabot, J., Wimmer, M.: Model-Driven software engineering in practice. Synth. Lect. Softw. Eng. **1**(1), 1–182 (2012). https://doi.org/10.2200/S00441ED1V01Y201208SW E001
22. Stahl, T., Völter, M., Bettin, J., Haase, A., Helsen, S.: Model-Driven Software Development - Technology, Engineering, Management. Pitman (2006)
23. Bibbo, L.M., Pons, C., Giandini, R.: Model-Driven Development of Groupware Systems. Int. J. e-Collab. **18**(1), 1–28 (2022). https://doi.org/10.4018/IJeC.295151
24. Salisbury, K., Conti, F., Barbagli, F.: Haptics rendering: Introductory concepts. IEEE Comput. Graphics Appl. **24**(2), 24–32 (2004). https://doi.org/10.1109/MCG.2004.1274058
25. Kuchenbecker, K.J., Romano, J., McMahan, W.: Haptography: Capturing and recreating the rich feel of real surfaces. In: Robotics Research, pp. 245–260. Springer (2011). https://doi.org/10.1007/978-3-642-19457-3_15

26. Seifi, H., Zhang, K., MacLean, K.E.: VibViz: organizing, visualizing and navigating vibration libraries. IEEE World Haptics Conference (WHC) **2015**, 254–259 (2015). https://doi.org/10.1109/WHC.2015.7177722

27. Triyason, T., Tassanaviboon, A., Kanthamanon, P.: Hybrid classroom: designing for the new normal after COVID-19 pandemic. In: Proceedings of the 11th International Conference on Advances in Information Technology, pp. 1–8 (2020)

28. Eid, M.A., Al Osman, H.: Affective haptics: current research and future directions. IEEE Access **4**(1), 26–40 (2015)

29. Hoggan, E., Brewster, S.: New parameters for Tacton design. In: CHI '07 Extended Abstracts on Human Factors in Computing Systems, New York, NY, USA, pp. 2417–2422 (2007). https://doi.org/10.1145/1240866.1241017

30. Yoo, Y., Yoo, T., Kong, J., Choi, S.: Emotional responses of tactile icons: effects of amplitude, frequency, duration, and envelope. IEEE World Haptics Conference (WHC) **2015**, 235–240 (2015)

31. Zhang, S., Wang, D., Afzal, N., Zhang, Y., Wu, R.: Rhythmic haptic stimuli improve short-term attention. IEEE Trans. Haptics **9**(3), 437–442 (2016)

An Overview of Brazilian Companies on the Adoption of Industry 4.0 Practices

Maria Amelia Eliseo[(✉)] [ID], Ismar Frango Silveira [ID], Valéria Farinazzo Martins [ID],
Cibelle Albuquerque de la Higuera Amato [ID], Daniela Vieira Cunha [ID],
Leonildo Carnevalli Junior [ID], Gabriel Batista Cristiano [ID], Felipe Chuang [ID],
and Fabio Tanikawa [ID]

Universidade Presbiteriana Mackenzie, São Paulo, SP 01239-001, Brazil
{mariaamelia.eliseo,ismar.silveira,valeria.farinazzo,
cibelle.amato,daniela.cunha}@mackenzie.br,
gabriel.cristiano@mackenzista.com.br

Abstract. Industry 4.0 brought a series of changes in the production model world-wide by inserting information technologies as a central element of its proposed revolution. This ecosystem of trends and technologies encompasses concepts such as greater flexibility and optimization of production resources, through the interaction of human factors and technology. However, the advances and benefits achieved since the establishment of this model are unevenly arranged among countries, where those considered peripheral from the point of view of capitalist development have little access to technologies and transformations, being at a competitive disadvantage compared to more developed countries. This article presents an analyze the stage of development of industry 4.0 in Brazil based on the literature and records of technologies and processes implementation responsible for digital transformation in Brazilian companies. The results show that, in addition to the process of adopting practices towards the evolution of Industry 4.0 being embryonic in the Brazilian context, there is little research that addresses the digital maturity of Brazilian companies.

Keywords: Industry 4.0 · Brazil · Digital transformation

1 Introduction

Production processes are being updated as new technologies emerge, and the three industrial revolutions over the last 200 years make this evident. The First Industrial Revolution, which occurred in 1780, began with mechanical looms powered by steam engines and culminated in the centralization of the production process in factories, significantly increasing productivity. The Second Revolution started about 100 years later with the development of continuous production lines based on the division of labor and the introduction of conveyor belts, resulting in another productivity burst. The Third Industrial Revolution, in 1969, was marked by the presentation of the first programmable logic controller, which allowed the programming of digital systems leading to industrial

V. Agredo-Delgado et al. (Eds.): HCI-COLLAB 2022, CCIS 1707, pp. 15–27, 2022.
https://doi.org/10.1007/978-3-031-24709-5_2

automation systems [1]. The Fourth Industrial Revolution, or Industry 4.0, is based on the inclusion of ICTs (Information and Communication Technologies) and the Internet of Things (IoT) in production processes, enabling Human-Computer Integration (Hint).

"The era of human-computer interaction (HCI) is giving way to the era of human-computer integration (Hint) - integration in the broad sense of a partnership or symbiotic relationship in which humans and software act with autonomy, giving rise to patterns of behavior that must be considered holistically" [2]. In the context of Hint, humans and computer systems are linked and coupled in a more extensive system in a physical and social context and work together, in partnership, in a symbiotic way.

Although Industry 4.0 can directly impact all value chains, strengthening sectors concentrated in large multinational companies with the capacity to incorporate technologies and their developments and increase productivity, small and medium-sized companies remain oblivious to the possibilities of integrating ICTs due to the limitation of economic resources, the adaptability of their workers, as well as the scarcity of knowledge about technologies. This situation worsened with the COVID-19 pandemic, which generated a significant drop in industrial production on a global scale, with a direct impact on the productive sector [3]. The post-pandemic will accelerate the fourth industrial revolution conversion process in large companies with high technical capital, which are conducting this revolution, leaving out many micro, small and medium-sized enterprises producers that, far from adopting technology, continue to develop their processes manually and will not be able to convert.

On the one hand, the software industry has grown remarkably in recent decades in emerging countries, generating a total absorption of human resources trained in these areas. On the other hand, its development has focused on consolidating the productivity of the world's most vigorous and concentrated sectors, generating a technological gap within the productive sectors.

It is worth noting that adopting technologies opens up a wide range of business opportunities for the industry. In a recent survey conducted by the Brazilian Agency for Industrial Development (Agência Brasileira de Desenvolvimento Industrial [ABDI]), medium and large Brazilian companies are still not open to using ICTs to generate innovative businesses. The research shows that, although 94% of Brazilian companies have their area and/or outsource IT (Information Technology) activities, there is a mismatch between the importance given to new technologies and the level of use of them by companies. Around 73% of companies do not have projects for IoT adoption. Within this group, the majority (44%) say they do not see the need to use this technology for their business. However, almost all companies that have adopted an IoT project say they are satisfied with the results: 40% above expectations and 50% within expectations. The biggest obstacle to implementing IT and connectivity projects is the high cost (already faced by 78% of companies). In second place comes the lack of skilled labor (69%). About 57% of companies say they have ill-prepared employees to deal with the connectivity needs in the industry [4].

In 2018, the Ministry of Industry, Foreign Trade and Services (Ministério da Indústria, Comércio Exterior e Serviços [MDIC]), in partnership with the ABDI, launched a set of measures to help the productive sector, especially small and medium-sized industries, towards to the future of industrial production. This set of measures involves awareness, assessment and business opportunities, factories of the future (innovations and development of new technologies), financing for the modernization of production plants, production of machinery or systems, the labor market (demands and offers by professionals), international trade and review and adequacy of standards for Brazilian companies to migrate to Industry 4.0 [5].

Small and medium-sized companies in Ibero-American economies, including Brazilian ones, constitute a source of employment for various social sectors and promote the productive development of other industries that make up the value chains. Still, most companies do not have technological updating strategies to improve competitiveness. At the same time, they do not become a demanding sector for the development of ICTs, which implies that with the technological transformation, the mass of workers excluded from this transformation will grow, as can be seen in studies by the Organization for Economic Cooperation and Development (Organização para Cooperação e Desenvolvimento Econômico) [6].

In this context, the convergence of integrated digital, physical and biological technologies determines the technological, the generation and processing of massive data, the installation of physical objects linked through networks for the Internet of Things, the development of learning algorithms, augmented and/or virtual reality, as well as the efficient use of energy resources will mark the acceleration of the fourth industrial revolution. In this scenario, the incorporation of innovative technologies is a process that requires a deep knowledge of the installed capacity that allows detecting the real needs of technological evolution for small and medium-sized companies.

This study aimed to investigate the situation of Brazilian companies concerning adopting industry 4.0 practices based on the literature. In the Brazilian reality, digital heterogeneity raises an alert for strategic planning and public and private policy actions. The research sought to understand the scenario and digital maturity of Brazilian companies to leverage a reflection on current and future levels of companies' digitalization.

2 Theoretical Reference

2.1 Industry 4.0 and Digital Transformation

The reference [7] defines Industry 4.0, or the Fourth Industrial Revolution, as an ecosystem of trends and technologies encompassing concepts such as greater flexibility and optimization of production processes through human and technology factors with a focus on low-cost production. This production model is born from a hypercompetitive scenario to equate manufacturing, mainly western, to the Asian competition level.

For an organization to be characterized as industry 4.0, it goes through the digital transformation process, which is the application of industry 4.0 technologies in the company's day-to-day operations. Consequently, the adoption of these new technologies follows a need for organizational transformation, which presents itself as a challenge to companies, introducing new approaches and techniques in the process of creating and obtaining value, organization and business model, digitizing business strategies and putting them at the center of how they achieve, serve and retain customers.

When considering the importance of human factors in Industry 4.0, which defines that no 100% automated system is completely reliable but that a better result is obtained through the combination of machines and human capacity, we conclude that digital transformation becomes a characteristic that is not entirely under the company's responsibility, as it requires "an adaptation to the demands of customers, partners, employees and competitors, who use and impose the use of new digital technologies" [8]. Thus, digital transformation is no longer a goal to be achieved by companies and organizations that intend to be part of Industry 4.0, to become the journey through which they will reach digital maturity.

The concept of digital maturity in Brazil is recent and was born as a response to the challenges imposed by the constant evolution of technologies, tools and trends in the digital environment in business models. Companies in Brazil face difficulties in reaching digital maturity, as it is not static, thus generating the adaptation of new technologies. As there is no standard way of classifying digital transformation in companies, some scholars have developed their methods based on the level of digital maturity of the companies themselves. There are several methods, but only one of them of Brazilian origin will be presented.

McKinsey & Company developed their tool to measure digital transformation in the researched company, considering four dimensions: Strategy, Capacity, Organization and Culture [9]. This tool measures digital transformation, resulting in a score that can have more advanced and less advanced characteristics:

- Digital leaders (51 points or more): high-level of digital transformation.
- Ascending (between 36 and 50 points, considering the extremities): medium-high-level of digital transformation.
- Emerging (between 35 and 26, regarding the extremities): medium-low level of digital transformation.
- Beginners (under 25 points): low level of digital transformation.

The above score considered all four dimensions, thus being the general performance of the companies. Yet, it is also possible to present analyses in each dimension separately, showing better disparities of the companies among each in detail [9].

2.2 Industry 4.0 Characteristics and Their Definitions

The concept of Industry 4.0 originated in Germany in 2011, which has one of the most competitive manufacturing industries in the world [10]. This term was first used at the Hannover Fair in 2011 to explore the potential of new technologies and concepts such as:

- Internet availability and the use of connected devices - IoT.
- Integration of technical processes and business processes in companies.
- Digital mapping and virtualization of the real world.
- Intelligent factories where production and products would have the smart concept.

According to the reference [11], the technological trends that are fundamental and outstanding in Industry 4.0 is its multidisciplinarity, since some areas that promote this revolution are the implementation of cyber-physical systems (CPS), cloud computing

(Cloud), Internet of things, Big Data, automatically guided vehicles (AGV), augmented and virtual reality, virtualization, digital twin, transparency, higher security, decentralized decisions, data processing, new business models, cost reduction, "green" production and the central role of the human factor.

The pillars of Industry 4.0, according to the reference [12], are summarized in Fig. 1 and detailed below:

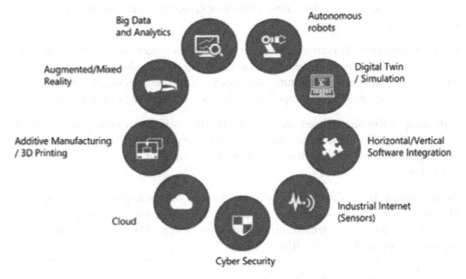

Fig. 1. Pillars of Industry 4.0, according to the reference [12].

Cyber-Physical Systems (CPS): They are interconnected systems where the cybernetic or computational part is tightly integrated with physical components, providing a union like embedded systems [13].

Internet of Things (IoT): IoT consists of a network of physical objects connected to the Internet, such as devices embedded in vehicles, sensors, computers and other objects/systems that exchange information/data with other objects/systems. It is a network of connected people and things that collect and share data about how they are used and their environment. Organizations across industries increasingly use IoT to operate more competently, better understand customers, deliver improved customer service, improve decision-making, and increase business value [14]. These devices are called IIoT or the Industrial Internet of Things in industries.

Cloud Computing: Cloud computing is a general vocabulary for anything that comprises streaming services hosted over the Internet. These services mean that the company no longer needs an IT infrastructure in its unit [14].

Big Data and Analytics (BDA): These are technologies such as database tools, mining and data analysis techniques that a company can use to study large-scale complex data in various applications to improve the company's performance in several dimensions [15].

Augmented Reality (AR): It is defined as a direct or indirect vision in real-time where the physical environment of the real world is portrayed but with virtual improvement (addition) of information. AR systems aim to improve the user's real-world interaction perceptively [13].

Additive Manufacturing (AM): AM was known before Industry 4.0 as 3D printing. This technology allows the construction of physical objects based on files, mainly from 3D CAD, to describe the consecutive addition of liquid materials, sheets or powders to form a real entity [13].

Cyber Security: With increased connectivity between objects and systems, factories have become much more vulnerable to intrusion threats by individuals, organizations and even governments. Cyber security has become much more relevant, requiring secure and reliable structures not to compromise systems and reduce their vulnerabilities [13].

Autonomous Robots: These systems are mainly used where repetitive, precision work is required and also in places that are restricted or dangerous to humans. Currently, the challenge is for these systems to work collaboratively with humans safely and learn from them [13].

System Integration: Characteristics of the industry 4.0 paradigm are the integration of 3 dimensions, a) horizontal integration across the entire value creation network, b) vertical integration and Manufacturing Execution Systems (MES), and c) end-to-end engineering across the product lifecycle [13].

2.3   Industry 4.0 in Brazil

A study by the National Confederation of Industry (Confederação Nacional da Indústria [CNI]) identified that the industrial sector corresponded to approximately 22,2% of the Gross Domestic Product (GDP) in 2021 [16]. It is an index that, compared to the history of Brazil since 1940, is the lowest. This sector is of great importance to the Brazilian economy as it generates jobs and wealth, but, on the other hand, there is investment and innovation.

To increase innovation and generate new technologies in the country, one way was to create the Brazilian Chamber of Industry 4.0 (Câmara Brasileira da Indústria 4.0), in which the Brazilian government aimed to increase the productivity and competitiveness of national companies, inserting the country into global value chains [17].

This initiative contains four working groups:

- Technological development and innovation.
- Human capital.
- Production Chains and Supplier Development.
- Regulation, Technical Standardization and Infrastructure.

According to expert consensus, the domestic industry is still largely transitioning from Industry 2.0 (assembly lines and electric power) to Industry 3.0 (expanded automation through electronics, robotics and programming) [18].

The country has the conditions for digital transformation but needs to risk more to make a technological leap like this. The Challenges related to implementation include: achieving innovative strategic policies; government incentives; bringing together industry managers with vision and courage; and having technological development and training of qualified professionals by academic and research institutions [19].

For the CNI, if Brazil inserts Industry 4.0 into its technology park, the possible consequences will be [20]:

- Cooperation among economic agents.
- Support the competitiveness among production systems (including environment, companies, suppliers and customers).
- Business chain development.
- Productivity gains with the adoption of new technologies.
- Implementation of new business models.
- Birth of new activities and professions.

In some countries, Industry 4.0 is already becoming a reality, even with the support of the governments of the leading economic powers, which have placed it at the center of their industrial policy strategies. This creates a double challenge for Brazil because, in addition to seeking the incorporation and development of these technologies, it is necessary to do so with relative agility to prevent the competitiveness gap between Brazil and some of its main competitors from increasing [20].

There are challenges for the public and private sectors, but there is a huge opportunity. Through digital technologies, the Brazilian industry has the chance to take a leap in productivity that will allow us to reduce the distance to developed nations. But a sense of urgency is needed, as major industrialized countries have placed these transformations at the heart of their industrial policy strategies [20]:

- Industry must streamline its production processes.
- The industry must re-qualify workers and managers.
- The insertion in industry 4.0 must start with available technologies and low cost.
- Industry must invest in research, development and innovation.

3 Research Methodology

To investigate the situation of Brazilian companies concerning the adoption of industry 4.0 practices and to understand this scenario, scientific databases were consulted in English and Portuguese. The research sought to broaden the understanding of the digital maturity of these companies. As inclusion criteria for the study, scientific publications in national and foreign journals based on pre-established descriptors and publication dates were considered.

To answer the research question, we established search criteria for scientific production. Keywords used both in Portuguese and translated into English were selected. The use of the English language aimed to expand access and considered that many Brazilian researchers have their productions published in international journals that use the

English language. The following keywords were used: "digital transformation", "industry 4.0", "digital maturity", "Brazil", and "Brazilian company". The period established was from 2017 to 2022. To access scientific publications, the search considered scientific text search engines, namely: Google Scholar and the CAPES Periodicals Portal (Coordination for the Improvement of Higher Education Personnel [Coordenação de Aperfeiçoamento de Pessoal de Nível Superior]). The choice of the research had as a criterion to be referenced for producing knowledge in digital transformation. The flowchart of the research procedure is shown in Fig. 2.

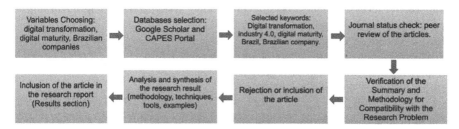

Fig. 2. The systematic analysis process of the literature

The criteria established for searching and selecting scientific publications significantly reduced the number of scientific articles included in this investigation. Although the initial search provided many publications, the requirements included only those studies that analyzed, in some way, the Brazilian panorama towards Industry 4.0 in the national context and with results description. Another relevant exclusion criterion was selecting full articles published in open access journals.

3.1   Research Technique

The methodological path of the research followed pre-established criteria described in detail. We established a research question, defined the search criteria, and selected and explained each of the studies analyzed. The analysis was performed according to the abstracts and description of the methodology used in the research. The established criteria' definition and detailing enable the study's reproducibility. The studies part of this research described the objectives, methodology and results obtained.

3.2   Search Limitations

This study suffers from many limitations that must be pointed out. Firstly, the research criteria adopted were quite restrictive, limiting the studies to be included in this analysis to those that dealt exclusively with Brazilian companies in the digital transformation process. Secondly, a significant amount of work may not have been covered by the academic databases (Google Academic and Portal CAPES, considered for this study) or excluded by some other criterion. It is essential to mention that relevant papers published in Brazil on Digital Transformation are often limited to master's or doctoral theses, books, book chapters or conferences without peer review, which were excluded from the results.

4   Results

The literature review involved the study of three articles that reflect the digital transformation among Brazilian companies. The search for information on research conducted in the last five years was performed through multi-source analysis of materials in digital format due to the dispersion of available articles. Based on the research results, it was realized that in Brazil, few papers still address the digital transformation of Brazilian companies. In this same sense, it is essential to emphasize that Brazil's literature on digital transformation issues is still embryonic.

In a first search in the selected databases, 4,059 articles were returned, 2,100 from Google Scholar and 1,959 from the Capes Portal. From this total, considering the title, year of publication and peer review, 12 articles were selected, 5 from Google Scholar and 7 from the Capes Portal. After reading the abstract, most of the articles were excluded because they addressed the management for the digital transformation, others addressed research on the maturity level measurement, and others did not bring the primary source, constituting bibliographic reviews of the literature, outside the scope of this investigation, which resulted in the three articles analyzed (1 from Google Scholar and 2 from Capes Portal).

The research highlights the digital transformation of Brazilian companies and the need to reflect on policies to implement this process. Brazil is still behind in the digital industry, human capital and research compared to other countries, especially in Europe. Below, Table 1 summarizes the systematic analysis results.

The study by [21] refers to a comparison between the main implications of Industry 4.0 technologies for production management in the universe of metal-mechanical and automotive companies in the Metropolitan Region of Curitiba (Brazil) and the Upper Bavaria Region (Germany). For the present investigation, only data referring to Brazilian companies were considered. The study included 63 companies in this mentioned sector above in the Metropolitan Region of Curitiba (Brazil), representing 80% of the regional companies, and 70% were micro and small companies. The results showed that technology adoption increases with the size of the company. Even with the constant adoption of Industry 4.0 technologies, not all technologies seem accessible in Brazil, especially for smaller companies.

The reference [22] analyzed the elements or dimensions that lead to higher levels of digital maturity. The sample involved 260 valid questionnaires answered by strategic-level managers from Brazilian companies in the retail sector, which involved 2.3% of small companies, 38.9% of medium-sized companies and 58.8% of large ones. The results indicated strong evidence that digital maturity manifests itself positively into a clear, dynamic digital strategy aligned with the business model. The operation dimension, related to collaboration and integration among companies, and the market capacity dimension were also impacted. Moreover, corporate culture must be treated as a fundamental dimension for conducting the digital transformation process, besides implementing digital assets, which characterize the use of technology involving managerial aspects such as leadership, culture, change management and governance.

The reference [23] presents the cultural, methodological and technological developments that one of the largest Brazilian private banks achieved in its digital transformation process. It shows a case study involving Banco Itaú Unibanco, highlighting the change

Table 1. Summary of the literature systematic analysis results.

Authors (year of publication)	Company branch	Research tools	Technologies used in the surveyed companies	Results
Brunheroto, Tomanek and Deschamps (2021)	Metal-mechanical and automotive companies in the Metropolitan Region of Curitiba (Brazil)	63 companies answered a questionnaire on the level of implementation of each technology and the improvements 76 responses Qualitative Analysis	Internet of Things Cloud Computing Cyber Security Big Data Analytics Virtually guided self-service 3D printing	The Internet of Things presented significant improvement levels for all performance objectives The average level of technology adoption increases according to the size of the companies. The results for large companies are significantly higher than other small ones
Salume, Barbosa, Pinto and Sousa (2021)	Brazilian companies in the retail sector, located in different regions of Brazil	The sample consisted of strategic-level managers from Brazilian companies in the retail sector who answered questions related to the digital maturity scale 260 valid questionnaires answered Regressive analysis technique	None	Communication and high-level engagement contribute to success in the digital transformation process, in addition to the company's internal analysis and broader market analysis in which it operates to maintain a better positioning
De Almeida Carlos (2020)	Banking sector	Banco Itaú Case Study Data were collected from company documents and results reports, updated to the 3rd. a quarter of 2019 Interview with a senior executive from the bank's technology area Qualitative Analysis	None	Communication and high-level engagement contribute to success in the digital transformation process, in addition to the company's internal analysis and broader market analysis in which it operates to maintain a better positioning

to agile methods in the performance of digital banks and fintech. As a result, we emphasize communication so that there is strategic alignment among all levels and agility dissemination in the company as a whole; the involvement of high-level leadership for the successful implementation and execution of Digital Transformation, as well as the company's internal analysis and broader market analysis in which it operates, to maintain a better positioning.

5 Discussion

Based on the content of the studies and research referenced in this article, some knowledge raises relevant discussion points. Considering that medium and small companies are responsible for a large part of the production in Brazil and that, in an inversely proportional way, they use little or no technology, software, or Internet of things structure, this entire productive sector has its potential committed for both productions and labors generation. In this way, public-private partnership initiatives aimed at promoting industry 4.0 in the country play a fundamental role in Brazil's search for alternative production models through investments in structure and professional training. It is also valid the participation of professionals specialized in HCI studies in the research and performance of such initiatives to facilitate the interaction of professionals from small and middle-sized companies as they integrate information technology into their daily business.

6 Conclusion

The literature review shows that the process of adopting practices toward an Industry 4.0 evolution is still too embryonic in the Brazilian context. Despite infrastructure barriers (for example, the slow and late adoption of 5G Internet in the country), issues related to the country's recent deindustrialization, economic crisis and inadequate skilled labor training are still limiting elements in the Brazilian context.

When considering the challenges brought by Industry 4.0 as opportunities for R&D, there is still a mismatch between academia and the demands of the market and society, which points to a need to intensify partnerships among the productive sector, universities and research centers in Brazil, since the demands in this sector tend to overgrow, becoming a determinant for the international competitiveness of the Brazilian industry.

Acknowledgment. This work was supported by MackPesquisa (Mackenzie Research and Innovation Fund [Fundo Mackenzie de Pesquisa e Inovação]), Project number 221006.

References

1. Drath, R., Horch, A.: Industrie 4.0: hit or hype? [Industry Forum]. IEEE Ind. Electron. Mag. **8**(2), 56–58 (2014). https://doi.org/10.1109/MIE.2014.2312079
2. Farooq, U., Grudin, J.: Human-computer integration. Interactions **23**(6), 26–32 (2016). https://doi.org/10.1145/3001896
3. Mon, A., Del Giorgio, H.R.: Analysis of industry 4.0 products in small and medium enterprises. Procedia Comput. Sci. **200**, 914–923 (2022). https://doi.org/10.1016/j.procs.2022.01.289
4. ABDI: Agência brasileira de desenvolvimento industrial, conectividade e indústria. Aplicação de tecnologias e inserção digital, 22/09/2021. Available in: https://api.abdi.com.br//file-manager/upload/files/Instituto_FSB_Pesquisa_-_ABDI_-_Conectividade_VF__2___1_.pdf (2021)

5. Brasil, Ministério da Economia, MDIC e ABDI lançam Agenda Brasileira para a Indústria 4.0 no Fórum Econômico Mundial. Available in: https://www.gov.br/produtividade-e-com ercio-exterior/pt-br/assuntos/noticias/mdic/mdic-e-abdi-lancam-agenda-brasileira-para-a-industria-4-0-no-forum-economico-mundial (2018)
6. Nedelkoska, L., Quintini, G.: Automation, skills use and training. OECD Social, Employment and Migration Working Papers, No. 202. OECD Publishing, Paris (2018). https://doi.org/10.1787/1815199X
7. Mercier-Laurent, E., Monsone, C.R.: Ecosystems of industry 4.0: combining technology and human power, In: Proceedings of the 11th International Conference on Management of Digital EcoSystems (MEDES '19), pp. 115–119. Association for Computing Machinery, New York, NY, USA (2019). https://doi.org/10.1145/3297662.3365793
8. Tadeu, H.F.B., Duarte, A.L.C.M., Chede, C.T.: Transformação digital: perspectiva brasileira e busca da maturidade digital. Revista DOM. Fundação Dom Cabral. Nova Lima, DOM, 11(35), 32–37. Available in: https://www.fdc.org.br/conhecimento/publicacoes/artigos-revista-dom-33389 (2018)
9. Martins, H., Dias, Y.B., Castilho, P., Leite, D.: Transformações digitais no Brasil: insights sobre o nível de maturidade digital das empresas no país. McKinsey & Company. Available in: https://www.mckinsey.com/br/our-insights/transformacoes-digitais-no-brasil (2019)
10. Rojko, A.: Industry 4.0 concept: background and overview. Int. J. Interact. Mob. Technol. (iJIM) 11(5), 77 (2017). https://doi.org/10.3991/ijim.v11i5.7072
11. Manavalan, E., Jayakrishna, K.: A review of Internet of Things (IoT) embedded sustainable supply chain for industry 4.0 requirements, Computers and Industrial Engineering, 127, 925–953 (2019). https://doi.org/10.1016/j.cie.2018.11.030
12. Foster, D., et al., Cloud computing: developing contemporary computer science curriculum for a cloud-first future. In: Proceedings Companion of the 23rd Annual ACM Conference on Innovation and Technology in Computer Science Education (ITiCSE 2018 Companion), pp. 130–147. Association for Computing Machinery, New York, NY, USA (2018). https://doi.org/10.1145/3293881.3295781
13. Vaidya, S., Ambad, P., Bhosle, S.: Industry 4.0 – a glimpse. Procedia Manuf. 20, 233–238 (2018). https://doi.org/10.1016/j.promfg.2018.02.034
14. Furtado, J.: Indústria 4.0: a quarta revolução industrial e os desafios para a indústria e para o desenvolvimento brasileiro. IEDI, , São Paulo. Available in: http://web.bndes.gov.br/bib/jspui/handle/1408/17621 (2017)
15. Kwon, O., Lee, N., Shin, B.: Data quality management, data usage experience and acquisition intention of big data analytics. Int. J. Inf. Manage. 34(3), 387–394 (2014). https://doi.org/10.1016/j.ijinfomgt.2014.02.002
16. CNI, Confederação Nacional da Indústria: A importância da Indústria para o Brasil. CNI, Brasília. Available in: https://industriabrasileira.portaldaindustria.com.br/grafico/total/producao/#/industria-total (2022)
17. Brasil, Ministério da Ciência, Tecnologia e Inovações, Câmara Brasileira da Indústria 4.0. Brasília: Ministério da Ciência, Tecnologia e Inovações. Available in: https://www.gov.br/mcti/pt-br/acompanhe-o-mcti/transformacaodigital/camara-industria (2020)
18. Firjan, Federação das Indústrias do Estado do Rio de Janeiro, Indústria 4.0, Rio de Janeiro: FIRJAN. Available in: https://www.firjan.com.br/publicacoes/publicacoes-de-inovacao/ind ustria-4-0-1.htm (2016)
19. Firjan, Federação das Indústrias do Estado do Rio de Janeiro, Indústria 4.0 no Brasil: oportunidades, perspectivas e desafios. FIRJAN, Rio de Janeiro. Disponível em: https://www.firjan.com.br/publicacoes/publicacoes-de-inovacao/industria-4-0-no-brasil-oportunid ades-perspectivas-e-desafios.htm#pubAlign (2019)

20. CNI, Confederação Nacional da Indústria, Desafios para Indústria 4.0 no Brasil. CNI, Brasília. Available in: https://www.portaldaindustria.com.br/publicacoes/2016/8/desafios-para-indust ria-40-no-brasil/ (2016)

21. Brunheroto, P.H., Tomanek, D.P., Deschamps, F.: Implications of industry 4.0 to companies' performance: a comparison between Brazil and Germany. Braz. J. Oper. Prod. Manag. **18**(3), 1–10 (2021). https://doi.org/10.14488/BJOPM.2021.009

22. Salume, P.K., Barbosa, M.W., Pinto, M.R., Sousa, P.R.: Dimensões´chave da maturidade digital: um estudo com empresas do setor de varejo no Brasil. RAM, Revista de Administração Mackenzie **22**(6) (2021). https://doi.org/10.1590/1678-6971/eRAMD210071

23. de Almeida Carlos, E.: Desafios culturais, metodológicos e tecnológicos da transformação digital: um estudo de caso no mercado bancário brasileiro. Revista Inovação, Projetos e Tecnologias **8**(2), 181–197 (2020). https://doi.org/10.5585/iptec.v8i2.18415

Analysis of Companies in Industry 4.0 to Characterize Their Users: The Cases of Argentina and Mexico

Alicia Mon[1]([⊠]) [iD], Horacio René Del Giorgio[1] [iD], César Collazos[2] [iD],
and Juan Manuel González Calleros[3] [iD]

[1] Universidad Nacional de La Matanza, Buenos Aires, Argentina
{amon,hdelgiorgio}@unlam.edu.ar
[2] Universidad del Cauca, Popayán, Colombia
ccollazo@unicauca.edu.co
[3] Benemérita Universidad Autónoma de Puebla, Puebla, México

Abstract. This article shows the results of a study carried out in Argentina and Mexico, which allows evaluating the level of technological development of the industry, identifying the products of Industry 4.0 that have been implemented by functional area and, from there, selecting the tasks that will characterize the specific users of each area according to the function they develop and the technologies that they must perform.

A survey in a set of companies in each country was conducted. The study is exploratory, on a non-probabilistic sample, applying a technological evaluation index introduced in this article, and the results allow to analyze the products of Industry 4.0 in the functional areas of the companies.

Finally, an initial identification of tasks by function is proposed that leads to a characterization of users in the different functional areas of a company.

Keywords: Industry 4.0 · ICT index · Industry 4.0 users

1 Introduction

The irruption of digital transformation in production systems, as well as the accelerated pace of the fourth industrial revolution, currently in progress, requires the horizontal integration of products and processes supported by collaborative networks in which workers cover multiple areas of a manufacturing industry. In this way, multiple production processes are carried out simultaneously with routes, merchandise flows, logistics, delivery, and distribution, drastically reducing production times, as well as operating costs, while the complexity of products and processes increases driven by the set of technologies that are implemented [1].

The transformation towards Industry 4.0 has a direct impact on workers in different sectors, producing the urgent need to adapt technological developments to the users of these new technologies. Users are forced to adapt their ways of working to the technological imprint and the use of a set of diverse devices and with heterogeneous sources of information. The processes of industrial transformation, collaborative work, and the interdisciplinary training of workers in an organization constitutes the necessary condition of adaptation to reach achievable production plans [2].

Although digital transformation is oriented to the use of specific technologies, it is inherent the combination of human capacity with the ease that allows the use of machines and in general of technological elements, requiring a plurality of skills of professionals who provide knowledge in the use of new technologies, such as the management of massive data, the control of specialized autonomous machines, the connectivity between objects, the management of virtual or augmented reality in the resolution of tasks as well as the sagacity to generate immediate solutions in all aspects.

In a dichotomous way, Industry 4.0 requires workers to become users of new technologies, performing multiple tasks to adapt to the needs of the industry, while requiring from them technological knowledge of a wide spectrum of technological platforms and software applications imposing production rhythms unknown until now.

2 Industry 4.0 in Latin America

The digitalization process deploys generating an increase in the technological heterogeneity of industries, deepening the structural gap previously existing in the fourth industrial revolution, accelerated by the Covid 19 pandemic. This transformation is projected as a negative effect on the different regions worldwide where many companies could disappear, depending on their size, the industry to which they are dedicated, as well as the geolocation and the socioeconomic context where they are located [3].

The gap in the digitalization of companies in Latin American countries is widely significant [4] and is at risk of increasing in the coming years with the accelerated evolution of Industry 4.0. The Inter-American Development Bank (IADB), in a recent study on the region, recommends public and private initiatives to support small companies in the use of technological solutions for their operations.

To analyze the level of digitalization that companies will face in in the next 5 to 10 years, the IADB has created a Conditional Digitalization Index (IDC) [5] based on three factors: the digital tools currently adopted by companies, the digital scenario in which each company hopes to be in the future, and the level of preparation to achieve the objectives. This IDC also assesses the use of technologies in company relationships with suppliers, in production management and in customer relationships. In this way, it allows evaluating the "perception" of companies about digitalization in 2030, what the impact of digitalization will be in the future, measured by current actions on a set of indicators that are not limited to the adoption of technologies. However, it does not detail which digital tools are available or which are adopted by companies, that is, it analyzes the current transformation process from the "perception" of the companies themselves, without determining the products that make up Industry 4.0. Its application is carried out with a survey through which companies indicate which of the descriptions of 4 possible digital generations best fit the practices to perform most of the routines of each function.

With these instruments, the IADB carried out a comparative study between Argentina and Brazil, taking 256 Argentinian companies and 474 Brazilian ones in the period 2019–2020, the results of which expose a worrying panorama about the perception of the companies themselves towards digital transformation, given that the vast majority manifest a high ignorance about the available technologies, the adoption processes, the capabilities in human resources as well as the technological potential for their business [5].

From this perspective, given the speed of the transformation process and the ignorance of companies about the decisions to be made, it is necessary to know what the specific technological products are being part of industry 4.0, what are the functional areas in which these products are adopted to identify the different capacities of the human resources that operate them who will be the end users of the new technologies.

The impact of technological transformation requires particular attention to the ways of interaction between the specific user working in the industry, with the diversity of equipment and technologies with which they must work and adapt.

To detect the specific characteristics of this type of user, a study has been carried out to assess the current state of technological development of companies in the Latin American context, identifying the technological products currently implemented by functional area.

For this purpose, a work has been done on the InTICs® Index [6] that evaluates the Level of technological development of each industry according to the Software, Hardware, and Infrastructure products that it has currently implemented fulfilling specific tasks in the different functional areas. This index allows to detect the specific products and select the subset of technologies that make up the Industry 4.0 implemented in each company.

The index was applied by surveying a group of companies in Argentina and Mexico to evaluate the current level of technological development, identify the Industry 4.0 products implemented and detect the functional areas where they are operated.

3 Model Structure

The index used is structured from the technological products differentiated into 3 ICTs components: Software, Hardware, and Infrastructure [7] grouped according to the specificities of each type of technology and implemented in the functional areas where these technologies fulfill specific tasks within the industries.

The generic functional areas that differentiate the index are based on Michael Porter's Value Chain Model and are shown in Fig. 1.

The functions that are performed in these areas are as follows:

- Logistics: Includes logistics activities, both inbound and outbound.
- Production: Includes operations activities.
- Sales: This area includes marketing and sales activities, as well as service activities.
- Management: This area is included in the support activities of company infrastructure and human resources.
- Accounting and Finance: This area is also part of the company's infrastructure support activities.
- Engineering: This area includes technology development activities. This includes product and process design features.
- Purchases: Includes the homonymous activities of the value chain.

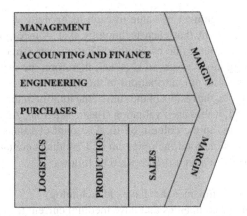

Fig. 1. Simplified model for the Value Chain. Source: Own elaboration

Once the functional areas of a company have been identified, the index allows to detect the technological products at their intersection with each functional area, from which it generates an assessment of 3 Levels, weighting each product according to its degree of development in terms of the time of validity in the market of each of them, allowing to distinguish by company at what level it is according to the technology implemented.

The index proposes a cross between the two identified typologies (ICTs and Production processes) to be able to identify precisely the specific products that are used for the correct performance of the functions in the different areas. Once these technological products have been identified, an assessment is assigned by levels according to: their degree of development in terms of the time they exist as tools used in the market, if the type of support they provide contributes with information that is sensitive to companies, the complexity of the problem they solve, if their use impacts on an improvement of processes or on the control of processes, if it improves efficiency in the use of resources, if it improves productivity in processes, if it reduces operating costs, and the degree of innovation generated by its implementation and application in the field of industry.

In this way, 3 levels of current products are established, according to whether they result from a basic technology, medium current technology, or more advanced technology, tending to the transformation of industry 4.0. This qualification has been instrumented from a double-entry table, where the specific products corresponding to each grouping of ICTs, in the types of Software, Hardware or Infrastructure are crossed with the functional areas, and a weighting is assigned at each crossing according to the present relevance of each identified product. To do this, a scale with the values of 1; 5 and 10 was used.

In Fig. 2 an extract from the Matrix Table of the index is shown, which defines the crosses to determine the relationship between ICTs and Industrial Processes and indicates the valuation defined for each specific product. Rows present each product ICTs grouped by type and colored according to the classification within each grouping.

According to this assignment of value to each technology, the proposed form of evaluation takes into account that each technology that is incorporated includes the previous ones, does not replace one by another. That is, every time new technology is incorporated, something more advanced is added; therefore, the result achieved in this instance responds to the sum of contributions of the values.

From the Matrix Table, the results of the sum of the totality of the products according to their level are derived, where each valuation (Basic, Medium, Advanced) has several boxes that are represented in the column of Total amount of values. The sum of these values indicates the possible total including all ICT products contained in each of the levels, from which the Levels are differentiated as follows:

- *Basic Level* for those companies that have old technology
- *Medium level* for those companies that have medium current technology
- *Advanced level* for those companies that have advanced technology

	Management	Finnance and Accounting	Engineering	Purchases	Logistics	Production	Sales
WEB Technologies - WEB Page (External Site)	1						1
WEB Technologies - Intranet (Internal Site)	1	1	1	1	1	1	1
WEB Technologies - Extranet (Transactional)				5	5		5
WEB Technologies - Online Advertising	5						5
Collaborative Systems - Video Conference	10		10				10
Collaborative Systems - IP Telephony	5	5	5	5	5	5	5
Collaborative Systems - Instant Messaging	1	1	1	1	1	1	1
Collaborative Systems - Email	1	1	1	1	1	1	1
Collaborative Systems - Social Networks	1						1
Collaborative Systems - File Synchronization	5	5	5		5	5	5
Collaborative Systems - Mobile Applications	5	5	5	5	5	5	5
Office Tools - Word Processor	1	1	1	1	1	1	1
Office Tools - Spreadsheet	1	1	1	1	1	1	1
Office Tools - Presentations	1	1	1				1
Office Tools - Database Manager		5	5	5	5	5	5
Office Tools - Calendar and Email Manager	1	1	1	1	1	1	1
Office Tools - PDF File Manager	5	5	5				5
Office Tools - PDF File Reader	1	1	1	1	1	1	1
Management Systems - Enterprise Resource Planning	5	5	5	5	5	5	5
Management Systems - Customer Relationship Management	5	5					5
Management Systems - Customer Claims Support							5
Management Systems - Dashboard / Balanced Score Card	10						10
Management Systems - Business Intelligence	10	10	10	10	10	10	10
Management Systems - Big Data	10	10	10	10	10	10	10
Management Systems - Machine Learning	10		10			10	
Management Systems - Energy Control Software			10			10	
Management Systems - Logistics / Supply			5	5	5	5	
Management Systems - Quality Management System	5	5	5	5	5	5	5

INDUSTRIAL PROCESSES → ICTs↓ (SOFTWARE)

Fig. 2. Matrix Table. Source: Own elaboration [6]

The ICT products identified by the index are 74 in the different functional areas, within which, those corresponding to the Basic Level are 20, those of Medium Level are 30 and those of Advanced Level are 24. The products included in this last Advanced level are not all the latest generation, but they are essential for the integration and operation of the others. Therefore, on this set it is possible to extract the subset of specific products of industry 4.0.

Figure 3 shows the specific products of the index that, in their integration, make up the subset of products of industry 4.0.

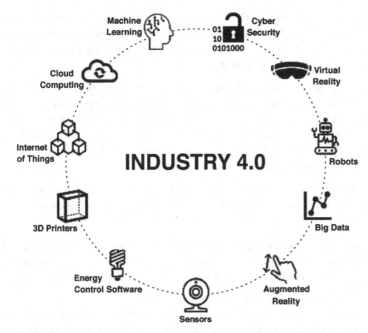

Fig. 3. Enabling ICT Products for Industry 4.0. Source: Own elaboration

The subset of products identified within Industry 4.0 require a process of integration between them, as well as with technologies of an earlier level of development.

Below are the Advanced Level ICT products that integrate a subset of 11 enabling technologies that make up Industry 4.0.

Virtual Reality: Virtual Reality is a three-dimensional environment generated by computers that create in the user the sensation of being immersed in it. This environment is visualized through Virtual Reality glasses, and sometimes accompanied by other devices, such as gloves or special suits, which allow greater interaction with the environment, as well as the perception of different stimuli that intensify the sensation of reality [8].

Robots: The equipment that performs some function of physical movement through artificial mechanics are considered Robots and are made up of computers that contain an electromechanical system composed of microprocessors and software that orders the development of automatic repetitive tasks independent of human control.

Big Data: Big Data is understood as a set of techniques tending to make decisions in real time that involve a large volume of data typically coming from different sources, usually characterized by three attributes: volume, variety, and speed [9].

Augmented Reality: Augmented Reality is the real-time visualization of visual and/or auditory virtual elements superimposed on a real-world environment; that is, adds virtual elements to an existing reality, rather than creating that reality from scratch [8].

Sensors: These are interconnected devices that take data as signals or measured values and send them to software that processes them.

Energy Control: It is a software that allows to control the energy consumption through electrical devices or sensors that, in a centralized and automated way, from any personal desktop computer, relieve the consumption data allowing the integral control of luminaires and electrical equipment in general.

3D Printers: 3D printers are made up of a set of technologies of manufacturing by addition, where a three-dimensional object is created by overlapping successive layers of material. One of the main benefits is associated with flexibility, since specific machinery whose function is limited to a particular product is replaced. They allow to improve product communication, by having a realistic 3D model in full color to convey much more information than with a computer image [9].

Internet of Things: It is an infrastructure based on cellular communication or through Wi-Fi networks that allows communication between different equipment, devices, and systems.

Cloud Computing: These are applications and computer services hosted externally, and typically accessed via the Internet, which allows dispensing with the own infrastructure necessary to execute applications: servers, eventual databases, or even the application itself, requiring only connectivity with the Internet [9].

Machine Learning: Software that contains a data analysis method that automates the construction of analytical models. It constitutes a branch of artificial intelligence based on the idea that systems can learn from previous data, and thereby identify patterns and make decisions with minimal human intervention from the programming of an algorithm.

Cyber Security: The implementation of techniques and applications with the aim of ensuring the integrity, privacy, confidentiality, and availability of assets belonging to the Information Systems of organizations against internal and external threats [9].

4   Case Studies in Argentina and Mexico

The introduced ICT Index was applied to carry out the survey in a set of 40 companies in Argentina and 8 companies in Mexico, taking a non-probabilistic sample of companies, to evaluate the current level of technological development and identify the products of Industry 4.0 implemented in the different functional areas where they are operated. The study is exploratory and the quantitative data it yields are used only to represent the qualitative analysis of both countries, without making statistical comparisons of companies, technologies, levels of development or functional areas.

The results of the study allow us to analyze a distinction by size in the companies surveyed in Argentina, where 70% are Micro and Small Enterprises, 17.5% is made up of Medium Companies, and 12.5% is in the category of Large Company. Meanwhile, of the companies surveyed in Mexico, 64% is Micro and Small Enterprises and 36% is Medium Enterprises.

From the application of the index in the companies surveyed, it can be observed that in Argentina 62.50% is in the Basic Level, 35% is in the Medium Level, and only 2.50% in the Advanced Level. While, in Mexico, of the 8 Companies surveyed, 25% are in the Basic Level, and 75% in the Medium Level, as shown in the following Fig. 5.

Fig. 5. Distribution according to Score. Source: Own elaboration

Performing the analysis by functional area of each company, it is observed that in the Purchasing area the companies of Argentina have implemented 30 products of Industry 4.0, while the companies of Mexico have 10 products distributed as shown in the following Fig. 6.

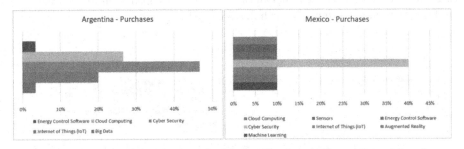

Fig. 6. Distribution of ICTs in Argentina/Mexico (Purchases). Source: Own elaboration

As for the Logistics area, companies in Argentina have implemented 34 products of Industry 4.0, while companies in Mexico have 4 products distributed as shown in the following Fig. 7.

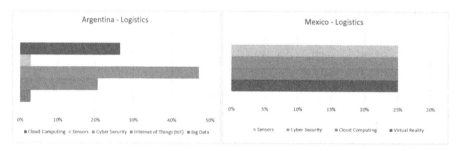

Fig. 7. Distribution of ICTs in Argentina/Mexico (Logistics). Source: Own elaboration

Regarding the Sales area, companies in Argentina have implemented 54 products of Industry 4.0, while companies in Mexico have 4 products as shown in the following Fig. 8.

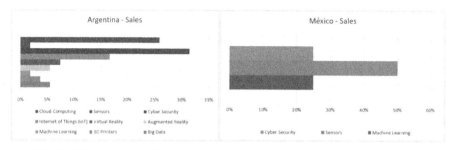

Fig. 8. Distribution of ICTs in Argentina/Mexico (Sales). Source: Own elaboration

As for the products implemented in the Management area, companies in Argentina have implemented 53 products of Industry 4.0, while companies in Mexico have 12 products distributed, as shown in the following Fig. 9.

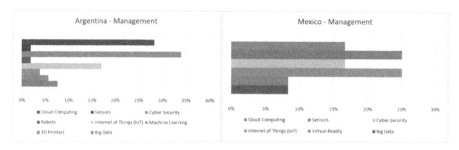

Fig. 9. Distribution of ICTs in Argentina/Mexico (Management). Source: Own elaboration

Regarding the area of Accounting and Finance, companies in Argentina have implemented 42 products of Industry 4.0, while companies in Mexico have 9 products as presented in the following Fig. 10.

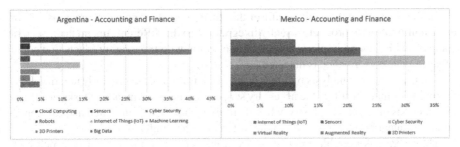

Fig. 10. Distribution of ICTs in Argentina/Mexico (Accounting and Finance). Source: Own elaboration

In the area of Engineering, companies in Argentina have implemented 42 products of Industry 4.0, while companies in Mexico have 8 products, distributed as shown in the following Fig. 11.

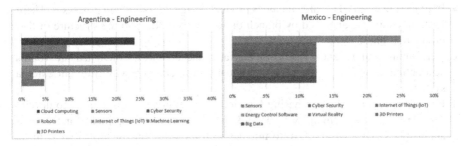

Fig. 11. Distribution of ICTs in Argentina/Mexico (Engineering). Source: Own elaboration

5   Results and Discussion

Analyzing the implementation of the subset of ICT products that make up Industry 4.0 in the universe of companies surveyed, it is observed that the products that are implemented in few companies and are distributed in all the functional areas of a type of industry. That involves interaction between different types of users depending on the role they play. The software that is implemented is multiplatform and is integrated into the different contexts of each company (management, production, logistics, engineering).

The interusability [10] that implies distributed usability between different devices turns out to be the significant thing about these products of Industry 4.0, promoting multitasking distributed in different functional areas and located in different environments, the performance of asynchronous tasks and the integration of multi-user technologies.

On the other hand, it is observed that about 70% of the companies surveyed have some Industry 4.0 product implemented in the different functional areas, highlighting those applied to Cyber Security, followed by Cloud Computing and in third place by the Internet of Things. Far from these 3 products appears, very scarcely, some of the remaining 8 products that are part of Industry 4.0.

In this sense, it is possible to affirm that there are some typical characteristics for the usability of these products, usually integrated into the different functional areas of a company, although no implementation or integration with the other products that could enhance their performance is detected.

Finally, from this analysis by functional area, it is possible to precisely identify those technologies that constitute the necessary support for the performance of tasks in each of the functions of a typical industry, while there are technologies integrated in the different tasks and integrated transversally in the different technological products.

However, it is possible to characterize users according to the area in which they conduct their tasks and diversified in the following functions:

- Users of management area: In this area it is necessary to distinguish those who analyze general data of the company and those who make decisions.
- Production Users: In this area, the activities of production operations by industry should be analyzed since the diversity of users is determined by each production line and the specific technologies for its operation.
- Engineering Users: This area includes product design activities and processes. Therefore, they must be analyzed by branch of activity according to the structure of their production lines.
- Accounting and Finance Users: In this area the activities conducted are routine accounting as well as finances of a company in interaction with different external systems.
- Purchasing Users: The purchasing functions of a company require users to develop their tasks in a systematic way according to the demand for inputs and internal acquisitions. These users have to interact with the different functional areas of the company.
- Logistics Users: In this area, the activities of entry of raw materials and inputs, as well as output and distribution, are conducted. Users must interact with agents external to the company in their daily operations.
- Sales Users: This area includes the activities of marketing and services, which implies an interaction with different market agents.

From this initial characterization of users by functional area, it is possible to analyze that the tasks are different in each function, that the technological products will be different according to the functions they perform in their daily operation, and that the technologies of Industry 4.0 are implemented in an integrated way in the different functions. However, users are people with different characteristics and knowledge, whose analysis is necessary to determine the usability needs of the products, and make the design according to them in such a way that they enjoy the full potential in their implementation.

6 Conclusions and Future Work

The analysis conducted allows us to conclude that the industry in Latin America is at a low level of technological development. The transformation towards Industry 4.0 is a process that develops slowly, disjointedly and with little information about existing technologies and their potential. The structure of SMEs in these productive sectors, analyzed with the survey, is limited in its economic capacity to incorporate knowledge and technological transformation compared to an accelerated pace observed in other sectors of the economy with a large concentration of capital and a structure of large companies.

The results of the study allow us to affirm that it is possible to identify the specific technologies that can be implemented to fulfill functions according to the area of the company in which they are located, which must be designed and developed for the specific users who fulfill the daily tasks, while the investment in technologies requires an approach towards the users in their real context of use to enhance the technological integration and the capabilities of the people.

However, the lack of knowledge of the potential offered by Industry 4.0 is common in all the companies surveyed. Even in companies that have a Medium level of technology use, they did not identify how they could improve their competitiveness, by digitizing some processes and automating some others.

Finally, as future work, based on the data of the survey of Argentina and Mexico with the identification of products of industry 4.0 and the initial distinction on users in the different functional areas of a company, a study will be carried out to characterize users in depth of an industry applying the *persona method* thus being able to identify usability attributes that should include the technological products that are developed for the users of industry 4.0 in the context of Latin American countries.

References

1. Ministerio de Ciencia, Tecnología e Innovación Productiva: Industria 4.0: Escenarios e impactos para la formulación de políticas tecnológicas en los umbrales de la Cuarta Revolución Industrial. Retrieved from http://www.infoplc.net/files/documentacion/industria4/infoPLC_net_0000038319.pdf (2015). 17 Nov 2022
2. Mon, A., Del Giorgio, H.R.: Herramienta de Evaluación de TICs para determinar el nivel de desarrollo tecnológico en la Industria. XIV COINI 2021 (Congreso Internacional de Ingeniería Industrial) – Universidad Tecnológica Nacional (FR Buenos Aires). Retrieved from https://indicetics.unlam.edu.ar/it/pdf/articulos/Herramienta-EvaluacionTICs-NivelDesarrolloTecno-Industria.pdf (2021). 17 Nov 2022
3. Mon, A., Del Giorgio, H.R.: Analysis of industry 4.0 products in SMEs. In: International Conference on Industry 4.0 and Smart Manufacturing (ISM 2021). Retrieved from https://indicetics.unlam.edu.ar/it/pdf/articulos/Analysis%20of%20Industry%204.0%20Products%20in%20Small%20and%20Medium%20Enterprises.pdf (2021). 17 Nov 2022
4. CEPAL: Datos y hechos sobre la transformación digital. In: Séptima Conferencia Ministerial sobre la Sociedad de la Información de América Latina y el Caribe. Retrieved from https://repositorio.cepal.org/bitstream/handle/11362/46766/1/S2000991_es.pdf (2021). 17 Nov 2022
5. Ferraz, J. C., Torracca, J., Urraca Ruiz, A., Britto, J., Schmidt, H.: Argentina vs. Brasil: la travesía por la digitalización. Banco Interamericano de Desarrollo - Instituto Para la Integración de América Latina y el Caribe. Retrieved from https://publications.iadb.org/publications/spanish/document/Argentina-vs.-Brasil-La-travesia-por-la-digitalizacion.pdf (2021). 17 Nov 2022

6. Del Giorgio, H.R., Mon, A.: Las TICs en las industrias. Ed Universidad Nacional de La Matanza. Retrieved from https://indicetics.unlam.edu.ar/it/pdf/libros/Las_TICs_en_las_Ind ustrias.pdf (2019). 17 Nov 2022

7. Novick, M., Ritondo, S.: El Desafío de las TIC en Argentina. Crear Capacidades para la Generación de Empleo. CEPAL, Santiago (2013)

8. Barraco Mármol, G., Bender, A., Mazza, N.: nTIC 2017. Retrieved from http://www.susten tum.com/nTIC/nTIC2017.pdf (2017). 17 Nov 2022

9. Mazza, N.: Gestión estratégica de recursos informáticos. Retrieved from http://www.susten tum.com/sustentum/pubs/geri.pdf (2014). 17 Nov 2022

10. Rowland, C.: Cross-device interactions and interusability. Designing for the Internet of Things. O'Reilly Media, Inc. Retrieved from https://www.oreilly.com/library/view/design ing-for-the/9781491971468/ch05.html (2015). 17 Nov 2022

Bootstrapping Safe IVIS Development with an Affordable Testing Suite

Leonel Mandarino[1] , Carlos Carvajal[1] , Andrés Rodriguez[1] ,
and Alejandro Fernandez[1,2]( )

[1] LIFIA, Facultad de Informática, UNLP, Calle 50 y 120, La Plata, Argentina
{andres.rodriguez,alejandro.fernandez}@lifia.info.unlp.edu.ar
[2] Comisión de Investigaciones Científicas de la Provincia de Buenos Aires, La Plata, Argentina

Abstract. In-vehicle information systems (IVIS) represent a growing industry. IVIS were originally built and deployed by car manufacturers, which ensured that they complied with the safety regulations of the car industry. Nowadays, IVIS enter the vehicle in the driver's and passenger's phones. These "nomadic IVIS", which sometimes interact with the car's entertainment system, can escape important safety checks. Any software developer, without training in vehicle safety, can build and distribute IVIS. This reality calls for tools and methods that help software developers conceive safe applications. This article proposes an affordable and reliable testing suite that provides support to developers of nomadic IVIS. The suite takes the form of a simulation and data collection environment, oriented to the rapid prototyping of IVIS. It considers security requirements while maintaining a low technological and economic threshold, to provide easy access to developers compared to expensive physical environments with real vehicles.

Keywords: IVIS · Safety · Prototyping · Evaluation

1 Introduction

The Strategic Highway Research Program (SHRP 2) [1] project obtained video and audio data from more than 3500 drivers over a 3-year period using information collected by the Naturalistic Driving Study [2]. This project was able to capture information on more than 35 million miles driven, comprising 905 automobile accidents with property and passenger damage. With this information, reports were obtained that indicate a 3.53% prevalence of accidents caused using native car apps, and a 6.4% prevalence of accidents caused by the use of cell phone apps. Therefore, it is estimated that 10 percent of the time, accidents are caused by drivers who are operating electronic devices while driving. It can also be noted that accidents are more frequent in connection with the use of mobile applications [3].

Typically, native car app developers work for large automotive companies and are trained to consider factors such as driver vision, time spent on the app, distracting elements, and colors in the interface, among others. However, there is an increase in the

V. Agredo-Delgado et al. (Eds.): HCI-COLLAB 2022, CCIS 1707, pp. 41–50, 2022.
https://doi.org/10.1007/978-3-031-24709-5_4

number of applications for smart devices that are intended as information systems for in-vehicle use[1]. For companies not specialized in the automotive industry, it is difficult and costly to tackle the development of tests on specialized tracks and with physical vehicles, especially if they want to work on multiple prototypes and new ideas. To contribute to the solution of this challenge, this article presents and evaluates an affordable and reliable IVIS testing suite.

The rest of this article is organized as follows. First, we provide a brief discussion of related work. We also introduce concepts and mechanisms used to determine the level of cognitive load of a driver. Then, we describe the proposed testing suite. Following, we present the results of a preliminary evaluation of the suite, focused on comparing two different IVIS in terms of cognitive load and driver distraction. Finally, we present the conclusions of the work done, summarize the main contributions and discuss future work.

2   Related Work

The Naturalistic Driving Study (NDS) collected information on 3,362 private vehicles, all driven by citizen volunteers who were observed over a 3-year period. The NDS project was mainly based on the belief that a better understanding of driving safety issues can be gained by studying drivers, their behavior and the different factors that affect them, such as weather conditions, the driving environment, electronic devices present in the car, etc. Participants' vehicles were fitted with cameras, radar, and hidden sensors to capture data as they went about their normal activities. Information was obtained on 6,650,519 trips, totaling almost 50 million miles traveled [2]. A study [3] following the DNS project sought to answer "why" and "how" a task is distracting. The authors concluded that most dangerous visual distractions are those in which the driver is exposed to the risk of a situation with abrupt and rapid changes. This is related to the duration of the distraction, being that the longer the driver loses sight of the road, the greater the possibility of finding himself in a difficult situation to face. Among the recommendations to reduce the risk when driving, they considered important to design interfaces that minimize the need for visual interaction on the part of the driver. Another aspect to keep in mind is that the elimination of long glances (more than 2 s) will not eliminate distraction problems, since most accidents are the result of small distractions at inopportune moments.

Comprehensive and realistic studies like NDS are valuable and only available to a handful of organizations. They are extremely costly in terms of time and necessary resources. The suite we present in this article incorporates the lessons documented by the NDS study but aims at the individual IVIS developer or to the small development company.

In the study "Steering Control in a Low-Cost Driving Simulator: A Case for the Role of Virtual Vehicle Cab" [4], an analysis is made regarding the credibility of the results obtained with low-cost simulators, based on the lack of a driver's cab. Depending on the initial investment for building a simulation environment, they can be classified into three general categories:

---

[1] https://www.statista.com/statistics/271644/worldwide-free-and-paid-mobile-app-store-downloads/.

- Low cost: they have a gaming wheel, with pedals, several screens, and no cockpit.
- Medium cost: large projection, fixed base, partial or full cockpit, etc.
- High cost: 360° view of the simulator, cockpit of a real vehicle mounted on motion sensors, etc.

The credibility of the results obtained with driving simulators, in general, has been a cause of concern and debate in the scientific community [5, 6]. Some studies have shown that the results obtained in simulators are of the same order and direction to those of real-world data [7, 8]. Other studies have compared low-cost simulators with more expensive and complex simulators to determine whether the former are sufficiently valid to be taken into account [9]. The results indicate that low-cost simulators are good indicators for studying the effects of IVIS on driver behavior.

Skyline [10] is a prototyping platform for user experience development based on a driving simulation. It was developed at Intel Labs, following principles of flexibility, integration, and customization, to enable rapid prototyping of in-vehicle user experiences. The main difference between Skyline and the platform presented in this article is the scope and focus of the simulation environment. In our case, facial recognition sensors are available, and mechanisms were implemented to measure the cognitive load of the driver. Thus, with this information, a more detailed profile of the driver and his behavior can be obtained, to develop safer interfaces oriented to his context of use.

3   Platform Overview

As previously discussed, visual distractions of 2 or more seconds prior to the occurrence of an unexpected event such as deceleration and/or braking of another vehicle are significantly more dangerous than distractions of less time or when a precipitating event does not occur. We conclude that the determinants of risk are the presence of an unexpected event and the time we keep our eyes off the road. This is directly related to the level of uncertainty and the reaction time available to the driver, i.e., once he/she regains concentration on the road after a distraction.

With this background in mind, we focused the design of the test suit in the core components depicted in Fig. 1. The test suite consists of two computing nodes, one used by the driver (subject of the test) and one used by the experimenter. The driver's computing node runs the driving simulation environment, the test instruments, and a test controller service. The driving simulation environment offers a first person, 3D, immersive simulation where the test subject drives a vehicle. The gaze tracker detects when the driver looks away from the road and towards the UI of an IVIS. The Detection Response Tasks instrument is used to assess the cognitive load of using an IVIS while driving in a simulated scenario. The simulation environment and the instruments are configured and controlled via the test controller service. The test controller service is also responsible for collecting data from the simulation and the instruments and making it available to the experimenter. The experimenter's node connects to the test controller in the driver's node to plan, launch and monitor experiments. The following subsections discuss the some of these components with more detail.

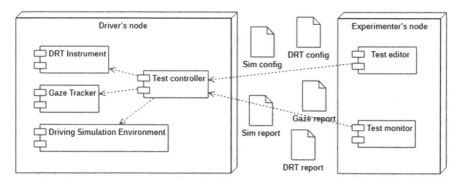

Fig. 1. Architecture overview

3.1   Driving Simulation Environment

The driving simulation environment executes the driving simulation, where tests take place. In addition, it is the element to which the other components subscribe to configure testing scenarios and to obtain information about the events and actions that occur during tests.

Among the different options available to use as the basis for the simulation environment, it was decided to use CARLA [11]. This simulator, developed at Intel Labs, has the advantage of being a recognized and constantly growing project. The project is Open Source, which made it very easy to integrate it into the suite and then exploit it for the development of new functionalities. In addition to the simulation engine, CARLA provides a vast catalog of digital resources such as urban designs, buildings, vehicles, and pedestrians that enrich the experiments and make them more attractive compared to other simulators. CARLA uses Unreal Engine for the execution and layout of the simulation. The control and configuration of the simulation is given through an API. CARLA allows you to control the amount of Non-Playable Characters (NPCs) distributed around the map; these are cars and pedestrians which CARLA internally calls "actors". Actors are important for the simulation because they bring life, dynamism and a higher degree of difficulty when walking around the map and they can be used to induce risks in the tests.

The simulation environment offers several sensors that allow it to react to events and to know the characteristics of the driving environment. The collision sensor records an event every time the vehicle collides with something in the simulated world. The GNSS (Global Navigation Satellite System) sensor tells the exact location of the vehicle. The lane encroachment sensor records an event every time the vehicle crosses a given street or surface. The different surfaces are defined at the time of map construction. Finally, the RGB cameras stream and/or record the images of the different scenes during the simulation.

3.2   Detection Response Tasks Instrument

Detection Response Task (DRT), standardized by ISO 17488:2016 [12], is a method to assess the potential for cognitive distraction introduced by a secondary task performed while driving. DRT consists of a visual stimulus that drivers must respond to while simultaneously driving and performing a secondary task. To assess the cognitive load of the secondary task, one compares the response to the visual stimulus (e.g., response time, hits, and misses) while driving with and without performing the secondary task.

The proposed suite implements the DRT visual stimulus as a small circle of a high contrast color, in the screen, simulating a light on the windshield. The driver must respond to the stimulus by pressing a button on the driving wheel, which causes the stimulus to disappear. The tool records the time it took the driver to respond to the stimulus. Failing to respond while the stimulus is active, will cause the tool to record it as miss. Responding when there are no active stimuli causes the tool to record an error.

The DRT component is configurable. The options to configure are:

- The radius of the circle determined in pixels.
- The color expressed in hexadecimal.
- The time in seconds that the light is on before it turns off (and a miss is recorded).
- The execution mode: this can be manual if you want to turn the light on and off at will, or random if you want the light to appear after a randomly selected number of seconds. An interval can be set for time selection.
- The location of the light; you can choose a fixed location on the screen determined by coordinates on the Cartesian axis. As an alternative to this option a random position on the screen can be chosen. To avoid obstructing the driver's view while moving through the world, you can choose quadrants of the screen where the light can appear.

3.3 Gaze Tracker

DRT helps isolate the impact of a secondary task on the driver's attention. The various sensors offered by the simulation (e.g., the crash sensor) help assess the impact of a secondary task on driving. However, none of them can help us tell where the driver was looking at. The Gaze tracker is a low-cost instrument that can record this information. It monitors the user's gaze using a camera. This is very valuable since it complements the objective of the DRT tasks and helps to identify the driver's attention during the tests.

For the development of the Gaze tracker we used the OpenCV library, which provides a great amount of functionalities for the detection of elements and people in real time. Thus, using the mechanism of the Haar Cascade Classifier, it is possible to identify objects in images or videos, regardless of their location or size. In addition, this algorithm is very fast, which makes it possible to detect elements in real time. Thus, with a pre-trained Haar Cascade model and using the functionalities provided by OpenCV, it is possible to detect the driver's movements in real time.

The gaze tracker attempts to continuously detect the face and eyes of the driver (see Fig. 2), and records as loss of attention the moments in which detection is not possible. This can occur, for example, when the driver is distracted by checking an application on an external screen and takes his eyes off the windshield.

One of the goals of this work is to achieve a rapid and inexpensive prototyping and testing environment, so that it is available to as many developers as possible. It should be noted that it is not necessary to have a high-quality camera for proper operation. It is

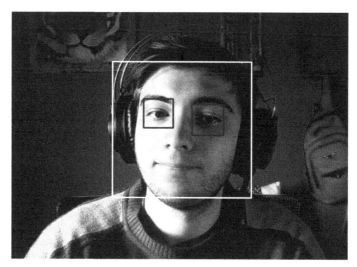

Fig. 2. Gaze recognition in real time

even possible, by means of mobile applications, to establish a connection between the camera of a cell phone and the computer, thus effectively turning it into a webcam.

4   Evaluation

The goal of the evaluation was to assess whether the proposed test suite helps developers understand and interpret driver behavior in different automotive environments while using an IVIS application. To do so, we used the testing suite to assess the impact of operating two different mobile applications while driving. This was done under the hypothesis that more complex interfaces require a higher level of attention and engagement from the driver, thus using the test suite should help us reach such conclusions.

The experiment was run with two different applications, with different levels of complexity: Facebook and Google maps. The Facebook mobile app was chosen under the hypothesis that it would result in a high cognitive load and source of distractions (as it was not designed to be used while driving). In contrast, Google maps was expected to be less demanding and suitable for in-car use. The working hypothesis is that using Facebook would yield considerably higher distraction time and more DRT misses.

4.1   Evaluation Setting

Five subjects with an age range of 21 to 56 years (median = 24) participated in the experiments. All subjects had a valid driver's license, and none had visual or hearing impairments.

Subjects seated in an ergonomic office seat in front of three adjacent 23-in. screens, which served as car windshields. They controlled the simulation using a steering wheel and pedals.

A smartphone was placed at the height of the steering wheel so as not to obstruct the driver's view of the windshield, in a position that is common to many drivers. The application under test was running on the phone.

The DRT light was displayed (turned on) for 2 s, in a random position, at random intervals (between 1 and 3 s). The driver had to press the "R2" button on the steering wheel as soon as he saw the light. In case of not pressing the button in time, the light automatically disappeared, and a miss was recorded. In case the "R2" button was pressed when the light was off, an error was recorded.

4.2 Tasks

Participants were asked to make a short tour of the city for 5 min, trying to respect all traffic rules (stop at red lights, avoid colliding with other cars, always maintain control of the car and stay in the corresponding lane). In addition, they were instructed on the tasks to be performed with a mobile application while driving through the city. In addition, while driving and using the app, they should respond to the DRT stimulus.

Participants were given a set of tasks to complete with each app. In the case of the use of Facebook, participants should read and like 8 publications, and access a person's profile. In the use of Google Maps, the trip to a destination must be configured, an intermediate stop must be added after starting the trip and finally an alternative route must be selected.

Each participant performed 3 simulation rounds of 5 min each with each of the applications (6 simulations in total). To avoid learning bias, the order in which the different applications are presented was randomized.

All tests were conducted on the same day with a half-hour separation between users. Before starting the tests, each driver was given 2 min to get used to operating the controls in the simulation. The series of 6 rounds was conducted with a 5-min separation between each round, totaling a test load of 55 min (30 driving, 25 rest) per user session. Instructions were repeated prior to each start of running an application.

At the end of each session, a survey was conducted based on the Driver Activity Load Index (DALI), which is a method for measuring subjective user workload. The DALI questionnaire consists of a 6-item Likert scale (0 to 5, low to high) on: global attentional demand, visual, auditory, tactile demand, stress level, temporal pressure, degree of secondary task interference over driving.

4.3 Results and Discussion

Figure 3 summarizes the observed results. The orange bar (upper bar) corresponds to Google maps, whereas the blue bar (lower bat) corresponds to Facebook. The row labeled "DRT miss" indicates the number of DRT stimuli that were not attended in time and disappeared. The row labeled "DRT Error" reports the number of times the "R2" button was pressed and there was no DRT stimulus (this is counted to prevent the driver from constantly pressing the DRT button while the notification is not on the screen). The row labeled "Distraction time" indicates the average time (in seconds) that the driver kept his/her eyes off the simulation. For the calculation of this variable, the average of each driver was obtained and then the results of all participants were averaged.

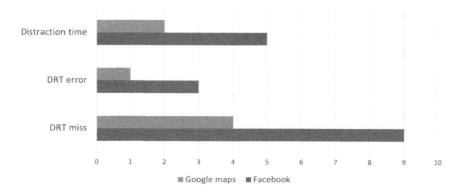

Fig. 3. Average observations for DRT errors, DRT misses, and total distraction time

As expected, distraction time was twice as much for Facebook than for Google maps. Similarly, DRT errors and misses were significantly more while using Face-book than while using Google maps.

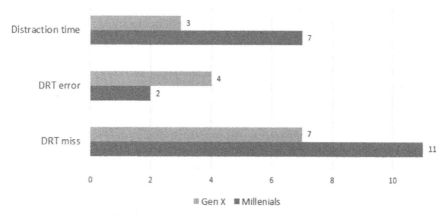

Fig. 4. Average DRT errors, DRT misses, and TDT by age group, while using Facebook

We wondered whether the suite could help us find any differences between millennial participants (that grew up using mobile apps) and Gen X participants (who adopted mobile apps during adulthood). At the risk of a reduced validity of the results (given the size of the sample), we partitioned results in two age groups: millennials (10 to 41 years old, to include both Gen Z and millennials) and Gen X (42 to 57 years old). We present two graphs, one for Facebook (Fig. 4) and one for Google maps (Fig. 5). In both graphs the lighter bar (upper bar) represents generation X, and the darker bar (lower bar) represents millennials (including Gen Z).

It is notable that millennials have longer total distraction time and more missed DRTs but make fewer errors for both applications. Perhaps one explanation is related to the persuasive power of applications in adolescents. This preliminary result may offer a hint of an interesting question worth of further analysis with a larger user base.

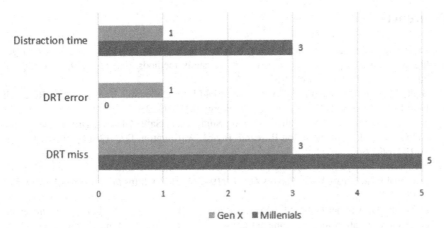

Fig. 5. Average DRT errors, DRT misses, and TDT by age group, while using Google Maps

All participants reported high levels of DALI for Facebook, particularly in terms of degree of interference on driving. In addition, subjects in Gen X commented on the difficulty of reading the application and loading interface elements.

These results indicate that the data collected with the three core elements of the testing suite (the simulation environment, the DRT instrument, and the Gaze Tracker) offers an indication of the impact of the IVIS app on the driver's attention. Moreover, as expected, the observed results match the expected results in the case of the two applications under study. However, comprehensive studies (specially including more subjects) are required to better assess the usefulness, and precision of the test suite.

5   Conclusions and Future Work

As development and distribution of IVIS become possible for any software developer, the need for affordable methods and tools to test how these systems impact the driver's attention becomes more important. Testing tools based on simulated environments have shown to be effective and low cost. We have built a low-cost testing suite that combines a simulated driving environment, a DRT instrument, and a Gaze Tracker. Preliminary experiments with the tool and with two applications whose impact on attention can be easily assessed, show that the data obtained with the test suite matches what is expected. The evaluation reported in this article is based on a small user sample and aimed only to assess the direction and magnitude of the results. Future work will improve evaluation with a larger user base and comparing against a more adequate and more detailed baseline. Moreover, future evaluation will also cover the perspective of the experimenter as well. This additional evaluation perspective will tell us whether the suite is usable and useful for application developers.

References

1. Antin, J.F., Lee, S., Perez, M.A., Dingus, T.A., Hankey, J.M., Brach, A.: Second strategic highway research program naturalistic driving study methods. Saf. Sci. **119**, 2–10 (2019). https://doi.org/10.1016/j.ssci.2019.01.016
2. Blatt, A., et al.: Naturalistic Driving Study: Field Data Collection. Transportation Research Board, Washington, D.C. (2014). https://doi.org/10.17226/22367
3. Victor, T.: Analysis of Naturalistic Driving Study Data: Safer Glances, Driver Inattention, and Crash Risk. Transportation Research Board, Washington, D.C. (2014). https://doi.org/10.17226/22297
4. Mecheri, S., Lobjois, R.: Steering control in a low-cost driving simulator: a case for the role of virtual vehicle cab. Hum. Factors **60**(5), 719–734 (2018). https://doi.org/10.1177/0018720818769253
5. de Waard, D., van der Hulst, M., Hoedemaeker, M., Brookhuis, K.A.: Driver behavior in an emergency situation in the automated highway system. Transp. Hum. Factors **1**(1), 67–82 (1999). https://doi.org/10.1207/sthf0101_7
6. Farber, E.I.: Comments on driver behavior in an emergency situation in the automated highway system. Transp. Hum. Factors **1**(1), 83–85 (1999). https://doi.org/10.1207/sthf0101_8
7. Bella, F.: Driving simulator for speed research on two-lane rural roads. Accid. Anal. Prev. **40**(3), 1078–1087 (2008). https://doi.org/10.1016/j.aap.2007.10.015
8. Godley, S.T., Triggs, T.J., Fildes, B.N.: Driving simulator validation for speed research. Accid. Anal. Prev. **34**(5), 589–600 (2002). https://doi.org/10.1016/S0001-4575(01)00056-2
9. Jamson, S.L., Jamson, A.H.: The validity of a low-cost simulator for the assessment of the effects of in-vehicle information systems. Saf. Sci. **48**(10), 1477–1483 (2010). https://doi.org/10.1016/j.ssci.2010.07.008
10. Alvarez, I., Rumbel, L., Adams, R.: Skyline: a rapid prototyping driving simulator for user experience. In: Proceedings of the 7th International Conference on Automotive User Interfaces and Interactive Vehicular Applications, pp. 101–108 (2015). https://doi.org/10.1145/2799250.2799290
11. Dosovitskiy, A., Ros, G., Codevilla, F., Lopez, A., Koltun, V.: Carla: an open urban driving simulator. In: Conference on robot learning, pp. 1–16. PMLR (2017)
12. I.O. for Standardization: Road vehicles—transport information and control systems—detection-response task (DRT) for assessing attentional effects of cognitive load in driving. Tech. Rep. ISO 17488:2016. International Organization for Standardization (2016)

Building a Usability Guide for the Design of Interactive Mobile Applications

Carlos A. Casas[1] (ID), Luis Garzón[2] (ID), Pablo H. Ruiz[1] (ID), Luis Freddy Muñoz[3], and Vanessa Agredo-Delgado[1](✉) (ID)

[1] Unicomfacauca, Popayán, Colombia
{carloscasas,pruiz,vagredo}@unicomfacauca.edu.co
[2] SENNOVA, Centro Comercio y Servicios, Servicio Nacional de Aprendizaje – Sena, Popayán, Colombia
gvluis@misena.edu.co
[3] Fundación Universitaria de Popayán, Popayán, Colombia
lfreddyms@fup.edu.co

Abstract. Usability is the degree of ease of a product to be used, it is the quality of the experience that a user has when interacting with a software product, determining the efficiency of the interface and the effectiveness of the tasks. Currently, there is a lack of knowledge, lack of what and how to apply usability in specific contexts, therefore, considering its importance, this paper shows the process of building a usability guide for the design of interactive mobile applications in the context of learning mathematics for children aged 6 and 7 years. For its construction was used the methodology of multi-cycle action research with bifurcation, with which the conceptualization, construction, and validation of the usability guide was performed. It was obtained that the guidelines and the guide to support the use of these guidelines are complete, useful, and easy to use.

Keywords: Usability guidelines · Usability guide · Interactive mobile applications

1 Introduction

For the last twenty years or so, computing has provided the world with countless general and specific purpose computer systems to perform almost any task that a human must carry out in his or her social, work, and even leisure context [1, 2]. The use of mobile devices has considerably increased the use of software tools in different environments of everyday life. In particular, the continuous advance of mobile technologies is leading to a new generation of software tools, called mobile applications, which are those applications developed to be used on any mobile device. However, some of the success factors of software applications have to do with: the ease with which users can interact with them, the ease with which users can interact with them, and the ease with which they can use them [1–3], the accessibility [4, 5], and the effectiveness in the performance of tasks, among others. The existence or absence of these factors determines the success or failure of each of the developed systems, which is why, in the design of any computer system, it is necessary to pay special attention to the elements that must contemplate the interface [6]. But most mobile applications are difficult to use, inflexible, and not robust [7]. In addition, it is necessary to have methodologies and tools that consider specific usability elements for the development of applications used on mobile devices [7]. Currently, there is a lack of knowledge, lack of what and how to apply usability in specific contexts, therefore, considering its importance, this paper shows the process of building a usability guide for the design of interactive mobile applications in the context of learning mathematics for children aged 6 and 7 years, for which the methodology of multicycle action research with bifurcation was used, with which the conceptualization, construction, and validation of the usability guide was performed.

2   Related Works

In [8] guidelines for incorporating usability in Interactive Television (ITV) and evaluation methods are defined. In [9] the usability recommendations to be considered in order to improve student interaction with educational Web sites are mentioned. On the other hand, in [10] guidelines were defined for the development of interactive educational tools for psychomotor development in children. In [11] determines the elements, components, and factors that are key when designing interactive interfaces for augmented reality environments. In [12] best practices for usability in the design of the virtual learning environment interface are identified, similarly, in [13] systematizes the design and development of M-Learning applications by defining design and development guidelines for mobile educational applications. In [14] defines principles and guidelines on the design of 3D user interface applications. On the other hand, in [15] describes a study of the principles and requirements of user interface design using mobile devices as a tool for mobile learning purposes. At [16] a game for children was designed based on the data obtained in surveys on the mathematics axis and color preferences. Similarly, in [17] a mobile application was designed to support learning in the subject of Mexican history, whose purpose was to be a form of didactic support for teachers who teach this subject at the elementary school level.

3   Methodology

This work was developed following the multi-cycle action research methodology with bifurcation [18], which is detailed below:

3.1   Conceptual Cycle

Considering that for this work children are the end users of the applications to be designed with the usability guide, it was necessary to define their main characteristics and needs in the context. For this purpose, the user-centered design (UCD) methodology was used as a basis [19]. The UCD involves the user from the first steps of the development process and the type of user determines the design, where the scope of dissemination, the age of the user, and the user's needs must be determined. Thus, in order to identify the characteristics and needs of children, it was necessary to conduct a survey with teachers who teach mathematics, since they are the ones who directly know the needs that must be solved through the applications that are developed using the usability guide. The chosen age range of 6–7 years was due to the fact that the Colombian Ministry of Education establishes that children of this age must be in the first grade of primary school and is in the pre-operational stage, it is at this time where the child begins to develop its logical and cognitive stage and understand the basic elements of the different areas of education, this combined with its rapid adaptation to the technological world today makes children have other options to learn faster and more agile the nature of the subjects [20] The survey was conducted with a total of 23 first-grade teachers (grade in which the principles of mathematics are taught and the children are on average between 6–7 years old).

Some of the most relevant results obtained from the survey were as follows:

- 70% of the teachers assure that the highest rate of the problem at the moment of learning is covered by addition and subtraction, given that children do not know at what moment to add and at what moment to subtract, in the same way, many times they do not recognize numbers or find it difficult to count numbers of 2 digits or more, so it can be determined that for applications the subject to be treated should be one of these two topics.
- The most used and accepted method to make a better study environment is the use of tangible media (60%), which contributes to knowing how to adapt this to the final mobile prototype.
- 65% agreed that the final prototype to validate the usability guide should be oriented to the development of a game, given that as they are children the best way to make this type of operations arrive.
- 95% of the teachers felt that the use of mobile applications helps to learn and that it can be a powerful tool to reach children.
- 60% of the teachers suggest that the application should have an activity that lasts 15 min on average and that it should include some process that helps the instruction of the class.
- 60% of the teachers suggest that they should be logical thinking applications.

3.2 Methodological Cycle

The following steps were followed to define and adapt the guidelines:

Literature Review. First, an analysis of the literature on usability guidelines applied to any context was made. A large number were found, mainly those defined by Nielsen [21], where most of them are oriented to the design of web applications, which are recommendations to take into account in applications without a specific context [22]. Despite the boom of mobile applications and their massive use, one of the pending issues is the definition and classification of guidelines and appropriate metrics to ensure usability in these applications, since they do not follow metrics, are not considered or there is simply no way to guide their application [23]. From the literature analysis, a list of general usability guidelines was obtained, the problem is that these are not focused on the mobile part, in addition, they were disorganized and in different sources, so it was necessary to structure them and adapt them to the mobile part.

First Version of the Guide. In order to define the first version of the guide, the guidelines analyzed from the literature and the study of the needs of the end user were taken into account. This made it possible to define that mathematics topics and ages between 6-7 years old are characteristics that need to be supported in the definition of the guidelines. As a mechanism to standardize the description of the guidelines, a brochure format was designed, as shown in Table 1.

Table 1. Structure of the guidelines

ID	1
Name	**Thematic scope (MANDATORY)**
Category	Pedagogical strategies, content
Description	Refers to the amount of information that will be displayed and taught to the user corresponding to his/her age in the application (Data provided by the mathematics curriculum standards stipulated in Colombia) [24] [25].
Application steps	1. To study the topics in which there are more needs or difficulties (MANDATORY). 2. Consider the curricular standards of mathematics stipulated in Colombia (MANDATORY). 3. Choose a maximum of two topics on which the app will focus, considering the previous results and data (MANDATORY). 4. Emphasize the app on the selected topic to obtain positive results and not saturate the child with too much information (MANDATORY). Focus the application on a single topic, a maximum of two, to avoid the massive load of information and divert the attention and progress of the child, according to interviews with teachers specialized in the area, the most difficult topic for children between 6-7 years is the sum, create interactive problems in the application of this topic, as shown in the image.
Example	

Table 2 shows a summary of the list of guidelines with the identifier and name of each guideline and its source.

Classification According to Standard 9241-11 Usability

Once the guidelines were defined in their first version, the efficiency, effectiveness, and satisfaction factors of the ISO 9241-11 standard were used as a classification tool, thus obtaining a list of the guidelines that contribute to each of these factors. In order to classify the guidelines, it was necessary to ground the above factors in the context in which the guidelines are used, which is why they were redefined: Effectiveness: Degree of precision with which the interactive mobile application allows supporting the learning of mathematics (The sum) in children between 6–7 years old, in addition to generating in children the need for the use of the application. Efficiency: Degree to which the interactive mobile application supports the learning of mathematics (The sum) in children

Table 2. List of guidelines

ID	Name	Source
1	Visibility of system status	[21, 24]
2	Correspondence between the system and the real world	[21, 24]
3	Control and freedom for the user	[21, 24]
4	Consistency and standards	[21, 24]
5	Error prevention	[21, 24]
6	Recognize rather than remember	[21, 24]
7	Flexibility and efficiency of use	[21, 24]
8	Dialog aesthetics and minimalist design	[21, 24]
9	Supporting users in error recognition, diagnosis, and recovery	[21, 24]
10	Promoting access to the social environment	[21, 24]
11	Provision of access to the natural environment	[21, 24]
12	Provision of access to the document environment	[25]
13	Management of attentional resources	[25, 26]
14	Management of attentional resources	[26]
15	Ease of learning	[25]
16	Processing capacity	[27]
17	Security	[25]
18	Capacity (Storage and memory)	[25, 28]
19	Performance	[25, 29]
20	General Guidelines	[30, 31]
21	Tabs	[32]
22	Slide menu	[25]
23	Compatibility	[25]
24	Icons	[33, 34]
25	Characters and scenarios	[35]
26	Information architecture evaluation	[35]
27	User location	[35]
28	Text justification	[35]
29	Colors	[21, 35]
30	Clean URLs	[36]
31	Logo placement	[36]
32	Neat and clean design	[36]

(*continued*)

Table 2. (*continued*)

ID	Name	Source
33	Content that looks like advertising	[36]
34	Child-friendly interaction styles	[35]
35	Thematic environment	[37–39]
36	Realistic mathematics	[37]
37	Interactivity	[39, 40]
38	Think like a child	Survey
39	Competitiveness	Survey
40	Encourages creativity	Survey
41	Thematic scope	Survey
42	User needs	[36]
43	Constant evaluation	[36]
44	Code quality	[36]
45	Mandatory fields	[36]
46	Controller model-view architecture	[36]
47	communication with device-specific aspects	[36]
48	Publishing	[25]
49	Proper use of white space	[25]
50	Horizontal scrolling	[36]
51	Style sheets for different formats	[36]
52	Dynamic data validation	[36]
53	Pop-up windows	[36]
54	Examples in form fields	[36]
55	Confirmation pages	[36]
56	Broken links	[36]

between 6 and 7 years old, taking advantage of the resources provided by mobile devices (interactivity, sound, interaction capacity, simplicity, multi-functions, motivation, gamification, processing, among others) to achieve its final objective. Satisfaction: The degree to which a user of the interactive mobile application (child between 6–7 years old) has positive attitudes, acceptability, or appreciation towards its use, in addition to the degree of ease of use presented by users at the time of use.

Once the usability factors were defined and grounded in the context, a classification was made according to the three factors as shown in the following table, in this work only the classification for the effectiveness factor is shown, see Table 3.

Table 3. Classification of guidelines considering effectiveness

Standard 9241-11 Effectiveness factor classification	
Id	Guideline name
1	Visibility of the system state
2	Correspondence between the system and the real world
3	Control and freedom for the user
9	Assisting users in diagnostic recognition and error recovery
11	Provision of access to the natural environment
14	Motivational resource management
15	Ease of learning
18	Ability
19	Performance
21	TABS
23	Compatibility
25	Characters and scenarios
29	Colors
34	Interaction styles suitable for children
36	Realistic mathematics
37	Interactivity
38	Think like a child
39	Competitiveness
40	Encourage creativity
42	User needs
43	Constant evaluation
57	Estimated time

Inclusion and Exclusion Criteria

Once the classification process was done and considering what was analyzed in the literature, the usability standard, and the experience, inclusion and exclusion criteria were created to filter and discard the guidelines that do not provide usability or do not apply directly to the mobile context as for learning mathematics, the criteria are shown below:

Criteria for inclusion of guidelines.

1. Does the guideline comply with the user-centered development?
2. Does the guideline provide functionality to the application?
3. Is the guideline adaptable to mobile design?

Exclusion criteria for guidelines.

1. Does the guideline does not comply with user-centered development?
2. Does the guideline does not bring functionality to the application?
3. Is the guideline not adaptable to mobile design?

Applying the above criteria, the guidelines shown in Table 4 were discarded, which shows the justification for their elimination.

Table 4. Guidelines that do not meet the criteria

Id	Guideline name	Guidelines that do not meet the criteria
		Justification
12	Provision of access to the document environment	Since it is an application for children, having a lot of information would saturate the application, which decreases satisfaction, effectiveness and efficiency
19	Performance	It is more focused on applications dedicated to high server consumption
22	Slide Menu	For our environment the slide menu is not used, so this guideline does not provide efficiency, effectiveness or satisfaction
26	Architecture evaluation	This guideline applies more to web page environments
27	User location	The guideline applies more to website URLs
28	Justification text	This guideline is more focused on text-intensive applications
30	Clean URLs	It contributes more to website design, not mobile application design
31	Logo location	It does not directly contribute to efficiency, effectiveness, or satisfaction
32	Neat and clean design	Focused for web pages, which consist of an infrastructure that must be complied with, it is not mobile oriented
33	Content that looks like advertising	There will be no content that looks like advertising
35	Thematic environment	Joined with the characters and scenery guideline
44	Code quality	Who decides what methodology or what type of coding will be the developer, so it does not provide or cannot say how it is the right way

(continued)

Table 4. (*continued*)

Id	Guideline name	Guidelines that do not meet the criteria
		Justification
46	Architecture of model view controller	This part is more of a development methodology than a guideline
49	Proper use of white space	Mobile applications or games are not relevant to handle white space, since they are more compact applications
50	Horizontal displacement	This guideline is intended for websites which require vertical scrolling
51	Style sheets for different formats	Applicable guidelines for web sites
54	Examples in form fields	Since it is an application for children, it will not have forms that are annoying or boring for them
56	Broken links	This guideline applies to websites

Once the entire process was completed, a second version of the guidelines was obtained, with which a series of validations and refinements were made, which are shown as part of the validation cycle.

3.3 Validation Cycle

To validate the second version of the guidelines obtained in the previous chapter, a series of tests were generated, including a proof of concept, an evaluation with experts and a case study.

Proof of Concept (PoC)
Objective of the proof of concept: to know the problems that may arise when using the guidelines and to verify if the guidelines really contribute and guide the user when designing an interactive mobile interface for learning mathematics in children between 6–7 years old. *Context:* it was decided to generate a series of mockups considering the usability guidelines. This validation was carried out by the members of the research team, who developed two prototypes. *Execution:* In the execution two prototypes were developed, in the development of prototype A was invested between 2 to 3 h and for the development of prototype B, 1 h. Some shortcomings were found in this process. In order to analyze and solve these shortcomings, a meeting was held with the team involved, which resulted in the following considerations:

- The material lacks ease of use since there are no guidelines to indicate the order of the guidelines or where to start using them.
- Some guidelines could complement each other, since there are some that were similar and therefore there is a repetition of information

Results of the Concept Test: From this test, the first measure obtained was the need to create a support guide for the management of the guidelines, which provides a series of steps and recommendations on how to apply the guidelines, for which it was considered that the guide should have a flow chart that would also support the management of the guidelines, in order to facilitate their use and provide a step-by-step textual and visual aid. In addition, the concept-to test identified the need to factor and refine the guidelines in order to solve the problem of repetition of information.

Expert Evaluation

The expert evaluation was carried out in order to obtain input, opinions and different points of view from experts in the area of usability to serve as a refinement mechanism and thus have a stable and reliable improved version. Objective: To validate with usability experts the completeness, suitability, ease of use and ease of learning of the guidelines and the guide. Context: The validation was carried out by means of questions addressed to six usability experts, in order to listen to suggestions that could be considered in subsequent versions of the guidelines. 66.7% of the experts have more than 5 years of experience in usability and 33.3% have between 3–5 years of experience. The survey was based on the Likert scale [41], and the questions were categorized according to the following variables: completeness, suitability, ease of use, ease of learning. Each of the experts was given the user's guide, the flow of use and the compendium of guidelines, as well as the link to the survey for validation. The results obtained from the expert evaluation are summarized in the following conclusions.

4 Conclusions

- According to the perception of the experts, it can be stated that more than 80% of the respondents agree that the guidelines have the necessary elements to be easy to learn.
- According to the perception of the experts, it can be concluded that the guidelines do not contain the necessary elements to affirm that they are easy to use, given that more than 50% neither agree nor disagree.
- According to the perception of the experts, it can be concluded that the guidelines contain the necessary elements to affirm that they are complete, since more than 80% of the respondents agree.
- According to the perception of the experts, it can be concluded that the guidelines do not contain the necessary elements to affirm that they are suitable, given that only 50% of the respondents agree with this statement.
- According to the perception of the experts it can be concluded that the guidelines contain the necessary elements to affirm that they are easy to learn, given that more than 80% of the respondents agree with this statement.
- According to the perception of the experts, it can be concluded that the guide contains the necessary elements to affirm that it is complete, given that more than 80% of the respondents agree.
- The guide contributes optimally and positively to the ease of use of the guidelines, but there are also points to improve, such as the organization to provide a better experience.

- The evaluation and interaction with experts in usability helped to positively improve the design of these, since they provided points of view that had not been considered, this experience provides greater feedback and improvement because the experts were willing to collaborate in different aspects.

According to the results and opinions of the experts, the following changes were made:

- Guideline No. 42 is merged with guideline No. 25, since they complement each other, thus making No. 25 complete.
- Guideline N°34 is eliminated, since it was repetitive with guideline N°38, which is more complete.
- Guideline N°41 thematic scope is reformed, since its structure was poorly focused and was more a definition of the context to be addressed than a guideline on how to define the thematic scope.
- A correction was made in the way the guidelines were written, most of the descriptions were changed since they were not very complete and clear.
- The application steps of the guidelines were completely reformed since it was one of the major shortcomings of the list of guidelines, they were organized by numbers to facilitate their application according to how they are listed.
- The steps that were mandatory and those that could be optional were placed, and their wording was improved since observations were made on the content of the description of the step.
- The guidelines were ordered with their id according to the proposed guide for their use in this way they are ordered and easier to use.
- The guidelines were classified into mandatory and alternative guidelines in order to provide flexibility in their use.
- The examples were adjusted to the specific context proposed, described in more detail and thus provide better guidance to the developer.
- The guide was supplemented so that each heading of the guideline explained in a general way about its content. In addition, the structure of the guide was organized by steps for a better description.

According to the results and changes considered in the expert evaluation, version three of the guidelines and its respective guide was generated. In addition, it was decided that in order to facilitate the use and understanding of the guidelines, a light version will be created, which only has the id, name and description of the guideline, so that there is a simple, more reduced, easy to use and understand version.

Case Study

The usability guidelines and their application guide were tested in the development of a case study, which allowed us to inquire their applicability.

Case Study Question: Based on the research question of the project, it was necessary to evaluate the applicability of the guidelines to ensure usability in the design of interactive mobile applications for learning mathematics in children between 6 and 7 years old.

Therefore, the question for the defined case study was: *is the support for the design of interactive mobile applications for learning mathematics in children between 6 and 7 years old, through the application of the usability guidelines and its respective guide, useful, easy to use and complete? Objective of the case study:* The objective of the case study was to verify that both the usability guidelines and the guide for their use were useful, easy to use and complete for the context they were developed. *Selection of the case study:* The practice of process definition, observation and execution of the case study is developed by the researchers, which consisted of evaluating the usefulness, ease of use and completeness of the proposal. The primary source of information is those responsible for applying the guidelines with the interest of ensuring usability in the final product, the case study is holistic type considering a unit of analysis with a research subject, the activity of using the guidelines and its guide was selected to emulate a real case in the development of mobile applications. *Context of the case study:* The development of the case study was conducted with a group of 15 students in their last semester of the systems engineering program at the Corporación Universitaria COMFACAUCA - Unicomfacauca. It is important to emphasize that the group that participated in the case study were students taking the elective in human computer interaction. *Planning of activities:* Table 5 shows a summary of the activities designed for the development of the case study and specifies the planned duration of the activities and the support instruments that were used for their development.

Table 5. Case study planning

Activity	Resources	Time
Introduction of the project and the practice to be performed	Power-Point Presentation	15 min
Contextualization on the use of the guidelines and their respective support provided by the guide	Power-Point Presentation	20 min
Questions and comments		10 min
Rest		20 min
Case study development	Case study execution guide document, requirements document, usability guidelines, mockup development sheets	2 horas
Survey application	Physical survey	20 min

Evaluation Instrument: For the evaluation of the case study different instruments were used, which are presented below:

- Survey: Establishes a communication between the researchers and the study subjects in order to obtain data in writing and thus know the states of opinion, characteristics or specific facts, which are related to the case study.

- Prototypes: Specification in mockups of the functionality of the outcome of the case study.

Observation Protocol: Through this method, an attempt was made to establish a concrete and intensive relationship between the researchers and the case study participants. This protocol allowed the collection of data and information through observation presented in the case study. Indicators and metrics: in order to objectively evaluate the case study and answer the question formulated, it was necessary to define a set of metrics and indicators, which are described in Table 6 below.

Table 6. Indicators and metrics

Case study question	Indicator	Metrics	Instrument
Is the support for the design of interactive mobile applications for mathematics learning in children between 6 and 7 years old, through the application of the usability guidelines and their respective guide, useful, easy to use and complete?	Utility	The perception of usefulness of the guidelines and their guide for the design of interactive mobile applications for learning mathematics in children between 6 and 7 years old, by the group of students	Survey
	Ease of use	The perception of the ease of use of the guidelines and their guide for the design of interactive mobile applications for learning mathematics in children between 6 and 7 years old, by the group of students	Survey
	Completeness	Perception of completeness of the guidelines and their guidance for the design of interactive mobile applications for mathematics learning in children between 6 and 7 years old, by the group of students	Survey

The detailed description of the indicators and how they are calculated through the identified metrics is as follows:

Usefulness: This is defined as the degree of usefulness that a person perceives of the guidelines and the defined guide. This variable represents a useful perceptual judgment of the proposal. The guidelines that have been established to determine usefulness are:

- The average degree of usefulness of the guidelines and the guide obtained from the students' perception that is between 1 and 5 (5 being the highest degree of usefulness) must be equal to or higher than 80%

Ease of Use: IT is defined as the degree of ease with which the person can understand the guidelines with their respective guide, this represents a judgment of perception of the effort required to understand what is proposed. The guidelines that have been established to determine the ease of use are:

- The average degree of Ease of use of the guidelines and the guide obtained from the students' perception that is between 1 and 5 (5 being the highest degree of ease of use) must be equal to or higher than 80%.

Completeness: This is defined as the degree to which a person perceives that the guidelines and their respective guide contain the necessary elements to be described. The guidelines that have been established to determine ease of use are:

- The average degree of completeness of the guidelines and the guide obtained from the students' perception that is between 1 and 5 (5 being the highest degree of completeness) must be equal to or higher than 80%.

Execution of the Case Study: For the execution of the case study, it was decided to apply the usability guidelines and their respective guide individually, while a group of student's design mobile interfaces for learning mathematics, in order to analyze the pros and cons found by the end users in the guidelines. The students were asked to make a prototype with the necessary interfaces to meet a specific requirement, which was the following: *"A school located in the city of Popayán, is looking for a group of developers in order to make a mobile application that provides support or help for math class, since it is one of the classes in which there is some difficulty in learning in students, teachers say that the difficulties occur in addition and subtraction so the application will be focused on these issues, the application seeks to motivate and encourage students for their progress in the app, teaching in a fun, didactic and creative way, the interface should be friendly and simple since this will be directed to children of 6 and 7 years old which have basic knowledge in reading and identification of numbers, the school wants to know the idea of the developers before selecting a final development so it is requested to make the Mockups corresponding to the app that will be offered to the institution".*

The development of the case study was carried out according to plan, but it is important to highlight that the time of some of the activities was exceeded.

Conclusions of the case study:

- According to the perception of the students it can be concluded that 86% agreed on the usefulness of the guidelines in the activity.
- According to the perception of the students 86% agreed on the completeness of the guidelines, therefore, it is affirmed that the guidelines are complete.
- According to the students' perception, 92% approve of the ease of use of the guidelines, largely because of the examples stipulated in the format, since these give a clearer vision of what is intended to be understood and expressed with the guidelines.
- According to the perception of the students, it can be concluded that 96% agreed with the usefulness of the guide, since it complements the list of guidelines.

- According to the perception of the students, 86% agreed with the completeness of the guide since it facilitates the understanding and gives a brief description of the guidelines, therefore the application and justification of the order of the guidelines is understood.
- According to the perception of the students, more than 96% agreed with the ease of use of the guide since it provided the guidelines, steps to follow and the terms used in the guide were adequate.
- It can be concluded that the purpose of the guidelines is fulfilled given that despite the fact that each of the attendees had a different idea, the usability guidelines were applied in the same way in their Mockups.
- From the development of the case study a positive response was obtained from the students, they were satisfied with the use of the guidelines in the development of their Mockups, there were no problems and they felt correctly instructed by the guide, finally, they stated that the guidelines really provide a support to develop interactive mobile applications with usability elements, in the learning of children between 6 and 7 years old.
- It was noted that the students did not necessarily read all the information to understand and apply the guidelines; in some cases, they only relied on the examples to understand them.
- It was noted that the graphic that contains the guide to explain how to use the guidelines was omitted in the development of the activity.
- Some students were confused at the beginning of the activity because they thought that the guidelines provided the idea to be developed, when in fact the objective of the guidelines is to guide an idea with concepts that provide usability.

From the results and opinions of the students, the following changes were made:

- Guideline N°10 lacks an example to better understand its application.
- Guideline N°4 has an example, but it does not have a guiding image alluding to what is being said.
- It was suggested to change the name of step 2 of the guide (refine) to a synonym or a more technical term.

Conclusions

This paper presents the process of construction of usability guidelines for the design of interfaces in interactive mobile applications in the context of mathematics learning in children between 6–7 years old, which were built from a constant validation that was performed in several phases, the first was to check if the content of the guidelines were framed in the concept of usability proposed by the categories of the ISO 9241–11 standard, In the next phase, a proof of concept was evaluated, which allowed to analyze missing elements when applying the guidelines and difficulties that arose in this process, which generated a new version of the guidelines and the creation of a guide to help with the use of these guidelines to generate an order of application, With these elements in a third phase, their completeness, suitability, ease of use and ease of learning were evaluated by usability experts, who gave their points of view and it was obtained that the guidelines were easy to learn, complete, but they were difficult to use and suitable in the context, on the other hand, the guide contains what is necessary to be easy to use, complete and easy to learn, With these results the guide and the guidelines were refined, which were finally validated through a case study, which sought to analyze their usefulness, ease of use and completeness through the development of a prototype of an interactive mobile application, developed by a group of students using this proposal, where it was obtained that the guidelines are complete, useful and easy to use on the other hand the guide is also easy to use, useful and complete.

References

1. Abud, M.: Calidad en la industria del software. Norma ISO-25000 (2012)
2. Carvajal, M., Saab, J.: Lineamientos y metodologias en Usabilidad para el gobierno en línea (2010)
3. Oneto, F., Diaz, V.: Usabilidad producto para las necesidades de los usuarios (2014)
4. S. Engineering: Software product Quality Requirements and Evaluation (2008)
5. ISO 25000: [En línea]. Available. https://iso25000.com/index.php/normas-iso-25000/iso-25012. Último Acceso 21 Mayo 2019
6. León, A.V.L.: Diseño de interfaces de Usuario como apoyo a las estrategias de diseño de interfaces de usuario como apoyo a las estrategias de aprendizaje (2009)
7. Enriquez, J.G., Casas, S.I.: Usabilidad en aplicaciones móviles. Tecnicos UNPA (2018)
8. Collazos Ordóñez, C.A., Arciniegas Herrera, J.L., Mondragón, V.M., Garcia Peñeda, X.: Lineamientos de usabilidad para el diseño y evaluacion de la television digital interactiva. Avances en Sistemas e Informática, pp. 213–218 (2008)
9. Castillo Bautista, R., Bautista Alvarado, S.D., Juarez Anguiano, A.: Usabilidad para sitios Web educativos. Revista académica ISEG (2006)
10. Ruiz, A., Cortés, A.D., Gómez, J.I.: Lineamientos para el desarrollo de herramientas educativas interactivas para la estimulación temprana a nivel psicomotriz en niños de 3 a 5 años de edad validados a través de un prototipo experimental. Ing. Compet. **16**(1), 283–293 (2014)
11. Videla Rodriguez, J.J., Sanjuan Perez, A., Martinez Costa, S., Seoane Nolasco, A.: Diseño y usabilidad de interfaces para entornos educativos de realidad aumentada. Digital Education Review, 61–79 (2017)
12. Tello Valle, J.A., Yautibug Apugllón, M.E.: Implementación de Mejores Prácticas de Usabilidad en el Diseño de la Interfaz del Entorno Virtual de Aprendizaje de la Universidadd Nacional de Chimborazo. Universidad Nacional de Chimborazo, Riobamba (2018)
13. Ocsa, A., Herrera, J., Villalba, K., Suero, G.: Propuesta para el diseño y desarrollo de aplicaciones M-Learning: caso, apps de historia del Perú como objetos de aprendizaje móviles. Nuevas Ideas en Informática Educativa 873–878 (2014)
14. Wenjun, H., Xiudong, B.: HCI in real-time strategy games: a study of principals and guidelines for designing 3D user interface. In: de 7th International Conference on Computer-Aided industrial Design (2006)
15. Seraj, M., Wong, C.Y.: A study of user interface design principles and requirements for developing a mobile learning prototype. In: de 2012 International Conference on Computer & Information Science (ICCIS) (2012)
16. Aquino Acevedo, Z.A.: El aprendizaje de las Matematicas en Segundo Grado de Primaria por Medio de Dispositivos Móviles. Universidad Tecnológica de la Mixteca (2007)

17. Garcia Lucas, P., Gómez Pérez, V.A., Benítez Hernández, A., Cruz Ahuactzi, J.: Propuesta de desarrollo de una aplicación móvil interactiva para apoyar el aprendizaje en educación básica: Historia De México, Una Necesidad. Pistas Educativas 268–284 (2016)
18. Lencinas, V., et al.: Investigacion-accion: una oportunidad para generar conocimiento desde la práctica profesional de bibliotecatios y archiveros. Cordoba (2017)
19. Gil, E.P., Tatjer, E.d.L., Monjo Palau, A.: Usuarios y sistemas interactivos. Universitat Oberta de Catalunya (2018)
20. R.P.: Los niños ya son adddictos al contenido móvil y esta mas expuestos a la publicidad que nunca (2017)
21. Nilsen J., *Usability Engineering,* Morgan Kaufmann Publishers INC, 1993
22. Ramírez, Y., Arturo, C., Luna, O., Enrique, J.: Medición de la usabilidad en el desarrollo de palicaciones educativas móviles. Revista Virtual Universidad Católica del Norte (2016)
23. Aziz, N.A.A.: Children interacts with Tablet Applications Gestures and Interface Design (2013)
24. Cáceres, J.: Heurísticas de Nielsen. . [En línea]. Available: https://blooming-coast-9431.her okuapp.com/heuristics/1 (2015). Último Acceso 15 Ago 2019
25. Chacon, L.C.: Norma para el desarrollo de aplicaciones para dispositivos móviles en la universidad de costa rica, 2018
26. Leguízamo, L., A.V.: Diseño de interfaces de usuario como apoyo a las estrategias de diseño de interfaces de usuario como apoyo a las estrategias de aprendizaje (2009)
27. Google: Android Developers. [En línea]. Available: https://developer.android.com/topic/per formance/memory. Último Acceso 19 Ago 2019
28. Smartface: Smartface. [En línea]. Available: https://smartface.io/smartface-memory-manage ment/. Último Acceso 19 ago 2019
29. Nielsen, J.: Website response times. 21 06 2010. [En línea]. Available: https://www.nngroup. com/articles/website-response-times/. Último Acceso 19 ago 2019
30. Gay, P.: Best practices for designing mobile applications. Growth from Knwledge, 26 08 2009. [En línea]. Available: https://blog.gfk.com/2009/08/best-practices-for-designing-mob ile-applications/. Último Acceso 2019 ago 20
31. Cerejo, L.: The elements of the mobile user experience. Smashing Magazine, 12 07 2012. [En línea]. Available: https://www.smashingmagazine.com/2012/07/elements-mobile-user-experience/. Último Acceso 20 ago 2019
32. Foro: Iphone side navigation vs. Tab bar Navigation. 22 10 2013. [En línea]. Available: https://ux.stackexchange.com/questions/40204/iphone-side-navigation-vs-tab-bar-nav igation. Último Acceso 21 ago 2019
33. Sasa, W., Aguilar, E.: Manual de Indentidad Visual. Costa Rica, San Jose (2015)
34. Flarup, M.: Designing android product icons. 2 07 2015. [En línea]. Available: https://applyp ixels.com/. Último Acceso 21 ago 2019
35. Carrera Díaz, M. : Lineamientos para el diseño de un sitio web de interés educativo dirigido a niños (2005)
36. Carvajal, M., Saab, J., Lineamientos y metodologias en usabilidad para el gobierno en línea (2010)
37. Villa Ochoa, J.A., Ruiz Vahos, H.M.: Modelación en educación matemática: una mirada desde los lineamientos y estándares curriculares colombianos. Revista Virtual Universidad Católica del Norte (2009)
38. Ausubel, D., Novak, J., Hanesian, H.: Psicología Educativa. Un Punto de Vista Cognoscitivo, Trillas (1998)
39. U. d. l. Andes, *Matemática interactiva: ¿Otra forma de enseñar la matemática?,* Mérida, 2003
40. Starico, M., Los proyectos en el aula. hacia un aprendizaje significativo en una escuela para la diversidad (1999)
41. Joshi, A., Kale, S., Chandel, S., Pal, D.K.: Likert scale: explored and explained. Br. J. Appl. Sci. Technol. **7**(4), 396–403 (2015)

Building Shared Understanding
with THUNDERS

Vanessa Agredo-Delgado[1,2](✉) ⓘ, Pablo H. Ruiz[1,2] ⓘ, and Cesar A. Collazos[2] ⓘ

[1] Corporación Universitaria Comfacauca – Unicomfacauca, Street 4 #8-30, Popayán, Colombia
{vagredo,pruiz}@unicomfacauca.edu.co
[2] Universidad del Cauca, Street 5 #4-70, Popayán, Colombia
ccollazo@unicauca.edu.co

Abstract. Collaborative work focuses on the interaction between a group of participants and the corresponding search to achieve a better-shared understanding of a problem, while they perform common tasks cooperating towards the achievement of the same objective. In this search for shared understanding, the differences in the experiences, knowledge, and other characteristics of the participants, make it complex to consider all opinions, points of view and also, that everyone understands and agrees with the topic of the activity and with the central idea of what is going to be solved. While trying to tackle these problematics, we defined THUNDERS, a process for building shared understanding in problem-solving activities. This work presents THUNDERS process as well as the quality validation of its process model SPEM 2.0, and an experiment with which its viability and usefulness was validated. The THUNDERS process enables to design, execute, and verify collaborative activities by using a set of phases, activities, tasks, work products, roles, and workflows in a planned way. The multi-cycle action-research methodology with bifurcation was used in the construction of the process. According to the results of the validations, it can be said that THUNDERS is feasible and useful for the building of shared understanding. However, some aspects to be improved were identified, such as the cognitive overload generated by its use and some elements of its formalization in SPEM; likewise, the need to incorporate mechanisms to monitor and assist the permanence of understanding throughout the execution of the activity was identified.

Keywords: Computer supported collaborative work · Shared understanding · Problem-solving activity · Validation process

1 Introduction

The collaborative work (CW) according to [1] is "a web of coordinated actions, performed by the participants to achieve a joint outcome". In this sense, the interaction will allow true collaborative work to arise, and this will encourage the efforts of the group members to bear fruit, facilitating the success of each member to achieve the common goal [2]. This is where the importance of a quality dialogue (active listening and participation) is essential for the interaction in order to encourage understanding

V. Agredo-Delgado et al. (Eds.): HCI-COLLAB 2022, CCIS 1707, pp. 68–87, 2022.
https://doi.org/10.1007/978-3-031-24709-5_6

among the participants and therefore, the collaborative work [3]. This dialogue must go beyond by simply exchanging meanings since a true dialogue promotes active listening skills (listening carefully to others and giving feedback), generate empathy, that is, put yourself in somebody else's place, be motivated, understand and inquire on what is being communicated, respond with the appropriate words, understand and make others understand what to do and how to apply the topic of the activity [4].

One way to achieve this quality dialogue, is to seek the achievement of shared understanding among the participants of the collaborative activity, that is, to achieve a stage in which people concur on topics, the interpretation of the concepts, so that the group members may share a perspective (mutual agreement) or act in a coordinated manner [5]. The shared understanding is a cognitive process, which is known that its existence in the collaborative work process among all involved actors it is one requirement for its successful implementation [6, 7]. Also, this is a collective way of organizing the relevant knowledge and might have a significant impact on the ability of teams in order to coordinate work by improving its implementation and increase the team members' motivation [8]. However, it can be difficult to achieve, because, in this dialogue among the participants, there are either lack of experience or different experiences, differences in knowledge, variety of contexts, and the actors' language [9]. In addition, the complexity of considering all opinions, points of view, and also, that everyone understands and agrees with the topic of the activity and with the main idea of what is going to be solved [10]. For these reasons, this paper presents THUNDERS (collaboraTive work through sHared UNDErstanding in pRoblems-solving activitieS) process definition as well as the quality validation of its process model SPEM 2.0 [11] by using the AVISPA visual analysis method [12]. Furthermore, an experiment is shown where both its viability and usefulness are validated. The THUNDERS process enables to design, execute, and verify collaborative activities by using a set of phases, activities, tasks, work products, roles, and workflows in a planned way. The multi-cycle action-research methodology with bifurcation [13] was used in the construction of the process. According to the results of the validations, it can be said that THUNDERS is feasible and useful for the building of shared understanding. However, some aspects to improve were identified, such as: the cognitive overload generated by its use and some elements of its formalization in SPEM; likewise, the need to incorporate mechanisms to monitor and assist the permanence of understanding throughout the execution of the activity was identified.

This paper is structured as follows: Sect. 2 contains related works. Section 3 contains the methodology to define the process proposal. Section 4 has conclusions and future work.

2   Related Works

2.1   Shared Understanding

Most research have focused on the shared understanding measurement, but not on how we can construct it [14, 15]. Below, some research about shared understanding measurement are presented: Smart [16] used a cultural model, where the nodes of the model represent concepts and their links reflect the ideas of each group member. Similarly, Rosenman et al. [17] worked with interprofessional emergency medical teams, where they measure the shared understanding through team perception and a team leader effectiveness measurement. On the other hand, White et al. [18], describe a range of techniques, the use of concept maps, relational diagrams, and word association tests by adopting them for specific application contexts that might obtain measurements of understanding so they may be compared across multiple individuals. Sieck, et al. [19] determined that the similarity of mental models might provide a shared understanding measurement. Bates et al. [20] developed and validated the Patient-Knowledge-Assessment tool questionnaire that measured a shared clinical understanding of pediatric cardiology patients.

2.2 Shared Understanding in Empirical Studies

As part of the developed work in [21], an empirical study is shown where both group learning and shared understanding are explored in a globally distributed engineering team. In [22], has the purpose to research the role that plays an organizational structure with communication responsibilities and a Knowledge Management practice, in the shared understanding of the requirements in Global Software Development. A controlled experiment was conducted in an academic setting where it revealed that this kind of organizational structure helps improve the shared understanding. In [23], it is addressed how the distribution of the team influences the success of projects by using a shared understanding approach, and an empirical study is carried out in a software product development company. Dossick et al. in [24], show the first findings of an empirical study that seeks to explore the use of Photo Elicitation techniques in combination with Ethnography to assess the amount of shared understanding in multidisciplinary teams working on a building design project. An experiment with students and a pilot field study with practitioners using a content validity survey instrument to measure shared understanding in the IT business are shown in [25].

Previous works show different methods for measuring shared understanding and empirical studies that explore its achievement, but none is related to build it in collaborative activities, in such a way that they do not guide its materialization. That is why in this work, the proposed process supports this construction.

3   Methodology

The research shown in this paper was developed following the multi-cycle action-research methodology with bifurcation [13]. This methodology allows to management and development of research projects based on various research cycles that address different problems that arise throughout the development of the project:

3.1 Conceptual Cycle

This cycle consisted of a conceptual analysis, where the problem is initially identified, determining that one of the main collaborative work problems is that collaboration success is hard to achieve [26]. At the same time, Rummel and Spada [27] argue that collaboration does not occur as easily as it may be expected. Therefore, there is a need to find a way to promote it. According to this, a review and literature analysis was carried out, which is briefly shown in this paper. The review was aimed to identify the existing elements in the literature that could be included in the THUNDERS process definition. In addition to keeping in mind the needs of the context of collaborative problem-solving activities, computer-supported collaborative work, and heterogeneous groups.

Literature Review. The review sought to characterize and identify the different existing approaches (process, activities, phases or steps, techniques, and strategies) that allowed the THUNDERS definition according to the literature.

The literature review work was addressed through the next research questions:

- What approaches have been used to execute computer-supported collaborative work?
- Do the approaches consider the shared understanding construction in their definitions?
- Do the approaches use any formal measurements to validate shared understanding?

The data sources that were used for literature review development are: IEEE Computer Society Digital Library and Scopus. In the search strategy, the keywords were identified with their respective synonyms, and through the combination of these keywords and their association, the search string was developed.

To make the study selection, a set of inclusion and exclusion criteria that allowed us to verify their quality and guarantee that they were studies related to the computer-supported collaborative work were defined.

Then, the identification and selection of the primary studies were based on two main steps:

Step 1: Consisted of applying on each of the data sources the search string; in this way, we obtained for IEEE = 10 papers and for Scopus 263 papers. In this step, we also carried out a debugging process of the recovered studies, which consisted of identifying the studies that were repeated and others that we consider as useless.

Step 2: In order to reduce the application subjectivity of the inclusion and exclusion criteria, several researchers participated in this step (Two from the Universidad de la Plata and one from the Universidad del Cauca). In the first iteration of this step, the criteria application was done by reading the paper title, abstract, keywords, and conclusions. In this process, each researcher reads these sections, and in the end, a meeting where each researcher presented their results was held, and in those papers that did not have the same classification to include or exclude it, the reasons for the made decision were presented, and later among all the participants, a consensus was reached. As a first iteration result, 30 papers were gathered as possible primary studies. In the second iteration, the criteria were applied by reading the full content of those 30 papers. In this iteration, the same review dynamic was maintained by the authors as in the first iteration, and as the result was obtained a set of 12 papers were classified as primary studies.

From all this process, it was evidenced that in most of the found literature there is no complete approach that ranges from the design of the activity to the complete verification of compliance with it. In addition to not considering shared understanding, as a strategy to improve collaboration, an aspect that will be considered in this work, is what and *how* to achieve it. With these 12 primary papers, it was possible to identify elements that served as the basis for the creation of the THUNDERS process here proposed.

3.2 Methodological Cycle

According to Bittner and Leimeister [28], it is determined that little is known about what leads to shared understanding, besides that the actors need guidance on how to evoke processes deliberately and repeatedly to achieve it. Considering the above, this work defines a process that can determine how to achieve a shared understanding. In this sense, this cycle consisted of the THUNDERS definition, where initially the components that would be part of the process were identified, starting from the analysis of the information previously obtained in the literature review. After this identification, a definition was made out of all the components that would make up the process, those obtained from the review and those that should be created- This, in order to create the initial version of THUNDERS, with phases, activities, tasks, steps, and work products that will allow to execute a collaborative work in problem solving activities seeking to achieve a shared understanding.

For this, this work is based on the concept of software process to determine the outcome of this research, a definition that refers to a sequence of steps arranged with some kind of logic that focuses on achieving some specific results [29]. With this, it is determined that the process obtained will be defined at a conceptual level, which will be an ordered set of methods and activities, tasks, practices, guidelines, strategies, rules, steps, roles, inputs, and outputs.

In order to define this THUNDERS process, the collaboration engineering design approach is followed [30], which addresses the challenge of designing and deploying collaborative work practices for high-value recurring tasks and transferring them to practitioners to execute them by themselves without the ongoing support from a professional expert in collaboration [31]. To model THUNDERS, it is used SPEM 2.0 meta-molding (Software Process Engineering Meta-Model) [11]. The process concept will determine the context on which this research will be worked. This refers to small and heterogeneous groups, in addition to applying the process in problem-solving activities.

From this point of view, the objective is to address this challenge by providing a structured collaboration process based on theory-grounded-design guidelines that can be used to support heterogeneous groups to develop a shared understanding of a task. With this, it is intended to contribute to making the construction of shared understanding more predictable and manageable.

Process Formalization. According to the THUNDERS process, the computer-supported collaborative work is divided into 3 phases, Pre-Process, Process, and Post-Process, which were taken from Collazos' work [32], these phases were updated and adapted to collaborative work. The first Pre-Process phase begins with the specific design of the activity and the necessary elements to be carried out; in the Process phase, the collaboration activity is executed in order to achieve the objectives based on the interaction among group members and with necessary resources. In the end of the activity, in the Post-Process phase, the activity leader (the person in charge of guiding the activity) performs an individual and collective review to verify the achievement of the proposed objectives and the problem that was solved in the activity.

Pre-Process Phase. Each activity was assigned its respective description and workflow to achieve its objective. The following Table 1 shows the process elements of the Pre-process phase as activities, tasks, roles, and work products of inputs and outputs.

Table 1. Process elements of the Pre-Process phase

Activity	Role	Tasks	Inputs	Outputs
Define the population	Information collector	Determine grouping characteristics	–	Grouping characteristics to be considered
		Apply characterization mechanisms	Grouping characteristics to be considered	Results of analyzed characteristics in the participants
Define pre-conditions for group members	Information collector	Define prior knowledge	Grouping characteristics to be considered	List of previous knowledge
		Analyze the prior knowledge	List of participants	List of participants with their previous knowledge
			List of previous knowledge	
Design the roles	Activity designer	Determine the roles of the groups	–	List of roles to use
		Define responsibilities for each role	List of roles to use	Responsibilities for each role
		Assign roles to each participant	List of participants	List of each participant with their respective role
Decisions on the members grouping	Activity designer	Define the groups' information	List of each participant with their respective role	Groups' information
		Selection and distribution of the groups	List of each participant with their respective role	List of each group with its respective participants

(continued)

Table 1. (*continued*)

Activity	Role	Tasks	Inputs	Outputs
			Responsibilities for each role	
Determine and design problem-solving activity	Activity designer	Determine the topic of the activity	List of each group with its respective participants	Activity topic with its information
		Determine the problem of the activity	Activity topic with its information	Activity problem with its information
		Define activity information	Activity topic with its information	Activity information
			Activity problem with its information	
		Structure the tasks to be executed	Activity information	Specific tasks with their respective information
Define the objectives	Activity coordinator	Specify the activity objectives	Specific tasks with their respective information	List of objectives to be achieved in the activity
		Design a verification method of compliance	List of objectives to be achieved in the activity	Verification method of the objectives
Define success criteria	Activity coordinator	Define conditions, requirements or expected results	List of objectives to be achieved in the activity	List of activity success criteria
		Design a verification mechanism of compliance	List of objectives to be achieved in the activity	A mechanism to verify compliance with the success criteria
			List of activity success criteria	
Specify activity rules	Activity coordinator	Define activity restrictions	Activity problem with its information	List of activity rules

(*continued*)

Table 1. (*continued*)

Activity	Role	Tasks	Inputs	Outputs
			List of objectives to be achieved in the activity	
		Design the follow-up verification	List of activity rules	Rules verification mechanism
Selection and/or design of materials	Activity designer	Select the activity resources	Activity problem with its information	List of resources to use in the activity
		Design the resources to use	List of resources to use in the activity	Designed resources to be used
		Design the resource distribution strategy	List of resources to use in the activity	Specification of the resource distribution strategy
			List of each participant with their respective role	
Design the verification method of problem-solving	Activity designer	Define activity completion criteria	Specific tasks with their respective information	List of criteria for the completion of the activity
			List of objectives to be achieved in the activity	
		Define compliance criteria of the problem	Activity problem with its information	List of verification criteria for problem solution
		Design a mechanism to verify completion of the activity	List of criteria for the completion of the activity	A mechanism to verify the completion of the activity
		Design a mechanism to verify the solution of the problem	List of verification criteria for problem solution	A mechanism to verify the solution of the problem

Process Phase. This phase is where the collaborative work interactions take place and obtains shared understanding through different strategies. The following Table 2 shows the process elements of the Process phase.

Table 2. Information about the process activities

Activity	Role	Tasks	Inputs	Outputs
Organization	Activity organizer	Describe the activity	Activity information	–
		Group formation	List of each group with the respective participants	–
		Assignment roles	List of each participant with the respective role	–
		Material distribution	List of resources to use in the activity	–
			Specification of the resource distribution strategy	
Shared Understanding	Participants	Tacit Pre-Understanding	Activity problem with its information	Individual understandings
			Activity information	Individual questions about the activity
		The construction	Individual understandings	Individual questions or disagreements about others' understandings
		The Collaborative Construction	Individual questions or disagreements about others' understandings	Clarification of individual questions
				Classification of individual questions into conflictive and non-conflictive

(continued)

Table 2. (*continued*)

Activity	Role	Tasks	Inputs	Outputs
		The Constructive Conflict	Clarification of individual questions	Group's understandings
Collaborative activity	Participants	Start the collaborative activity	Group's understandings	–
		Selection of the solution to implement	Activity problem with its information	The chosen solution to the problem
		Implement the solution	The chosen solution to the problem	Step by step of the implemented solution
		Verify the solution	Step by step of the implemented solution	The solution applied in a scenario of the problem to be solved
Collaborative knowledge building	Participants	Concept artifact creation	Step by step of the implemented solution	Concept artifact created by group
				Questions about the conceptual artifact
		Debates generation	Questions about the conceptual artifact	Concept artifact with adjustments
		Presentation of the artifact	Concept artifact with adjustments	–

Considering the importance of the Shared Understanding activity, the tasks and steps that are part of its definition are detailed below. This activity seeks to have the group members agree on what the problem is in the collaborative activity; they must understand it before starting its development, this activity is formed by the *Tacit Pre Understanding* task which is, the people's ability to understand individual representations when they make use of them [33], The *Construction* task happens when one of the group members inserts meaning by describing the problematic situation and deals with it, hereby tuning in fellow teammates. These fellow teammates are actively listening and trying to grasp the given explanation [34], the *Collaborative Construction* task is a mutual task of building meaning by refining, building or modifying the original explanation [35], and finally, the *Constructive Conflict* task, which is where the differences of interpretation among the group members are treated through arguments and clarifications [5]. Considering these tasks, it is defined for each a series of steps that will allow to achieve the objectives (See Table 3).

Table 3. Steps of each task of the shared understanding activity

Task	Steps	Description
Tacit Pre-Understanding	1: Appropriation – Tacit Knowledge	Read the task individually
	2: Express – Explicit Knowledge	Members write what they understood
	3: Clarify Pre-Understanding	Each member writes questions
Construction	4: Construction of meaning	Share their individual understanding
	5: Listening to others	Listen to others' understanding
	6: Understanding others	Write the questions or disagreements about what you hear from others
Collaborative Construction	7: Clarifying different understandings	Each member asks clarification questions
	8: Identifying conflicts	Classify their own questions in conflicting and non-conflicting
Constructive Conflict	9: Solving conflicts	Discuss conflict differences until everyone agrees
	10: Group voting	Voting to agree with the shared description
	11: Expressing the shared understanding	The group writes a new understanding where everyone agrees

Post-Process Phase. The phase seeks to verify that the objectives proposed in the activity were achieved and if the problem was solved, in addition to verifying the participants' performance. The following Table 4 shows the process elements of the Post-Process phase.

Table 4. Information about the Post-Process activities

Activity	Role	Tasks	Inputs	Outputs
Review the success criteria	Activity leader	Measure each success criterion	List of activity success criteria	List of accomplished criteria
			List of verification criteria for problem solution	
			A mechanism to verify compliance with the success criteria	List of unaccomplished criteria
			A mechanism to verify the solution of the problem	
		Analysis of possible compliance with the criteria	List of accomplished criteria	Actions to fulfill the missing criteria
			List of unaccomplished criteria	
Verify compliance with the problem	Activity leader	Evaluate the achievement of objectives	List of criteria for the completion of the activity	List of achieved objectives
				List of unaccomplished objectives
			A mechanism to verify the completion of the activity	Actions to fulfill the missing objectives
		Evaluate the problem resolution	List of verification criteria for problem solution	Criteria list of the solution of the fulfilled problem
			A mechanism to verify the solution of the problem	Criteria list of the solution of the unfulfilled problem
			Step by step of the implemented solution	Actions to solve the problem properly

(*continued*)

Table 4. (*continued*)

Activity	Role	Tasks	Inputs	Outputs
Do performance evaluation	Activity leader	Evaluate individual performance	The solution applied in a scenario of the problem to be solved	Analysis of individual's performances
			Concept artifact with adjustments	
		Evaluate group performance	The solution applied in a scenario of the problem to be solved	Analysis of group's performances
			Concept artifact with adjustments	
End the collaborative activity	Activity coordinator	Give feedback on the activity	–	Information on the results obtained in the activity
		Close the activity	Information on the results obtained in the activity	Lessons learned from the participants

3.3 Evaluation Cycle

This cycle consisted of the evaluation of THUNDERS. This evaluation was divided into two parts, initially the quality of its SPEM 2.0 specification was validated using AVISPA, identifying some errors in the definition and formalization of the model, which were discussed and analyzed to determine the solutions that were incorporated from its design and formalization, after applying these improvements, it was inquired about the feasibility and utility of the proposed initial process for the shared understanding construction, through an experiment. It is important to clarify that before these two evaluations; the process was subjected to several reviews in which two members of the IDIS research group of the Universidad del Cauca and a member of the GIS group of the Universidad de la Matanza participated. Also, we created a focus group with two experts on group work and collaboration engineering to review the process, before they should be implemented in practice. The experiment is presented in a summary way in the following sections.

Validation of the THUNDERS Specification
In order to have a more reliable and valid version from the viewpoint of the formalization in SPEM 2.0 of THUNDERS process model, before its experimentation, an initial

assessment was executed where AVISPA-Method (Incremental method for visual analysis of process models) was used [12], which allows the assessment of the process models at a lower cost than its assessment in the real application. AVISPA-Method uses a tool for the analysis and Visualization for a Software Process Assessment called AVISPA [36] and defines the following set of activities to guide the assessment: a) To design the process model: a process model version (SPEM version) is designed and formalized. b) To export the process model: the process model SPEM version is exported to an XML version. c) To examine the process with AVISPA-Method: the process model (XML version) is loaded in the AVISPA tool. In each of the views generated in AVISPA and with the help of error patterns [12], potential problems, and opportunities for model improvement are identified and located. d) Analysis and results report: the identified problems in the process model are reviewed and discussed. This analysis requires reviewing the process model in its original format (SPEM version). In the end of the review, the real problems on the process model are identified, as well as the possible improvements to be made. e) Adjust: adjustments are made to the process model according to the errors and suggestions for identified improvement. In the following section, an analysis of the results obtained from applying the AVISPA-Method in the THUNDERS process model assessment is shown. The results are detailed from the three graphic views (tasks, roles, and work products) provided by AVISPA, each view deals with a particular aspect of the process model [37].

Task View of the THUNDERS Process Model. The task view provided by AVISPA shows the process from the perspective of the tasks performed during the execution of the process model. In this view, each rectangular node represents a specific task of the process and the attributes of each node provide information about the process that is being analyzed [37]. Figure 1, presents the results obtained when assessing THUNDERS regarding the tasks, which shows that several possible errors were found in the specification of the process model. According to the error pattern, independent sub-projects [12] groups of isolated nodes can be identified in the task view. In Fig. 1, it can be seen that there are two disconnected set of tasks (subgraphs at the top of the figure), which refers to the fact that these sets of tasks do not add value to the process objective and therefore they act in isolation and do not help achieve the objective of the process. The first set (task group in blue color) of disconnected tasks is formed by "Determining group's characteristics, Defining prior knowledge, Applying characterization mechanisms, and Analyzing the prior knowledge", and the second set (task group in yellow color) by the tasks that "Give feedback on the activity and Close the activity". Furthermore, in this view it can be seen that the tasks with the numbers 1, 2 correspond to Evaluate the problem resolution, and Evaluate the achievement of objectives, respectively. Taking into account that the width of the nodes represents the outputs produced by the tasks, in the specific case of tasks 1 and 2, their width exceeds the average with respect to the others, which allow to identify the possible existence of the error-pattern-multipurpose task, which refers to the fact that a task must focus on achieving a specific purpose, instead of generating work products that misled the task that is the basic work unit of the process.

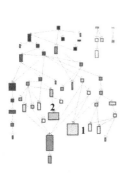

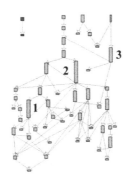

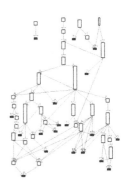

Fig. 1. Task view

Fig. 2. View about
over-demanded work products

Fig. 3. View about
unnecessary work products

Fig. 4. Roles's view

Work Products View. To verify the process model regarding the work products, AVISPA provides a view for this purpose, allowing to see over-demanded work products [12]. Figure 2, shows that the work products with the numbers 1, 2, and 3, correspond to the List of objectives to be achieved in the activity, Activity problem with its information, and the List of each participant with their respective role. Considering that, the height of the nodes represents that they are over-demanded products, that is, they are inputs to multiple tasks of the process. In this specific case, their height exceeds the average with respect to the others, which made it possible to identify the existence of the error pattern in over-demanded work products. Furthermore, in the upper part of Fig. 2., there is an isolated subgraph, formed by the set of work products in green color, Information on the results obtained in the activity and Lessons learned from the participants, this isolated graph allowed to identify the possible existence of the error pattern of independent subprojects. In Fig. 3, the nodes also represent a work product, but this view emphasizes on the nodes that may be useless, showing that the dark blue nodes identify the possible existence of the Waste work products pattern, that refers to work products that are neither deliverable nor input for any task.

ROLES'S View. In the view role, each node identifies a role and each of the lines among nodes specifies collaboration [37]. Figure 4 presents the obtained results when assessing THUNDERS with respect to their roles, where none of the nodes collaborates with the others, which allows to recognize the presence of the Isolated Role error pattern [12], since as far as possible it is necessary to define roles that collaborate with each other [38].

Validation of the THUNDERS Viability and Usefulness

To validate the THUNDERS viability and usefulness, an experiment that is presented in summary in the following section was carried out.

Experiment Context. The experiment was conducted in a university environment in which 45 last-semester students of Universidad de la Matanza – UM (Argentina) participated with a well level of experience in the activity topic, for this group the proposed process was applied. Moreover, 15 students of Universidad Nacional de la Plata – UP (Argentina), enrolled in the last year, participated with a well level of experience in the topic, to whom the proposed process was not applied. The groups were formed using a software tool called Collab [39] that analyzes the learning styles and organizes the group through a Genetic algorithm described in [40], where heterogeneous groups of 5 participants were formed and allowed learning styles to complement each other and thus obtain better results.

The problem-solving activity consisted of each group assuming that they were part of the engineering team process of a company, where they had to establish the software development processes that best adapted and supported the projects in the company. To solve the problem, they had to follow an execution guide called SpeTion-SPrl, where information about the projects and processes is defined, and with this, the scope could be determined.

Experiment Planning. The research question was defined as: how feasible and useful is this proposed process? This study had one analysis unity, which was the academic context, where a problem-solving activity about the Scope definition in Software Process line was carried out.

Hypothesis. Considering the objective, it is intended to evaluate the following hypotheses:

- The proposed initial process is feasible for the construction of shared understanding in a problem-solving activity
- The proposed initial process is useful to achieve the objectives of the problem-solving activity

Execution of the Experiment. The UM groups applied the entire process, while the UP groups simply met to develop the proposed activity. Therefore, the UM in the pre-process phase for each activity used a software tool MEPAC [41], which provided the step by step through forms, with the design and definition of necessary elements. The Process phase used a software tool collab [39] for group formation; also in this phase formats were used to write the individual's understanding about the problem, to write the questions or disagreements, to classify the understanding of the other members, to classify their own understanding, the group also wrote the understanding where everyone agreed the groups solved the problem and used a survey format with 24 questions to analyze the results.

The time used to apply the proposed process in UM was 3 h 55 min, and for the UP it was 2 h and 40 min.

Analysis Results

With the observation made by the researchers while the activity was being carried out, it was possible to determine that those groups that obtained poor results in the evaluations were those that did not perform well in the application of the process and did not generate internal discussions to resolve doubts. Therefore, it was observed that following the process was exhausting for the participants and that this generated a lack of commitment to the rest of the activity and a high cognitive load. On the other hand, to guarantee that the found results are not only observational and apparent but statistically significant, the student's t-distribution was used [42], which allowed to validate the hypotheses (The details of the results obtained in the validation can be seen in [43]). With this statistical analysis, and all the specific alternative accepted hypotheses, it can be determined that the process is feasible for shared understanding to be built. In addition, with 3 out of 4 specific alternative accepted hypotheses, it can be determined that THUNDERS is useful to achieve the objectives of the problem-solving activity.

With the statistical comparison of the results with the use of the process and without its use, it was verified that the THUNDERS process improves the participants' individual understanding enhances the group's understanding and generates a homogeneous understanding of the activity, it does not generate a discrepancy of each participant regarding the group understanding, the shared understanding activities generated better results and were better fulfilled among the participants. Also, it was determined that the use of THUNDERS process generates final products with better quality levels. THUN-DERS allowed to obtain better achievement participants' satisfaction with the objectives proposed by the activity. Conversely, it cannot be determined that the THUNDERS elements are satisfactory for the participants and in the same way, with the outcomes of the activity.

4   Conclusions and Future Work

This paper presents the first version of the THUNDERS process for the shared understanding construction of problem-solving activities, which was constructed from elements found in the literature review, and the analysis of the context and its needs.

THUNDERS was validated in two parts, in the first one, the quality of its SPEM 2.0 specification was validated using AVISPA, this validation allowed to identify of some error patterns in the definition and formalization of the model, which were discussed and analyzed to determine solutions that were incorporated from its design and formalization. This validation made possible direct efforts improve the definition of THUNDERS and thus have a more stable and validated version, from the point of view of its formalization. In the second part of its validation, an experiment was carried out to inquire about the viability and usefulness of the proposed process for the construction of shared understanding. The results obtained in the experiment from the statistical analysis allowed us to conclude that THUNDERS is a feasible process for shared understanding construction and useful to achieve its objectives. However, according to the specific null hypotheses that were accepted, it cannot be determined that the perception of the participants' satisfaction with the elements of the process and the results of the activity improve. In addition, the need was found to improve the process in a way that is lighter and easier to be carried out, to avoid the cognitive burden at the beginning of the activity.

As future work, it was possible to identify that, although we use existing measurement elements for shared understanding, there is still a need to include in THUNDERS monitoring and assistance mechanisms that allow it to be maintained throughout the activity. In the same way, it is necessary to incorporate mechanisms into THUNDERS, that allow to achieve a better-shared understanding and easier use, by developing some techniques and elements to take advantage of their benefits. Elements such as specific templates that support the creation of an activity that builds a shared understanding, specific roles, and the additional elements that can be incorporated into the process for such construction.

References

1. Schmidt, K., Simonee, C.: Coordination mechanisms: towards a conceptual foundation of CSCW systems design. Comput. Support. Coop. Work **5.2**(3), 155–200 (1996)
2. Johnson, R.T., Johnson, D.W.: Active learning: Cooperation in the classroom. Ann. Rep. Educ. Psychol. Japan, **47**, 29 (2008)
3. Laranjeira, M.V.: Teoría y práctica del aprendizaje colaborativo asistido por ordenador. Sintesis, Madrid (2010)
4. Stigliano, D., Gentile, D.: Enseñar y aprender en grupos cooperativos: comunidades de diálogo y encuentro. Novedades educativas, Buenos Aires (2008)
5. Van den Bossche, P., Gijselaers, W., Segers, M., Woltjer, G., Kirschner, P.: Team learning: building shared mental models. Instr. Sci. **39**(3), 283–301 (2011)
6. Leeann, K.: A practical guide to collaborative working. Nicva, Belfast (2012)
7. Scott, B.B.: Creating a Collaborative Workplace: Amplifying Teamwork in Your Organization. Queen's University IRC, pp. 1–9 (2017)
8. HindsP.J., Weisband, S.P.: Knowledge Sharing and Shared Understanding in Virtual Teams, de Virtual Teams that Work: Creating Conditions for Virtual Team Effectiveness, pp. 21–36. Jossey-Bass (2003)
9. Hsieh, Y.: Culture and shared understanding in distributed requirements engineering. In: IEEE International Conference on Global Software Engineering (ICGSE'06), pp. 101–108 (2006)
10. Kleinsmann, M., Bujis, J., Valkenburg, R.: Understanding the complexity of knowledge integration in collaborative new product development teams: A case study. J. Eng. Technol. Manag. **27**(1–2), 20–32 (2010)
11. OMG: Software & systems process engineering metamodel (SPEM). OMG Std. 2, 18–71 (2007)
12. Camacho, M.C., Hurtado, J.A., Ruiz, P.: Un método incremental para el análisis visual de modelos de proceso software. Gerencia en Tecnologia Informatica **15**(43), 79–91 (2016)
13. Pino, F., Piattini, M., Horta, G.: Managing and developing distributed research projects in software engineering by means of action research. Revista facultad de ingenieria Universidad de Antioquia (2013)

14. Bittner, E.A.C., Leimeister, J.M.: Why shared understanding matters – engineering a collaboration process for shared understanding to improve collaboration effectiveness in heterogeneous teams. In: System Sciences (HICSS), vol. 46th Hawaii International Conference, pp. 106–114 (2013)
15. Gomes, D., Tzortzopoulos, P., Kagioglou, M.: Collaboration through shared understanding in the early design stage. In: 24th Ann. Conf. of the Int'l. Group for Lean Construction, Boston (2016)
16. Smart, P.R.: Understanding and Shared Understanding in Military Coalitions. Web & Internet Science, Southampton (2011)
17. Rosenman, E.D., et al.: A simulation-based approach to measuring team situational awareness in emergency medicine: a multicenter, observational study. Acad. Emerg. Med. **25**(2), 196–204 (2018)
18. White, R., Gunstone, R.: Probing Understanding. The Falmer Press, London (1992)
19. Sieck, W.R., Rasmussen, L.J., Smart, P.: Cultural network analysis: a cognitive approach to cultural modeling. Network Science for Military Coalition Operations: Information Exchange and Interaction, pp. 237–255 (2010)
20. Bates, K.E., Bird, G.L., Shea, J.A., Apkon, M., Shaddy, R.E., Metlay, J.P.: A tool to measure shared clinical understanding following handoffs to help evaluate handoff quality. J. Hosp. Med. **9**(3), 142–147 (2014)
21. Ingrid, M., Swaak, J., Kessels, J.: Assessing group learning and shared understanding in technology-mediated interaction. Educ. Technol. Soc. **5**, 35–47 (2002)
22. Humayun, M., Gang, C.: An empirical study on improving shared understanding of requirements in GSD. Int. J. Softw. Eng. Appl. 113–134 (2013)
23. Rosenkranz, C., Hummel, M., Holten, R.: The Role of shared understanding in distributed scrum development: an empirical analysis. In: Proceedings of the European Conference on Information Systems (ECIS) (2016)
24. Dossick, C., Osburn, L., Asl, B.A.: Measuring shared understanding: developing research methods for empirical research on interdisciplinary engineering team practices. In: 15th Engineering Project Organization Conference (2017)
25. Jentsch, C., Beimborn, D., Jungnick, C., Renner, G.: How to measure shared understanding among business and IT. In: Academy of Management Conference (2014)
26. Grudin, J.: Why CSCW applications fail: problems in the design and evaluationof organizational interfaces. In: Proceedings of the 1988 ACM Conference on Computer-supported cooperative work, pp. 85–93 (1988)
27. Rummel, N., Spada, H.: Learning to collaborate: an instructional approach to promoting collaborative problem solving in computer-mediated settings. J. Learn. Sci. **14**(2), 201–241 (2005)
28. Bittner, E.A.C., Leimeister, J.M.: Creating shared understanding in heterogeneous work groups: why it matters and how to achieve it. J. Manag. Inf. Syst. **31**(1), 111–144 (2014)
29. Humphrey, W.S.: The software engineering process: definition and scope. ACM SIGSOFT Softw. Eng. Notes **14**(4), 82–83 (1989)
30. Kolfschoten, G.L., De Vreede, G.-J.: The collaboration engineering approach for designing collaboration processes. In: de International Conference on Collaboration and Technology, Heidelberg (2007)
31. de Vreede, G.-J., Briggs, R.O., Massey, A.P.: Collaboration engineering: foundations and opportunities: editorial to the special issue on the journal of the association of information systems. J. Assoc. Inf. Syst. **10**(3), 7 (2009)
32. Collazos, C.A., Muñoz Arteaga, J., Hernández, Y.: Aprendizaje colaborativo apoyado por computador. LATIn Project (2014)
33. Stahl, G.: Group cognition in computer-assisted collaborative learning. J. Comput. Assist. Learn. **21**(2), 79–90 (2005)

34. Web, N., Palincsar, A.S.: Group Processes in the Classroom. Prentice Hall International (1996)
35. Baker, M.: A model for negotiation in teaching-learning dialogues. J. Interact. Learn. Res. **5**(2), 199–254 (1994)
36. Hurtado, J.A., Bastarrica, M.C., Bergel, A.: AVISPA: a tool for analyzing software process models. J. Softw. Evol. Process **26**(4), 434–450 (2013)
37. Hurtado, J., Bastarrica, M., Bergel, A.: AVISPA: a tool for analyzing software process models. J. Softw. Evol. Process **26**(4), 434–450 (2013)
38. Hurtado, J., Lagos, A., Bergel, A., Bastarrica, M.: Software process model blueprints. In: Conference on New Modeling Concepts for Today's Software Processes (2010)
39. Lescano, G., Costaguta, R.: COLLAB: conflicts and sentiments in chats. In: *Interacción 2018 Proceedings of the XIX International Conference on Human Computer Interaction*, Palma de mayorca (2018)
40. Lescano, G., Costaguta, R., Amandi, A.: Genetic algorithm for automatic group formation considering student's learning styles. In: 2016 8th Euro American Conference on Telematics and Information Systems (EATIS), Cartagena (2016)
41. Agredo, V., Ruiz, P., Collazos, C., Fardoun, H.: Software tool to support the improvement of the collaborative learning process. In: Colombian Conference on Computing (2017)
42. Neave, H.R.: Elementary Statistics Tables. Routledge, London (2002)
43. Agredo-Delgado, V., Ruiz, P., Mon, A., Collazos, C., Moreira, F., Fardoun, H.: Validating the shared understanding construction in computer supported collaborative work in a problem-solving activity. In: WorldCist'20 – 8th World Conference on Information Systems and Technologies, Budva (2020)

Driver Identification Using Machine Learning and Motor Activity as Data Source

Carlos H. Espino-Salinas[1] (ID), Huizilopoztli Luna-García[1](✉),
José M. Celaya-Padilla[2] (ID), Jorge A. Morgan-Benita[1] (ID), Wilson J. Sarmiento[3] (ID),
Hamurabi Gamboa-Rosales[1] (ID), Jorge I. Galván-Tejada[1] (ID),
and Carlos E. Galván-Tejada[1] (ID)

[1] Unidad Académica de Ingeniería Eléctrica, Universidad Autónoma de Zacatecas, Jardín Juárez 147, Centro, 98000 Zacatecas, Zac, Mexico
{carlosespino,hlugar,alejandro.morgan,hamurabigr,gatejo,
ericgalvan}@uaz.edu.mx
[2] CONACYT, Universidad Autónoma de Zacatecas, Jardín Juárez 147, Centro, 98000 Zacatecas, Zac, Mexico
jose.celaya@uaz.edu.mx
[3] Programa de Ingeniería en Multimedia, Universidad Militar de Nueva Granada, Cra 11, 101-80 Bogota, Colombia
wilson.sarmiento@unimilitar.edu.co

Abstract. Being able to have a system capable of identifying drivers offers many applications, among the most relevant being the ability to generate user personalized interfaces in automotive environments that can improve the user experience as well as their comfort. Currently proposed solutions include biometric data, global processing systems, driver images and data extracted from vehicle sensors. In these solutions, degree of invasiveness, noise in signals and large number of variables used are problem for their practical application. This document proposes a driver identification scheme to address these challenges. The scheme uses data extracted from steering wheel and the brake and acceleration pedals to learn driving patterns of each subject through some machine learning techniques in a simulated environment. Data extraction, analysis, processing, and results show that drivers could be identified with significant accuracy. To evaluate the depth classification models, validation metrics were applied where random forest algorithm obtained an accuracy of 83%. Thus, concluding that generated dataset can provide relevant information for driver identification.

Keywords: HCI · Driver identification · Machine learning · Motor activity · ADAS

1 Introduction

Today, driver identification has become an active field of study to customize advanced driver assistance systems (ADAS) in intelligent vehicles, provide security for ride-sharing services and prevent car theft [1]. ADAS systems provides additional information

V. Agredo-Delgado et al. (Eds.): HCI-COLLAB 2022, CCIS 1707, pp. 88–100, 2022.
https://doi.org/10.1007/978-3-031-24709-5_7

from the car surrounding environment to support a driver and assist in implementing critical actions. The synchronization of a driver's actions and the information from the environment is essential for the efficient performance of the various applications [2]. These systems have also introduced biometric-based infotainment technology for driver convenience, meaning that intelligent vehicles actively record driver behavior to provide user interface and lifelogging services focused on vehicle users [3]. To provide personalized services and human-vehicle interaction (HVI) to the driver, an authentication technology that uses driver bioinformation to prove identity with a biometric system is being studied. If the driver is authenticated in and out of the vehicle using the driver's biological information, a personalized telematics service is provided to the driver [4].

One of the biometric methods used for driver identification are those that use electrocardiogram (ECG) signals via sensors located on the vehicle seat or steering wheel. A driver identification system using an ECG signal determines the driver's status and provides recognition information through the classification of stress, fatigue, cognitive distraction, health and emotion steps [3]. Silva et al. [5]. Studied a driver identification system using ECG signal acquired from the driver's wrist. The driver's ECG lead-1 was acquired from steering wheel and identified with an error rate of 3 to 5% in stable status and 30% error rate in moving status.

Another very popular case of driver identification research is image processing which is a mature and effective technology for identification issue, but this requires an additional video equipment that occupies a lot of space in vehicles and expensive. In addition, images are affected by lighting, vehicle vibration, driver' skin colour, glasses, jewellery and other equipment to wear, which could make troubles for recognition [6].

Human Computer Interaction (HCI) development stars with the introduction of in vehicle entertainment with the use of the radio, telephone, and GPS navigation [7]. However, other research has focused its efforts on data collection and processing using other devices that are not necessarily the biological signals that a driver can produce, use of the global positioning system (GPS) data for characterize driving styles and distinguish driver [8], but this type of system tends to have a certain degree of error in locations where satellite signal can affect quality of the data.

Nowadays most of the vehicles have different sensors for a constant diagnosis that can help to have a car in optimum performance, one of these elements is the controller area network bus (CAN-bus) where different signals collected other sources can identify the driver. However, the use of CAN-bus means that required input measurements are not general in application for all vehicles [9]. Another method also used is the one based on vehicle telematics data called on-board diagnostics (OBD). OBD interface of a vehicle provides in-vehicle sensor reading such as vehicle speed, engine RMP, throttle position, engine load, break-pedal displacement, etc. OBD dongles can be used to extract these internal sensors data in real-time to infer information about the car and its driver. In-vehicle sensors data are directly or indirectly are influenced by divers driving style. The driving style of each individual varies depending on how they maneuver their vehicle [10].

Thanks to the rise of machine learning together with HCI systems advance allows to interrelate the human being with electronic devices to process large amounts of data which is capable of giving solutions to a great number of problems that can affect to vehicle users.

Today there is great interest in the development and improvement of ADAS systems, such as emotion recognition, improvement of personalized infotainment systems, driver identification, among others. Although there is a great variety of elements in a vehicle where important information can be extracted to identify a specific driver and to able to present personalized information in graphic interfaces of a vehicle improving the HVI, as well as user experience.

This research has main objective to use the data generated based on the frequency with which driver uses the brake an accelerator or how much pressure is applied on these pedals as well as how the steering wheel angle varies in a controlled environment through a simulator, to finally process this data and classify different driver through machine learning algorithms. The main contribution of this work is the generation of a model and new data set capable for driver identification in a simple and efficient way with the analysis and processing of data acquired. Thus, ruling out many variables that increase cost and time of computational processing, in addition to obtaining a minimally invasive model that affects styles of each driver. With this driving identification, it is intended in the future to design personalized information and entertainment systems that adjust to needs of vehicle user.

1.1 Related Works

This sub-section provides a brief review of the recent research that aims to identify drivers using machine learning for the generation of classification models by extracting and processing different data generated by the driver or the vehicle.

In the work of Girma et al. [10]. Proposed Long-Short-Term-Memory (LSTM) model to predicts the identity of the driver based on the individual's unique driving patterns learned from the vehicle telematics data. The model efficiently learns individual unique driving patterns from the data to identify the driver, this method is evaluated on a real-world dataset using different metrics maintains its accuracy above the acceptable value 88%. In the same way Kwak et al. [11]. Used vehicle telematics data extracted from OBD proposed and evaluate a driver-identification method based on wavelet transform by performing driving-pattern analysis for each driver. They compared the performances of three different machine learning techniques for performing driver identification, obtained an accuracy of 91.6% in multi-class classification using XGBoost classifier, in the case of an urban road, the support vector machine classifier achieves accuracy of 89.06% in multi-class classification. Also Nasr et al. [12]. Using HCRL dataset which includes various features extracted through in vehicle CAN-bus data and ODB proposed an architecture benefit from triplet loss training for driving time series in an unsupervised approach. An encoder architecture based on exponentially dilated causal convolutions is employed to obtain the representations. A support vector machine classifier is then trained on top of representations to predict the person behind the wheel with accuracy of more than 94%. In recent years other research [13–15] has emerged implementing different machine learning and artificial intelligence techniques using real driving datasets consisting of measurements taken from vehicle sensors to characterize driving styles and identify who is behind the wheel as it can be extremely valuable for different scenarios.

Simulated and naturalistic driving patterns have been studied in the literature using different features extracted mainly from the in-vehicle's CAN-bus (the steering wheel. The vehicle speed, and the engine speed, etc.). Using these features, different machine learning methods have been proposed to learn driving styles and identification the user. However, other works have used other means to solve this problem, such as Rahim et al. [16]. Proposed a driver identification scheme uses data from the global positioning system to learn individual's driving pattern, which is commonly deployed in car navigation systems and can also be found in general-purpose hand-held devices in the prevailing market. The consequent analysis and empirical results show that the scheme could identify drivers with significant accuracy given only GPS data. To assess the scheme in depth, they perform experiments both on the collected data and the real-world open datasets. The average accuracy approximates above 96% for up to 25 drivers.

The identification of drivers using ECG signal has also generated interesting results since it allows to know the status of driver and provides recognition information. Santos et al. [17]. Has been studied a driver identification system using ECG signals, proposed method presents a true positive rate of 96.25% for authentication, and 95.8% for identification using a decision tree based on Random Forest Algorithm. Choi et al. [3]. Proposed a driver identification system using a 2D spectrogram. It identifies a section where the resolution is optimally adjusted using a spectrogram that can simultaneously analyze the time-frequency features of an ECG. The experimental results show that the proposed method improved the identification performance compared to the existing multidimensional feature extraction methods such as Ensemble Empirical Mode Decomposition (EEMD) and Mel Frequency Cepstral Coefficients (MFCCs). The identification accuracy using the proposed 2D spectrogram with the optimized resolution was analyzed the highest at 97.1% in CU-DB, 100% in MIT-BIH NSR DB, 98.1% in QT DB and 98.7% in European DB.

Different driving styles lead to different driving data. The behavioral signs used for analysis and classification of drivers are several where the movement of the steering wheel and the amount of pressure applied to the pedals of a car are used for driver identification, as is the case of Li et al. [6]. Studied an applicable driver identification method using machine learning algorithms with driving information. The driving data are collected by a 3-axis accelerometer, which records the lateral, longitudinal and vertical accelerations. Four basic supervised classification algorithms are used to perform on the data set for comparison, among the four basic algorithms, random forest (RFs) algorithm has the greatest performance on accuracy (62.3%), recall (65.7%) and precision (65.3%). Finally, Nasr et al. [18]. Designed a deep learning-based system architecture that analyzes windows of 30 s of driving data to capture the unique underlying characteristics of the individual's steering behavior based on which it further distinguishes the drivers. The performance of the proposed systems is tested over a real-world dataset of 95 drivers. The evaluation results indicate that our system outperforms well-stablished benchmarks and baseline methodologies.

Although each of the works contribute significantly to the problem of driver identification, this research focusses on generating and processing a database generated from physical interaction (motor activity) that drivers have with basic elements of driving (accelerator, breaking and steering wheel) that favor the future development of a simple, non-invasive, and objective multimodal driver recognition system.

2 Materials and Methods

In this section, we wills explain in detail the methodology implemented for driver identification as shown in Fig. 1. Using motor activity exerted on some elements of vehicle in a simulated environment. In the first stage, data of the main elements necessary for driving were extracted, thanks to access provided by the simulator to the different sensors of the virtual vehicle. Then, these data went through a normalization process to avoid problems of outliers and overfitting at the time of training the identification models. Finally, driver identification models were generated and validated with different metrics each stage is explained in detail in next subsections.

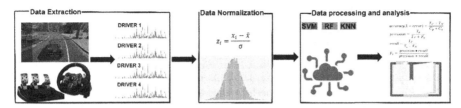

Fig. 1. Methodology for driver identification using machine learning and motor activity.

2.1 Data Extraction

For security reasons, data extraction was performed using CARLA 0.9.13 simulator, which is an open-source simulator developed to aid the creation, training, and validation of autonomous vehicles. CARLA attempts to meet requirements of several ADAS use cases, i.e. training perception algorithms or learning driving policies, CARLA is also free to use and sensor suite configurations provide signals that can be used to train driving strategies [19]. In the case of present study, signals extracted from the simulator are those generated through motor activity exercised by means of accelerator pedal, brake pedal and steering wheel, obtaining 3 features and 9,000 observations per driver in the data extraction phase as shown in Table 1. Where each driver was labeled with 0, 1, 2, 3 for driver one, two, three and four respectively.

We generated our data set on a machine with Intel Core i5-9400F at 2.90 GHz, 32 GB RAM and NVIDIA GeForce GTX 1070 Ti. Peripherals were Logitech G29 Driving Force built for today's driving games and simulation. The route and traffic established for driving was the same for each study subjects for 10 min (5 for driving adaptation and use of the simulator and res for recording and storing motor activity signal) to ensure replication in future research. Route established within the simulator is shown in Fig. 2.

Test subjects are students from the Universidad Autonóma de Zacatecas with ages between 27–37, who have an average driving time about 8.75 years, all subjects are male,

Table 1. Example of generating data by each driver

Sample number	Motor activity acceleration	Motor activity break	Motor activity steering wheel angle	Driver
1	0.679931302	0	−0.243051659	0
2	0.672789414	0	0.301507503	0
3	0.669198607	0	−0.104604312	0
⋮	⋮	⋮	⋮	⋮
9001	0	0.549534057	−1.439965432	1
9002	0	0.392749183	−0.079991518	1
9003	0.524402881	0	−0.590714625	1
⋮	⋮	⋮	⋮	⋮
18001	0	0.898714153	2.221737421	2
18002	0.476545161	0	−1.892375448	2
18003	0.402442758	0	3.758628905	2
⋮	⋮	⋮	⋮	⋮
31438	0.840223762	0	8.276900048	3
31439	0.639982157	0	−16.88071172	3
31440	0	0.290274153	−1.375341671	3

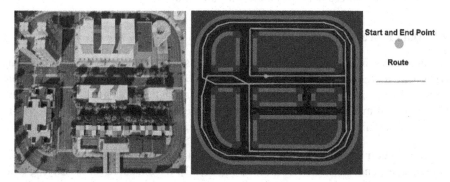

Start and End Point

Route

Fig. 2. Map of the CARLA simulator used for driving simulation and the established route.

and voluntary participated in our experiment at Laboratory of Interactive Technology and User Experience (LITUX) as shown in Fig. 3. Having sufficient explanation, including the purpose and procedure of our experiments and how the experimental data would be used.

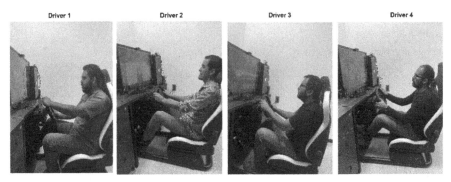

Fig. 3. Study subjects performing driving test in LITUX of UAZ

2.2 Data Normalization

Data Normalization it can be used to scale data in the same range of values for each input feature to minimize bias within the model from one feature to another. Data normalization can also speed up training time for each function within same scale. It is especially useful for modeling applications where inputs are generally at very different scales. Mean and standard deviation are calculated for each feature [20]. The transformation occurs in Eq. 1.

$$z_i = \frac{x_i - \overline{x}}{\sigma} \tag{1}$$

Using statical normalization avoids outlier problems as it handles outliers but does not produce normalized data with the exact same scale.

2.3 Data Processing and Analysis

For this research, multi-class classification models were used since data contain four types of drivers as output (driver 1, driver 2, driver 3 and driver 4). To compare the performance of different machine learning (ML) algorithms in driver identification problems, three classical machine learning algorithms are used on the data set, this initial part is known as classification analysis. Three algorithms are briefly mentioned below.

Support Vector Machine (SVM). SVM is a maximum margin classification rooted in both machine and statistical learning theory [21, 22]. It's a method for classifying both linear and non-linear data being primarily designed for two-class problems, it finds the hyper plane with a maximum distance to the closet point of the two classes; called the optimal hyper plane $f(w, x) = wx + b$ as shown in Fig. 4.

Random Forest (RF). In general, the process of RF follows the algorithm described below. A leaf is used for the expansion of the construction of the tree in each step. At the end, from decision trees built, they are merged into a single tree to obtain a higher prediction accuracy [23]. (1) Given a dataset M_1 of size $m \times n$, a new dataset A_2 is created from the original data, sampling and eliminating a third part of the row data. (2)

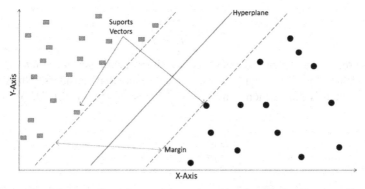

Fig. 4. Example of the operation of support vector machine for the classification of two classes

then, the model is trained generating a new dataset through reduced samples, estimating unbiased error. (3) At each node point (which are the pints where trees are growing simultaneously), column n_1 is selected from the total n columns. (4) Finally, when trees finish growing, a final prediction based on the individual decisions is calculated, looking for best classification accuracy.

K Nearest Neighbors (KNN). The principle of KNN algorithm is that the most similar samples belonging to the same class have high probability. Generally, the KNN algorithm first finds k nearest neighbors of a query in training dataset, and then predicts the query with the major class in the k nearest neighbors. Therefore, it has recently been selected as one of top 10 algorithms in data mining [24].

To know the different machine algorithms performance and compare their results, it is necessary to apply different validation metrics such as: confusion matrix, accuracy, precision, recall and F1-Score.

Confusion Matrix. Is typically used in machine learning to evaluate or to visualize the behavior of models in supervised classification contexts [25]. Contain de number of true positives (T_P), True Negatives (T_N), False Positives (F_p) and False negatives (F_N).

Accuracy (Acc). Is used to have certain performance criteria, which refers to degree to which the result of a calculation conforms to the correct value [26]. Shown in Eq. 2.

$$accuracy(1 - error) = \frac{Tp + Tn}{Cp + Cn} \tag{2}$$

where T_P are true positives, T_n are true negatives, C_p are truly positives and C_n are truly negative.

Precision and recall. The accuracy of a classifier also depends on the ratio between number of targets correctly detected and all detected targets, known as precision, and ratio between the number of targets correctly detected and all true targets, known as recall, shown in Eq. 3 and 4.

$$precision = \frac{Tp}{Tp + FP} \tag{3}$$

$$recall = \frac{Tp}{Tp + FN} \qquad (4)$$

Since precision and recall are both necessary for evaluating the detection capabilities of an algorithm, it is convenient to find a single measure that considers both, that is the F1-Score, which is the harmonic mean of the precision and recall [27]. As shown in Eq. 5.

$$F_1 = \frac{precision \cdot recall}{precision + recall} \qquad (5)$$

3   Results and Discussion

As result, a new dataset of motor activity signal was obtained from 4 different drivers where the motor variables obtained for each sample were angle movement exerted on the steering wheel (PosAng), amount of pressure exerted on the acceleration pedal (throttleCmd) and amount of pressure exerted on the braking pedal (breakCmd) a total of 9,000 observations were extracted for each driver for a total of 36,000 observations that can be used for different scenarios within an automotive specially for use in ADAS. In this research work sought to solve the driver's identification problem using data extracted. It can be seen in Fig. 5. That values of each study subject vary constantly in each sample; however, each signal is different from other which makes sense since each driver has different ways of driving which allows a first approach to establish that it is possible to identify drivers thanks to dataset obtained in this study.

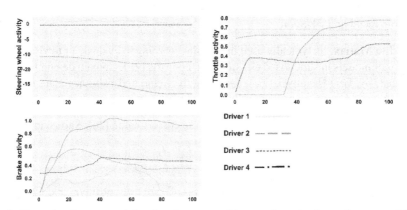

Fig. 5. Example of motor activity signals generated by steering wheel, accelerator, and brake during 100 samples out of 9000 obtained by each driver in a driving simulator (CARLA).

On the other hand, in the application and validation of machine learning algorithms proposed in this research, promising results were obtained as shown in Table 2. Where 80% (28,000 observations) of data was used to train models and 20% (7,200) for testing. The results presented are those obtained with test data set.

Table 2. Performance of machine learning algorithms for driver identification.

ML algorithm	Validation metric	Driver 1	Driver 2	Driver 3	Driver 4
SVM	Recall	0.74	0.75	0.87	0.82
	Precision	0.72	0.77	0.84	0.85
	F1-Score	0.73	0.76	0.85	0.84
	Accuracy	**0.80**			
RF	Recall	0.80	0.82	0.89	0.83
	Precision	0.79	0.80	0.86	0.88
	F1-Score	0.79	0.81	0.88	0.85
	Accuracy	**0.83**			
KNN	Recall	0.80	0.78	0.86	0.83
	Precision	0.73	0.81	0.87	0.88
	F1-Score	0.77	0.80	0.87	0.85
	Accuracy	**0.82**			

Random Forest obtained the best performance at time of identifying four drivers with accuracy of 0.83, however although it presents better results than previous research there are also studies that also obtain results above those obtained in this work, most of this works propose invasive methods such as electrocardiograms or encephalograms to mention a few, on the other hand use of systems for vehicle diagnosis used for data extraction is a very efficient proposal, minimally invasive and with good performance for driver identification but the number of features to evaluate are much higher which means higher cost and computational time without neglecting that there are features that may not provide relevant information for a classification model.

Finally, Fig. 6. Shows confusion matrix obtained by applying RF for the identification of drivers.

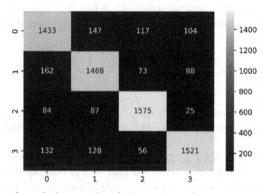

Fig. 6. Cross-sectional confusion matrix of the number of observations per driver classified correctly and incorrectly in the test data.

As can be seen, driver 1, 2, 3 and 4 were correctly identified 1,433, 1468, 1575 and 1,521 times, respectively. These results may be the consequence that some of subjects tend to generate more motor activity than others, as demonstrated in the graph presented above, which implies that they are more likely to be identified. These numbers are really promising since great discoveries can be made in simulated environments and solve real problems such as generating better interaction between ADAS and road users.

The HCI has been an important field of research that seeks to improve the user experience in the large number of systems that exist and automotive field is no exempt, that is why the behaviors generated by each driver could create adaptive and customized systems for each user, depending on their driving style, it could even guide future work as the detection of sudden movements, drowsiness and lack of driving ability, to mention a few.

4   Conclusion and Future Work

The aim of this paper was describing a process capable of creating a database of motor activity generated through basic elements of driving a vehicle that would allow the creation of models for driver identification using some machine learning algorithms. It is concluded that data obtained from different drivers are relevant to identify each one of them with a high degree of accuracy of 83%, it was also demonstrated that our dataset is quite useful with only a limited number of features compiled through a driving simulator. One of the main motivations to propose new ways to identify drivers is to be able to provide better and advanced forms of human-computer interaction personalized for each user in automotive environment which we call HVI, although this is a first approach to achieve our purpose, we can say that results can be improved in future work.

For future work we proposed to add a greater number of study subjects that help to diversify the dataset, in addition to extraction more variables from the simulator that may be useful to improve performance of the models, perform a univariate and multivariate analysis as well implementation of intelligent selection algorithms that allow to objectively determine the sensors that generate relevant information to classify different types of drivers.

Finally, it also suggests improvement of ADAS based on driver identification, establishing personalized systems for each subject an evaluating its performance based on a user-centered design.

References

1. Nasr Azadani, M., Boukerche, A.: DriverRep: driver identification through driving behavior embeddings. J. Parallel Distrib. Comput. **162**, 105–117 (2022). https://doi.org/10.1016/j.jpdc.2022.01.010
2. Ziebinski, A., Cupek, R., Grzechca, D., Chruszczyk, L.: Review of advanced driver assistance systems (ADAS). AIP Conf. Proc. **1906**, 1–5 (2017). https://doi.org/10.1063/1.5012394
3. Choi, G.H., Lim, K., Pan, S.B.: Identification system based on resolution adjusted 2D spectrogram of driver's ECG for intelligent vehicle. Mob. Inf. Syst. **2022**, 5404343 (2022). https://doi.org/10.1155/2022/5404343

4. Ahmad, B.I., Langdon, P.M., Liang, J., Godsill, S.J., Delgado, M., Popham, T.: Driver and passenger identification from smartphone data. IEEE Trans. Intell. Transp. Syst. **20**(4), 1278–1288 (2019). https://doi.org/10.1109/TITS.2018.2845113
5. Silva, H., Lourenço, A., Fred, A.: In-vehicle driver recognition based on hand ECG signals. In: Proceedings of the 2012 ACM international conference on Intelligent User Interfaces (IUI'12). Association for Computing Machinery. New York, NY, USA, pp. 25–28 (2012). https://doi.org/10.1145/2166966.2166971
6. Li, Z., Zhang, K., Chen, B., Dong, Y., Zhang, L.: Driver identification in intelligent vehicle systems using machine learning algorithms. IET Intell. Transp. Syst. **13**(1), 40–47 (2019). https://doi.org/10.1049/iet-its.2017.0254
7. Tepe, R.: What is the Role of HCI Within the Automotive Industry? (2020)
8. Dong, W., Li, J., Yao, R., Li, C., Yuan, T., Wang, L.: Characterizing Driving Styles with Deep Learning (2016)
9. Martínez, M.V., Echanobe, J., del Campo, I.: Driver identification and impostor detection based on driving behavior signals. In: 2016 IEEE 19th International Conference on Intelligent Transportation Systems (ITSC), pp. 372–378 (2016). https://doi.org/10.1109/ITSC.2016.7795582
10. Girma, A., Yan, X., Homaifar, A.: Driver identification based on vehicle telematics data using LSTM-recurrent neural network. In: Proceedings - International Conference on Tools with Artificial Intelligence, ICTAI (2019). https://doi.org/10.1109/ICTAI.2019.00127
11. Il Kwak, B., Han, M.L., Kim, H.K.: Driver identification based on wavelet transform using driving patterns. IEEE Trans. Ind. Inf. **17**(4), 2400–2410 (2021). https://doi.org/10.1109/TII.2020.2999911
12. Azadani, M.N., Boukerche, A.: Driver identification using vehicular sensing data: a deep learning approach. In: IEEE Wireless Communications and Networking Conference, WCNC (2021). https://doi.org/10.1109/WCNC49053.2021.9417463
13. Ezzini, S., Berrada, I., Ghogho, M.: Who is behind the wheel? driver identification and fingerprinting. J. Big Data **5**(1), 1–15 (2018). https://doi.org/10.1186/s40537-018-0118-7
14. Aslan, C., Genç, Y.: Driver identification using vehicle diagnostic data with fully convolutional neural network. In: 2021 29th Signal Processing and Communications Applications Conference (SIU), pp. 1–4 (2021)
15. Gallo, G., Bernardi, M.L., Cimitile, M., Ducange, P.: An explainable approach for car driver identification. In: 2021 IEEE International Conference on Fuzzy Systems (FUZZ-IEEE), pp. 1–7 (2021). https://doi.org/10.1109/FUZZ45933.2021.9494566
16. Rahim, M.A., et al.: Zero-to-stable driver identification: a non-intrusive and scalable driver identification scheme. IEEE Trans. Veh. Technol. **69**(1), 163–171 (2020). https://doi.org/10.1109/TVT.2019.2954529
17. Santos, A., et al.: ECG-based user authentication and identification method on VANETs. In: Proceedings of the 10th Latin America Networking Conference (LANC'18). Association for Computing Machinery, New York, NY, USA, pp. 119–122 (2018). https://doi.org/10.1145/3277103.3277138
18. Azadani, M.N., Boukerche, A.: Siamese temporal convolutional networks for driver identification using driver steering behavior analysis. IEEE Trans. Intell. Transp. Syst. **23**, 18076–18087 (2022). https://doi.org/10.1109/TITS.2022.3151264
19. Dosovitskiy, A., Ros, G., Codevilla, F., Lopez, A., Koltun, V.: {CARLA}: {an} open urban driving simulator. In: Proceedings of the 1st Annual Conference on Robot Learning, vol. 78, pp. 1–16 (2017). https://proceedings.mlr.press/v78/dosovitskiy17a.html
20. Jayalakshmi, T., Santhakumaran, A.: Statistical normalization and back propagation for classification. Int. J. Comput. Theory Eng. **3**, 89–93 (2011). https://doi.org/10.7763/ijcte.2011.v3.288

21. Meyer, D.: Support vector machines: the interface to libsvm in package e1071. ... *Syst. their ...*, vol. 1 (2014). https://doi.org/10.1007/978-0-387-77242-4
22. Zanaty, E.A.: Support vector machines (SVMs) versus multilayer perception (MLP) in data classification. Egypt. Inform. J. **13**(3), 177–183 (2012). https://doi.org/10.1016/j.eij.2012.08.002
23. Subudhi, A., Dash, M., Sabut, S.: Automated segmentation and classification of brain stroke using expectation-maximization and random forest classifier. Biocybernetics Biomed. Eng. **40**(1), 277–289 (2020). https://doi.org/10.1016/j.bbe.2019.04.004
24. Goyal, R., Chandra, P., Singh, Y.: Suitability of KNN regression in the development of interaction based software fault prediction models. IERI Procedia **6**, 15–21 (2014). https://doi.org/10.1016/j.ieri.2014.03.004
25. Caelen, O.: A Bayesian interpretation of the confusion matrix. Ann. Math. Artif. Intell. **81**(3–4), 429–450 (2017). https://doi.org/10.1007/s10472-017-9564-8
26. Zanella-Calzada, L.A., et al.: Feature extraction in motor activity signal: towards a depression episodes detection in unipolar and bipolar patients. Diagnostics **9**, 8 (2019). https://doi.org/10.3390/diagnostics9010008
27. AlBeladi, A.A., Muqaibel, A.H.: Evaluating compressive sensing algorithms in through-the-wall radar via F1-score. Int. J. Signal Imaging Syst. Eng. **11**(3), 1–8 (2018). https://doi.org/10.1504/IJSISE.2018.093268

Evaluation and Redesign Proposal of an Infotainment System: A Case Study with a Parked Vehicle

Juan S. Guzmán[1] , Andrés F. Agudelo[1(✉)] , Isabela Toledo[1] ,
Diego Bambague[1] , Huizilopoztli Luna-García[2] , and Cesar A. Collazos[1]

[1] Universidad del Cauca, Popayán, Colombia
{juanseguzman,andresfag,tbisabela,fbambague,
ccollazo}@unicauca.edu.co
[2] Universidad Autónoma de Zacatecas, Zacatecas, Mexico
hlugar@uaz.edu.mx

Abstract. This paper presents a process implemented for the analysis of the frontend design of an infotainment system through the evaluation of a set of heuristics in a parked vehicle. The guidelines used to evaluate the system cover design, interaction and connectivity dimensions, which are studied through the execution of a usability test whose objective is to identify the pain points that arise from the interaction of the characterized users (22 to 24 years and no experience in infotainment systems) with the vehicle. A redesign proposal is also made as a result of the vulnerabilities that were found through the observation technique in the usability test. Obtained results include a summary of the feedback from the usability test and the redesign proposal whose objective is to promote a better user experience and satisfy the passenger needs.

Keywords: Infotainment system · Driver eXperience · Usability · Parked vehicle · Redesign

1 Introduction

In recent years, the automotive industry has shown continuous growth in relation to the in-vehicle technology [1]. The growing demand for smart and more advanced vehicles is increasing the need for companies to incorporate greater advantages and options to their customers in order to improve their experience [2, 3]. One of the technological trajectories that has managed to emerge within the automotive industry growth is the incorporation of in-vehicle infotainment systems, also called IVIS [4]. Infotainment is a compound term that arises from the intersection between the words information and entertainment [5]. Thereby, an infotainment system corresponds to the set of components used to provide information and entertainment to the driver and other passengers in the vehicle, through interfaces with audio and video, and control elements such as touch screens, button panels, voice commands, and sensors to recognize gestures, among others [6]. Infotainment systems bring a world full of interaction opportunities for both the

V. Agredo-Delgado et al. (Eds.): HCI-COLLAB 2022, CCIS 1707, pp. 101–113, 2022.
https://doi.org/10.1007/978-3-031-24709-5_8

driver and other passengers to complete the tasks related to driving and other secondary activities such as tuning into a radio station, dialing the number of a contact, navigating the map and so on [7]. However, the increase in the number of gadgets that an IVIS can provide, and even the design under which these elements are distributed, can affect the User Experience (UX), and therefore, it could make it difficult to perform secondary tasks and in a worst case scenario affect driver and passenger's safety while driving [8]. In fact, according to [9], it has been proven that the improper use of advanced infotainment systems such as Android Au- to™ or Apple CarPlay® while driving can be more dangerous than doing it under the influence of alcohol or cannabis, which supports the hypothesis of the researchers of the referenced work, who argue that current approaches that guide the design of infotainment systems are not sufficient to achieve the necessary levels for safe driving. Another factor to take into account when referring to the IVIS user experience is the mental model of the users. The mental model can be understood as what the user believes about how a system works and it will define how the user interacts with the system itself [10]. When the user mental model doesn't match the way the system actually works, then the user experience could be affected, the number of errors can increase and there will not be an intuitive flow when executing the tasks [11]. Mental models are built based on the previous experiences of the users and they are even influenced by the culture in which the person operates, so they tend to predict the actions that the user takes in a particular scenario and is constantly in evolution, as it adapts over time and as new experiences are gained and more knowledge is acquired [12]. For these reasons, it is crucial that the designers and developers of these systems have reference points where the design focuses on the needs and the mental model of the users and not only in the number of tasks that can be executed with the product [13]. Consequently, we decided to describe a process that can provide a starting point for infotainment system interface designers in order to facilitate the identification of pain points on existing infotainment designs and thus encourage better user experience, understand the user's mental model and so, satisfy user needs. This paper presents a short compilation of a methodology carried out in order to evaluate the usability of an in-vehicle infotainment system when the vehicle is parked and also includes a redesign proposal based on the pain points that were identified during the usability test. In order to evaluate the system, the heuristics described in [14] were adapted according to the case study.

2   Heuristics Adaptation

In order to assess the usability of the IVIS, a set of proposed heuristics was identified with the aim of evaluating the system and have a point of reference when understanding the interaction of users within the vehicle. For this, we base ourselves on a set of guidelines described by Luna-García et al. in [14] and we choose the most convenient ones to carry out the case study. The original guidelines described 4 dimensions such as Design, Interaction, Security and Connectivity and a total of 17 proposed heuristics of which 12 were used, the most appropriate for the project. The chosen heuristics are displayed in Fig. 1.

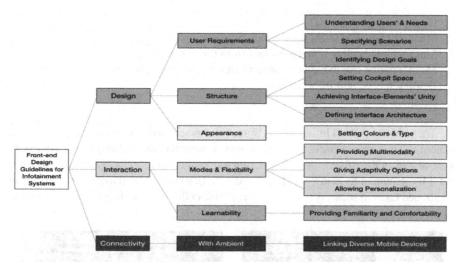

Fig. 1. Adapted heuristics from Luna-Garcia, H. et al. [14]

The chosen heuristics are classified in three levels: *Design, Interaction* and *Connectivity*. The Design level focuses on providing general aspects about the analysis, planning and conceptual design of infotainment systems to achieve a coherent user centered approach (*Understanding Users' & Needs*). Also, this Design level focuses on structuring design alternatives considering taking advantage of the space available in the vehicle cabin, organizing the interactive elements to form an integrated whole with an adequate distribution and location of these elements (*Structure*). Finally, this level also considers aspects related to typography, fonts and the color palette to con- vey content and information in a clear, legible and easy to understand way (*Appearance*). The Interaction level focuses on determining specific widgets and interactive elements to support the functionality requirements of the conceptual design and pro- mote a better user experience (*Modes & Flexibility*). In addition, this level promotes learning capacity, focusing on the familiarity and comfortability of the system (*Learnability*). On the other hand, the Connectivity level encourages some ideas to integrate widgets that allow connectivity between infotainment systems and the environment (*Connectivity with Ambient*). It should be noted that the heuristics related to Safety were discarded, since the study was carried out with a parked vehicle and it was not necessary to evaluate the interaction in motion. Also, the heuristics related to connectivity with intelligent elements on the roads were also discarded, as they also needed in motion activities

3 Case Study

First, with the purpose of evaluating the selected heuristics, a set of tasks was proposed based on the dimensions to be assessed and some related works task proposals described in [15–18]. These tasks were also proposed with the intention of being temporally measurable to calculate how users react to them and how much time they should spend on the system dashboard looking away from the road in a real life situation. The following list shows the simplified set of tasks users were asked to perform, subtasks are not described.

1. Play a song from the CD.
2. Manually tune FM radio station to a given frequency.
3. Make a phone call to a given contact from the contact list.
4. Make a phone call to a given contact using the voice command.
5. Display specific car information.
6. Set the interface language.

Then, the Audi MMI Infotainment System® was selected as the case study in-vehicle system as it was able to do every task proposed. Throughout the usability test, participants were seated in the driver's seat of a stationary Audi 1 vehicle equipped with the Audi MMI Infotainment System® (see Fig. 2 and Fig. 3), which allowed users to complete the mentioned tasks in sections such as media, phone calls, radio, setting up, among others.

Fig. 2. Audi MMI Infotainment System® dashboard

Fig. 3. Audi MMI Infotainment System® control center

After choosing the case study vehicle, a small group of users were selected based on the characterization. Only 5 users were selected following the recommendation made in [19] by usability expert, Jakob Nielsen, where he affirms that "the best results come from testing no more than 5 users and running as many small tasks as you can afford" (For reasons of not having enough people and cars, another technique was not used, such as "How Many Test Users in a Usability Study", to have a more adequate sample when taking averages) ... The users' ages ranged from 22–24 years, their current studies were undergraduate and they didn't have any relevant infotainment system experience, which leads to a better understanding of the learnability of the system.

Before actually evaluating the tasks with the characterized users, the tasks were performed by some experts and an average time for execution was measured for each task in order to have a point of reference when assessing the non-experienced users. Experts refers to people who have had more than 3 years of experience using the Audi MMI Infotainment System®.

4   Usability Test

After specifying the case study, the usability test was executed. In order to start, each user had 5 min of free interaction with the vehicle components. After these couple of minutes, every task was mentioned in order, and, by implementing the observational technique [20], some information related to the user-system interaction was gathered, such as the completion time for each task and some additional notes of the individual experience. The completion time per task and user is specified in Table 1, along with the experts' timing mentioned in the previous section.

Table 1. Users' and experts' timing table per task

Task/User	A	B	C	D	E	Experts
1	00:02:12	00:01:17	00:01:20	00:01:13	00:01:35	00:00:53
2	00:02:48	00:02:06	00:02:47	00:02:14	00:01:43	00:01:01
3	00:03:18	00:02:09	00:01:52	00:00:59	00:00:59	00:00:42
4	00:05:26	00:01:40	00:01:05	00:00:53	00:01:13	00:00:48
5	00:00:39	00:00:37	00:00:49	00:00:49	00:00:59	00:00:25
6	00:00:45	00:01:40	00:01:05	00:01:15	00:01:49	00:00:31

Table 1 shows the timing required per each user in order to complete every task and it can be compared to the results of the experts' average timing. Figure 4 displays a graphical representation of the difference between the average timing of the non-experience users and the experts.

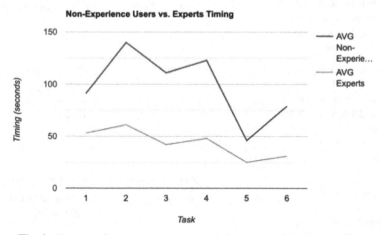

Fig. 4. Non-experience users vs. experts timing graph (color figure online)

As shown in Fig. 4, the non-experience users (blue line) and the experts (red line) have a relevant difference when it comes to the tasks completion timing. As expected, non-experience users take longer to complete tasks, to such a level that some of them take almost or even more than double the time it takes to the experts. This graph provides a first approach in the learnability of the system, comparing the time response from novice users and recurring users. After all of the tasks were performed by each user, some additional feedback was asked in order to really understand and comprehend the full experience and list factors that affected their interaction within the vehicle. This feedback led to summarizing the most relevant pain points encountered, as shown in Table 2. This table also categorizes each relevant vulnerability into the dimension and category that relates according to the heuristics adaptation mentioned above.

Table 2. Main pain points observed during test

Problem	Dimension	Category	Heuristic
There is confusion assimilating the buttons that allow you to select the options of the corners of the interface, because it is not intuitive that they are for that purpose	Dimension	Structure	Achieving interface elements' unity
	Interaction	Learnability	Providing familiarity and comfortability
There is difficulty in finding the option that corresponds to the manual configuration of the radio station, by using a term not according to its function	Interaction	Learnability	Providing familiarity and comfortability
There is disagreement with the search for contacts by last name, because the Colombian mental model suggests doing the search by name	Design	User requirements	Specifying scenarios
	Interaction	Model & flexibility	Giving adaptivity options
There is confusion between the volume wheel and the scroll wheel, because the mental model of Colombians suggests that the central and bigger wheel is used to vary the volume	Design	Structure	Achieving interface elements' unity
	Interaction	Learnability	Providing familiarity and comfortability
When a voice command is executed it is not specified that you should speak after the tone and users usually speak before it, generating the system to discard its command	Design	User requirements	Specifying scenarios
	Interaction	Learnability	Providing familiarity and comfortability

(continued)

Table 2. (*continued*)

Problem	Dimension	Category	Heuristic
Difficulty finding the option that corresponds to the language configuration of the interface, by using a term not according to its function	Interaction	Learnability	Providing familiarity and comfortability

5   Redesign Proposal

After executing the usability test, and having detected the problems that the users had when performing the different tasks, we developed a redesign proposal taking into account the heuristics that failed when evaluating them in some of the tasks. In order to do that, we were guided by usability principles and suggestions made by users after the usability test. A User Interface (UI) prototype was developed in order to evaluate the proposed new components of the infotainment system. Each of the changes in the design and the justification that leads to its implementation, is described below.

5.1   Selecting Corner Option

The infotainment system has a set of options located in the corners of the interface, however the buttons from the physical control that make possible the interaction with the UI were not labeled in a way that allowed users to easily perceive the correspondence between the buttons and the options that each one activates (see Fig. 5(a)). Therefore, the redesign consists in assigning a number to each of the options of the interface and labeling its corresponding button with the same number, as seen in Fig. 5(b). This numbering allows the user to easily associate the options with the physical control, thus they can perform tasks quicker and reduce the time they take their eyes off the road.

5.2   Tuning Radio Station Manually

During the second task, the user was requested to tune in a radio station manually, that is, establishing a specific frequency that is not among those already saved or those that the interface shows by high reception. In order to perform this action, the user must select the 'Funciones' (Functions in Spanish) option (See Fig. 6(a)). However, everyone exceeded the estimated time of completing the task because they didn't find an option that specified or resembled the word manual. In efforts to solve this problem, it has been proposed to change the word 'Funciones' to 'Manual', as it communicates clearly and simply in the user's own language what the option it's supposed to do and making this function easy to find regardless of the user's experience with the system. The previously described change can be seen in Fig. 6(b).

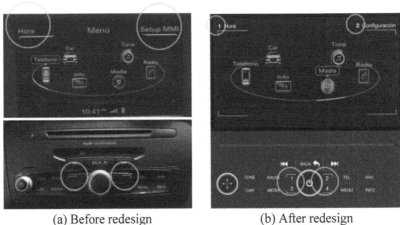

(a) Before redesign   (b) After redesign

Fig. 5. Selecting corner option redesign

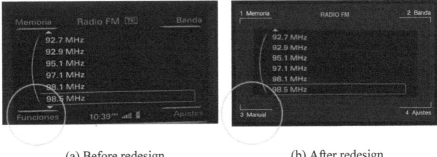

(a) Before redesign   (b) After redesign

Fig. 6. Tuning radio station manually redesign

5.3 Searching Contact by First Name Instead of Last Name

According to our evaluation, in the Colombian mental model the search for a contact from the directory is mostly done by first name, as opposed to the infotainment system's search organized by last name. According to this, it is proposed that by default, searching contacts must be done by the first name. Nonetheless, taking into account the heuristics of Adaptability Options, the proposal allows this configuration to be adapted as desired by the user. Thus, providing flexibility to the system to accommodate individual preferences and to support different input modalities. This change can be seen in Fig. 7.

5.4 Volume Wheel and Scroll Wheel

In aims to minimize errors and to avoid the user's constant confusion between the volume control wheel and the scroll wheel (See Fig. 8(a)), it was proposed that these elements should be arranged in a different way and an icon should be added to one of the wheels for

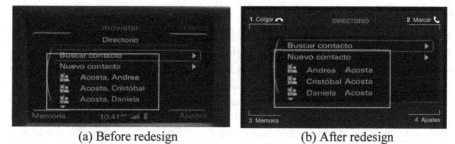

(a) Before redesign   (b) After redesign

Fig. 7. Searching contact by first name instead of last name

it to be easier to identify its function. In the new arrangement, the volume wheel should be installed in the center of the system control and the scroll wheel should be moved to the left corner in a smaller size and with a motion icon added on top (See Fig. 8(b)). This change was presented in this way because in the tests it was possible to see that in order to try to increase the volume of the song of task 1, all the participants tried to do it using the center knob instead of the left corner knob, this is because culturally it is where the volume control is generally located.

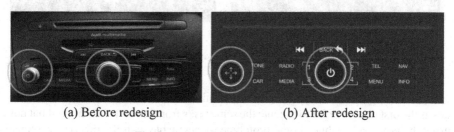

(a) Before redesign   (b) After redesign

Fig. 8. Volume wheel and scroll wheel

5.5 Voice Command Calling Instruction

From the reaction video we recorded of the users when interacting with the voice commands, we heard that the phrase that the infotainment system used to ask the user which phone line to call, confused one of our participants by not specifying WHEN the number should be said. In this case, we proposed that the default phrase used by the system should be modified from "indicate the line, please" to "indicate the line after the tone, please", and thus avoid the command being ignored because it wasn't said at the right time. This type of feedback messages provided by the system should inform the user of actions and expectations in an explicit way and in plain language, as these are relevant and of interest to the user for performing tasks or solving errors.

5.6 Selecting Corner Option

As mentioned in Table 2, it is difficult to find the option that corresponds to the configuration of certain interface elements, such as language. The interface initially uses the term "Setup MMI" (See Fig. 9(a)), however, it is considered that this isn't a term that fits the geographical context and mental model of the users evaluated, and it also breaks consistency within and across interfaces as this is the only term that is in a different language. This type of inconsistency can imply a longer time to learn the interface or can lead to unintended actions that may cause distraction to the driver. This is why it is decided to change the term "Setup MMI" to "Configuración" (Settings in Spanish), as shown in Fig. 9(b).

(a) Before redesign   (b) After redesign

Fig. 9. Selecting corner option redesign

A new usability test was performed with another five users with the same characteristics as the first ones in order to execute the same tasks from the first usability test but now using the proposed changes in the prototype. A new table with the time measurement from the new users' task execution is shown in Table 3.

Table 3. New users' timing table per task

Task/User	F	G	H	I	J	Experts
1	00:00:50	00:00:58	00:01:01	00:01:09	00:00:46	00:00:53
2	00:01:56	00:01:03	00:01:26	00:01:12	00:01:25	00:01:01
3	00:01:21	00:01:25	00:01:03	00:01:59	00:02:11	00:00:42
4	00:01:19	00:01:00	00:01:02	00:00:53	00:00:55	00:00:48
5	00:00:35	00:00:15	00:00:16	00:00:49	00:00:36	00:00:25
6	00:00:40	00:00:26	00:00:30	00:01:15	00:00:27	00:00:31

A decrease in the temporal values of Table 3 can be observed compared to Table 1, which gives us feedback on how positive the changes made to the interface were. Fig. 10

shows the difference between the completion time by the experts in the original design (red line), the average completion time by the users A–E in the original design (blue line) and the average completion time by the users F–J in the redesign proposal (orange line). It can be seen that the time in order to execute the tasks in the redesign proposal is less than the one in the original design.

An additional feedback was given by the new users, and they mostly agreed with the interface as a usable component to perform the given tasks. Also, the UI prototype was shown to the previous users and they agreed with the proposed changes. Fortunately, all six detected problems had a satisfactory solution and were approved by the new and previous tested users, based on their mental model.

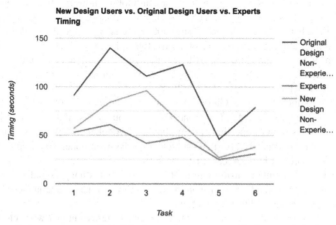

Fig. 10. New design users vs. original design users vs. experts timing graph (color figure online)

6   Conclusion and Future Work

In-vehicle infotainment systems are a field in constant development within the automotive industry, today the interaction with these systems within the vehicle is increasing at an accelerated rate. For this reason, it is important to start by focusing on a fundamental part that is the user when designing the interfaces and the entire system to achieve an adequate user experience and satisfy their needs. Thanks to the results obtained during this research, it was possible to provide a starting point for designers to approach the needs of users and their mental model and thus use it as a tool to pro- vide an adequate user experience. With the execution of the usability test within this case study, it was possible to identify some of the weak points that could occur during the performance of the tasks in the Audi MMI Infotainment System®. Likewise, it was possible to propose a redesign following the UX principles to address the vulnerabilities observed and, in general, satisfy the needs of users characterized based on their mental models. All the elements studied during the usability test allowed the redesign to become a much more coherent step and to have better results. This set of steps may soon help propose design patterns to provide a starting point for designers of new infotainment systems and make it easier to identify weak points in existing designs. There is still a lot of room in the field of infotainment systems to explore, as it is to apply techniques to approach users and evaluate heuristics, involve much more human factors, and analyze much more complex human behavior. It is also expected as future work to evaluate an infotainment system and propose adaptations in other case studies such as that of a moving vehicle.

References

1. Perri, A., Silvestri, D., Zirpoli, F.: Change and stability in the automotive industry: a patent analysis. Department of Management, Università Ca' Foscari Venezia Working Paper No. 5 (2020)
2. Uchil, S., Yazdanifard, R.: The growth of the automobile industry: Toyota's dominance in United States. J. Res. Mark. **3**, 265–268 (2014). https://doi.org/10.17722/jorm.v3i2.86
3. Krasova, E.: Characteristics of global automotive industry as a sector with high levels of production internationalization. Amazonia Investiga **7**(16), 84–93 (2018)
4. Shokoufeh, M.K., Gaffar, A.: Using artificial intelligence to automatically customize modern car infotainment systems. In: Proceedings of the 18th International Conference on Artificial Intelligence (ICAI'16: July 2016, USA) (2018)
5. Marqual IT Solutions Pvt. Ltd: Global In-Vehicle Infotainment Market By Installation Type By Form By Vehicle Type By Component By Region, Industry Analysis and Fore cast, 2019–2025. https://www.reportlinker.com/p05885917/Global-In-Vehicle-Infotainment-Market-By-Installation-Type-By-Form-By-Vehicle-Type-By-Component-By-Region-Industry-Analysis-and-Forecast.html. Accessed 1 Dec 2021
6. Garzon, S.R.: Intelligent in-car-infotainment systems: a contextual personalized approach. In: 2012 Eighth International Conference on Intelligent Environments, Guanajuato, pp. 315–318 (2012). https://doi.org/10.1109/IE.2012.70
7. Rohit, K.: What's driving in-vehicle infotainment systems? https://www.electronicspecifier.com/products/artificial-intelligence/what-s-driving-in-vehicle-infotainment-systems. Accessed 2 Feb 2021
8. Broccia, G.: Model-based analysis of driver distraction by infotainment systems in automotive domain. In: Proceedings of the ACM SIGCHI Symposium on Engineering InteractiveComputing Systems (2017). https://doi.org/10.1145/3102113.3102152
9. Rammanth, R., Kinnear, N., Chowdhury, S., Hyatt, T.: Interacting with Android Auto and Apple CarPlay when driving: The effect on driver performance, IAM roadSmart (2020)
10. Manktelow, K., Chung, M.C.: Psychology of Reasoning. Theoretical and Historical Perspectives (2004)
11. Soler-Adillon, J.: Principios de diseño de interacción para sistemas interactivos (2012)
12. Nielsen, J.: Mental models and user experience design. Nielsen Norman Group. https://www.nngroup.com/articles/mental-models/. Accessed 23 Jan 2021
13. Gaffar, A., Kouchak, S.M.: Minimalist design: an optimized solution for intelligent interactive infotainment systems. In: 2017 Intelligent Systems Conference (IntelliSys), pp. 553–557 (2017). https://doi.org/10.1109/IntelliSys.2017.8324349
14. Luna Garcia, H., et al.: Front-end design guidelines for infotainment systems. Dyna New Technol. **5**(1), 9 (2018). https://doi.org/10.6036/NT8655
15. Westlake, E.J., Boyle, L.N.: Perceptions of driver distraction among teenage drivers. Transport. Res. Part F: Traffic Psychol. Behav. **15**(6), 644–653 (2012). https://doi.org/10.1016/j.trf.2012.06.004
16. Strayer, D.L., Cooper, J.M., Goethe, R.M., McCarty, M.M., Getty, D.J., Biondi, F.: Visual and Cognitive Demands of Using In-Vehicle Information Systems (Technical Report). AAA Foundation for Traffic Safety, Washington, D.C. (2017)

17. Strayer, D.L., et al.: Visual and Cognitive Demands of Using Apple CarPlay, Google's Android Auto and Five Different OEM Infotainment Systems (Technical Report). AAA Foundation for Traffic Safety, Washington, D.C. (2018)

18. Young, K., Regan, M., Hammer, M.: Driver Distraction: A Review of the Literature. Distracted Driving (2003)

19. Nielsen, J.: Why you only need to test with 5 users. Nielsen Norman Group. https://www.nngroup.com/articles/why-you-only-need-to-test-with-5-users/. Accessed 2 Mar 2021

20. Ciesielska, M., Boström, K.W., Öhlander, M.: Observation methods. In: Ciesielska, M., Jemielniak, D. (eds.) Qualitative Methodologies in Organization Studies, pp. 33–52. Springer, Cham (2018). https://doi.org/10.1007/978-3-319-65442-3_2

Model-Driven User Interface Development: A Systematic Mapping

Juan Carlos Mejias[1] , Nemury Silega[2]([⊠]) , Manuel Noguera[3] ,
Yuri I. Rogozov[2] , and Vyachelav S. Lapshin[2]

[1] KPMG Uruguay, Edificio Torre Libertad, Plaza Cagancha 1335, 11200 Montevideo, Uruguay
`juancarlosmejias@kpmg.com`
[2] Department of System Analysis and Telecommunications, Southern Federal University,
347900 Taganrog, Russia
`{silega,rogozov,lapshin}@sfedu.ru`
[3] Departamento de Lenguajes Y Sistemas Informáticos, Universidad de Granada, Pdta. Daniel
Saucedo Aranda S/N, 18071 Granada, Spain
`mnoguera@ugr.es`

Abstract. Model-driven development (MDD) and user interface development (UID) are two interesting research areas in software engineering. While MDD is a paradigm which fosters the models as the main artifact in the software development life cycle, UID deals with methods and techniques for developing high-quality, highly productive user interfaces in terms of usability and reusability. Although research into the use of MDD for UID might well be of interest to the international research community, no such work has yet been published. The aim of this paper is to assess the state of the art in MDD for UID. It mainly focuses on identifying the features of MDD approaches that support UID; how these proposals impact the quality of the software; and what methodological aspects are considered by these proposals. We carried out a systematic mapping study. As a result, 110 papers were analyzed in terms of the criteria obtained from the research questions. This study allows our research questions to be answered. We would like to highlight firstly the predominance of research in purely academic scenarios; secondly, the lack of empirical proof to demonstrate the impact of the approaches; thirdly, the non-existence of methodologies to guide the MDUID process; fourthly, the wide number of tools adopted to support MDUID; and fifthly, the preference for using the task model in the approaches analyzed. This study enables us to determine the state of the art in the topic as well as to identify various problems worthy of future research.

Keywords: Systematic mapping · User interfaces · MDUID · Models · Model-driven development

1 Introduction

Nowadays, users are demanding an ever-increasing number of high-quality systems and their perception of system quality is strongly determined by their experience with the

V. Agredo-Delgado et al. (Eds.): HCI-COLLAB 2022, CCIS 1707, pp. 114–129, 2022.
https://doi.org/10.1007/978-3-031-24709-5_9

user interface (UI). UIs have significant requirements (e.g. multiplatform support and remote access) and their development requires a considerable effort: certain lines of research highlight the fact that UI code represents 48% of the entire system code and requires 50% of project time [1, 2]. These aspects have been corroborated recently.

Model-driven development (MDD) represents a relevant step for consolidating the software development industry in three main ways: by increasing the abstraction level, by using standards, and by exploiting development automation. In order to take advantage of MDD specifications in the user interface development field, the model-driven user interface development (MDUID) approach emerged. The main goal of MDUID is to provide the required insights for the professional, consistent and systematic design and implementation of user interfaces [1, 3–5].

Pinhero [3] identifies several benefits of MDUID, for example to provide an abstract description of a user interface than the descriptions provided by the tools traditionally adopted for UI development. In order to exploit the advantages of MDUID, various approaches have been proposed [6, 7]. Although OMG created IFML to support UI development in an MDD context, few studies examine the features of these approaches.

This work presents the results of a systematic mapping study to assess the state of the art of the MDUID-based approaches in the period 2004–2020. With this study, we intend to identify the main characteristics of MDD-based approaches that support UID; determine how these proposals affect the quality of the software (and the development process); identify the methodological aspects that these proposals consider. The results of this study could represent the starting point for future research.

The remainder of the paper is structured as follows: Sect. 2 describes the systematic mapping methodology; Sect. 3 presents the study results; Sect. 4 evaluates our mapping study; and Sect. 5 outlines our conclusions and future lines of research.

2   Research Method

A systematic mapping (SM) is a secondary study to create a classification scheme and structure an interesting field in software engineering [8]. An SM is considered a prior step for determining suitable areas for a more in-depth study [9]. A SM conceives the follow stages [10]: Definition of research questions; Search execution; Work selection and quality evaluation; Data extraction; Analysis and classification; and Mapping evaluation. The following sections present the results for each stage in our mapping.

2.1   Definition of Research Questions (RQ)

We formulated the following questions for this study:

RQ1: What quality attributes of the software development process improve with MDUID-based approaches?
RQ2: What quality characteristics of the software product improve with MDUID-based approaches?
RQ3: What technologies support MDUID-based approaches?
RQ4: What are the most common models or metamodels?

RQ5: What methodological aspects do these approaches deal with?
RQ6: What research types and research methods have been applied?
RQ7: What is the most common environment for applying the proposals?

2.2 Search

For the purposes of our study, we decided to search in Google Scholar, ACM, IEEE, Springer and Scopus databases. Springer, Scopus, ACM and IEEE are some of the most important databases in the field of software engineering while Google Scholar is a very popular search engine in the research community. Scholar is also widely applied in the execution of searches for systematic mappings [11].

The search string was created by combining keywords (and their synonyms) related to the research topics with Boolean operators. We used the following search string:

("user interface" OR "graphical user interface" OR GUI) AND ("model driven user interface development" OR "model-driven user interface development" OR MDUID) AND (software OR "software development")

For each database, we executed the search in keywords, title and abstract fields. Since it was from 2004 that MDUID gained acknowledged popularity [12], we conducted the search in the period from 2004 until 2020. Having conducted a search of all the databases, we selected 99 publications, as Table 1 shows. In keeping with our goal of obtaining a good sample [13], we also applied a variant of the snowball sampling strategy. With this strategy, 11 works were added. We finally selected 110 publications.

Table 1. Search results

Publications	Google Scholar	ACM	IEEE	Springer	Scopus	Total
Search results	15	20684	61	14206	3273	38374
Analyzed	148	241	61	271	106	827
Candidate	55	36	17	46	48	202
Selected	28	14	13	26	18	99

2.3 Selection Process

Article selection was based on the exclusion/inclusion criteria shown in Table 2.

The selection process included three steps (see the results in Table 2). In the first step, each reviewer applied the inclusion/exclusion criteria based on the title and abstract of randomly appointed publications. In the second step we applied the inclusion/exclusion criteria to the introduction, conclusions and references of the remaining papers. This new set of papers is called the candidate set. Finally, the candidate papers were analyzed by a shallow reading first and with a full reading for those that raised doubts.

Table 2. Inclusion/Exclusion criteria

Criteria	Description
Inclusion	The publication (journal article, conference paper, thesis) describes an MDUID-based approach for developing user interfaces
Exclusion	The publication is not a research paper but might, for example, be a technical document that deals with MDUID adoption
Exclusion	Visionary proposals which are not implemented (at least partially)
Exclusion	Full papers which are not available
Exclusion	Reviews about the state of the art about MDUID
Exclusion	The publication describes the results of either evaluating or validating a proposal that is not well described in the same paper

2.3.1 Reliability Evaluation of the Inclusion/Exclusion Criteria

To evaluate the reliability of the exclusion/inclusion criteria, we selected the first 50 references obtained from the Google Scholar search (34.97% of the total results obtained from this site and 40% of the finally selected publications). After applying the inclusion/exclusion criteria, the titles and abstracts of these 50 papers were used to classify the papers in a separate review by two independent reviewers. Cohen's Kappa coefficient [14] was applied to calculate inter-reviewer reliability. The reliability value was satisfactory (KA = 0.71). This result proves that the criteria are clearly defined and that there is no significant divergence among reviewers [15].

2.4 Classification Scheme

Figure 1 depicts the classification scheme that was defined for this mapping study.

Quality process: This refers to the attributes (productivity, efficacy, efficiency and cost) of the development process that are improved with MDUID-based approaches.

Product quality: In accordance with the standard ISO/IEC 9126–1 [16], the features are classified into functionality, reliability, usability, maintainability and portability.

Methodological proposal: This refers to the publications which mainly deal with the methodological aspects of a proposal.

Technologies to support the MDUID-based approaches: The most popular technologies are Eclipse Modeling Framework, Eclipse Plugins, WebRatio, IdealXML, etc.

Models/Metamodels: The most common are the task models, domain models, abstract UI models and concrete UI models.

Research type and research method: This classification is based on the scheme described by Petersen [10] and Wieringa et al. [17]. Research can either be classified as solution proposals, evaluation research or validation research. In evaluation research, it is possible to use either the industrial case study or the controlled experiment with practitioners research methods, whilst in validation research it is possible to apply either the academic case study or the laboratory experiment as the research method.

Application environment: The application environment could either be an academic environment or an industrial environment. Furthermore, we record the publication year and type (journal article, conference paper or thesis) for each publication.

We created a spreadsheet to record the data of each paper. This approach made it easier to process the data. Furthermore, as some authors [18, 19] recommend, the data extracted were reviewed by a third reviewer in order to reduce bias.

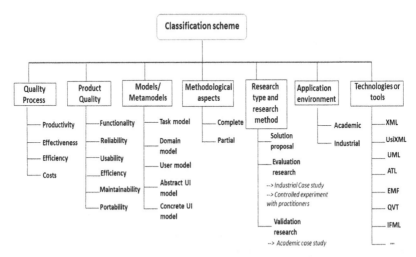

Fig. 1. Classification scheme

3 Results

Fig. 2. Publications per year

Figure 2 depicts the behavior of publications in the time period from 2004 until March, 2020. During the period 2004–2006 the number of publications was low, but from 2005 the number of publications in this research field was steady at between six and nine. The highest number of publications (12) was reached in 2018, whilst in 2019 we identified 9 publications, a number above the average (7). This behavior proves that MDUID remains as an attractive topic and there are still issues to be addressed. The research questions (RQ) that we defined in Sect. 2.1 are answered below:

RQ1: *What quality attributes of the software development process improve with MDUID-based approaches?*

We found 43 works (39%) which mention that productivity is improved [20–62], 5 works (4.5%) mention that costs are reduced [29, 39, 53, 63, 64], 7 works (6.3%) remark that efficiency and efficacy are increased as well [20, 37, 65–69]. One publication demonstrated that a MDUID-based approach improved the productivity of the user interface development by 90% [14]. Usually, however, the publications lack empirical evidence to demonstrate the positive impact of MDUID-based approaches.

RQ2: *What quality characteristics of the software product improve with MDUID-based approaches?*

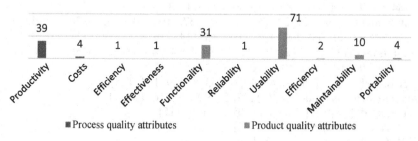

Fig. 3. Process and product quality

Usability and functionality are the quality features of the software product that are most often mentioned in the publications analyzed. The analysis yield that 71 (64.5%) works mention that usability is improved [12, 20, 26, 27, 29, 30, 33, 34, 37–42, 44, 47–52, 57, 59, 62–68, 70–107] while 31 (28.1%) works remark that functionality grow too [12, 21, 22, 28, 29, 35–37, 39, 46, 48, 51–54, 56, 57, 62, 65, 67, 90, 91, 96, 101, 107–113]. The remaining quality characteristics have been less studied. Figure 3 shows a graphical representation of the results for RQ1 and RQ2.

RQ3: *What technologies support MDUID-based approaches?*

The most adopted technologies in the analyzed approaches are:

- **XML** (35.8%) [20, 21, 26, 27, 31, 32, 36, 38, 42, 46, 48, 50, 51, 59, 60, 66, 70, 71, 74, 80, 83, 84, 86, 91, 97, 99–102, 110, 114–121].
- **UsiXML** and its respective tools suit (21.8%) [20, 26, 27, 31, 32, 36, 48, 51, 70, 71, 74, 79, 83, 84, 91, 101, 106, 107, 110, 114, 116–119].
- **UML** (22.7%) [21, 25, 26, 28, 35, 42, 43, 54, 56, 60, 61, 68, 69, 87, 89, 90, 96–98, 103, 105, 112, 113, 115, 122].
- **Eclipse Modeling Framework - EMF** (23.6%) [13, 30, 32, 37, 40, 44, 47, 53, 55, 62, 64, 66, 68, 77, 82, 90, 97, 102, 104, 105, 108, 112, 115, 119, 120, 123].
- **ATL** (12.7%) [37, 44, 62, 64, 66, 75, 77, 81, 82, 97, 98, 102, 115, 124].
- **CTT** (8.2%) [26, 50, 86, 88, 90, 93, 103, 119, 122].
- **QVT** (7.2%) [22, 25, 47, 55, 67, 109, 116, 118].
- **IFML** (9.1%)[45, 49, 53, 56, 59, 68, 97–99, 105].
- **CTT Environment – CCTE** (3.53%) [93, 119].

There are some technologies such as Aceleo [47, 66], IdealXML [20, 83] and Ontology [55, 100, 112] that are less adopted but are interesting options. On the other hand, others develop their own technology [15, 16, 19, 29, 30]. It is noteworthy that a low number of works adopt ATL (12.7%) and QVT (7.2%), two popular transformation languages. These evidences show that transformation languages are scarcely exploited.

RQ4: *What are the most common models or metamodels?*

Some of most adopted models in the analyzed approaches are:

- **Abstract UI model** (45.5%)[20, 22, 24, 26, 30, 32, 37, 38, 40, 41, 48–51, 56, 59, 61, 68–73, 75, 76, 79, 84, 91, 93, 95–101, 103–107, 110, 114–116, 119, 125, 126].
- **Concrete UI model** (33.6%) [20, 26, 30, 32, 37, 38, 40, 41, 49–51, 59, 68–73, 75, 79, 84, 91, 93–100, 103, 104, 114–116, 119, 126]
- **Task model** (31.8%) [20, 22, 23, 26, 27, 32, 37, 40, 46, 49, 51, 52, 70–72, 74, 76, 78, 83, 86, 90, 93, 99, 100, 104, 108–110, 113, 114, 116, 117, 119, 122, 124].
- **Domain model** (25.5%) [26, 29, 32, 37, 39, 40, 42, 46, 48–50, 53, 56, 68, 70, 71, 78, 83, 93, 95, 96, 101, 105, 107, 110, 112, 121, 122].
- **User model** (9.1%) [45, 46, 48, 49, 65, 68, 89, 99, 104, 125].
- **Business process model** (6.4%) [27, 57, 90, 95, 116, 117, 119].
- **Dialog model** (6.4%) [33, 34, 45, 46, 52, 108, 115].
- **UML Activity diagram** [25, 28, 42].
- **UML Class diagram** [28, 105, 122].

Some approaches define their own metamodels [23, 24, 42, 117]. Other approaches [36, 94] adopt metamodels proposed by relevant authors in this field. While surprisingly only three works adopted the popular UML class diagram and UML activity diagram. It is also noteworthy the low number of works that do not exploit models of other stages in the software life cycle to generate specific models for UI, for example data models.

RQ5: *What methodological aspects do these approaches deal with?*

Only 50 of the selected publications (45.5%) [12, 13, 20, 22, 24, 25, 27–30, 32, 36–38, 43, 45, 47–49, 53, 54, 63, 65, 66, 70–72, 77, 79–81, 83–85, 87, 92, 93, 95, 97–99, 103, 105, 106, 110, 116, 119, 120, 123–125] deal with methodological aspects and all of them do so to some extent. We did not find any publication that completely defines the roles, activities and artifacts required to adopt the approach.

RQ6: *What research types and research methods have been applied?*

The analysis yielded that solution proposal with 99 works (90%) is the most common research type, with evaluation research representing 8. 2% [27, 62, 67–69, 76, 101, 105, 107] and validation research 1.8% [65, 92]. Regarding research method, one work applied a controlled experiment with practitioners [69, 105, 107] and another applied an industrial case study. Finally, the evaluation research applied an academic case study.

RQ7: *What is the most common environment (either academic or industrial) for applying the proposals?*

The 96.4% of the approaches are applied in academic environments, only four approaches have been applied in real industrial environments [27, 56, 72, 87]. This means that the adoption of MDUID in industry is still marginal.

4 Conclusions and Future Work

In this work we have performed a systematic mapping to analyze 110 publications. With this study we have obtained useful insights for the research community about MDUID.

The mapping study enabled us to identify various issues in the MDUID research field. Possibly the most relevant of these is the lack of empirical evidence to assess the real impact of MDUID-based approaches on the software development process and on the software product. These elements are strongly related to the fact that only 4.4% of the publications have been applied in an industrial environment.

The identification of the most adopted models could be a useful insight for both researchers from MDUID and software developers. The researcher on MDUID can identify the gaps of the most common models and find solutions to solve them. Whilst, software developers can choose the right models according to their context or simply adopt the most common ones. On the other hand, we wish to highlight that only 44.5% of the works partially deal with methodological aspects.

Acknowledgement. This research is supported by a postdoc fellowship granted by the Institute of Computer Technologies and Information Security, Southern Federal University, project №. PD/20-02-KT.

References

1. Meixner, G., Paternò, F., Vanderdonckt, J.: Past, present, and future of model-based user interface development. i-com **10**(3), 2–11 (2011). https://doi.org/10.1524/icom.2011.0026
2. Martin, C., Braune, A.: Integration of a template system into model-based user interface development workflows. In: Kurosu, M. (ed.) HCI 2017. LNCS, vol. 10271, pp. 480–495. Springer, Cham (2017). https://doi.org/10.1007/978-3-319-58071-5_36
3. Silva, P.: User interface declarative models and development environments: a survey. In: Palanque, P., Paternò, F. (eds.) DSV-IS 2000. LNCS, vol. 1946, pp. 207–226. Springer, Heidelberg (2001). https://doi.org/10.1007/3-540-44675-3_13
4. Gomaa, M., Salah, A., Rahman, S.: Towards a better model based user interface development environment: A comprehensive survey. In: Proceedings of MICS, vol. 5 (2005)
5. Calvary, G., Coutaz, J.: Introduction to model-based user interfaces. Group Note **7**, W3C (2014). https://www.w3.org/2011/mbui/drafts/mbui-intro/
6. Martínez, Y., Castro, C.C., Beigbeder, S.M.: Evidencia empírica sobre mejoras en productividad y calidad en enfoques MDD: un mapeo sistemático. REICIS: Revista Española de Innovación, Calidad e Ingeniería del Software **7**(2), 6–27 (2011)
7. Mohagheghi, P., et al.: Where does model-driven engineering help? Experiences from three industrial cases. Softw. Syst. Model. **12**(3), 619–639 (2013). https://doi.org/10.1007/s10270-011-0219-7
8. Petersen, K., et al.: Systematic mapping studies in software engineering. In: Ease (2008). https://doi.org/10.14236/ewic/EASE2008.8
9. Mujtaba, S., et al.: Software Product Line Variability: A Systematic Mapping Study. School of Engineering, Blekinge Institue of Technology (2008)
10. Petersen, K., Vakkalanka, S., Kuzniarz, L.: Guidelines for conducting systematic mapping studies in software engineering: an update. Inf. Softw. Technol. **64**, 1–18 (2015). https://doi.org/10.1016/j.infsof.2015.03.007
11. Noruzi, A.: Google scholar: the new generation of citation indexes. Libri **55**(4), 170–180 (2005). https://doi.org/10.1515/LIBR.2005.170
12. Akiki, P.A., Bandara, A.K., Yu, Y.: Adaptive model-driven user interface development systems. ACM Comput. Surv. **47**(1), 9 (2014). https://doi.org/10.1145/2597999

13. Wolff, A., Forbrig, P.: Model-driven user interface development with the eclipse modeling project. In: 5 th International Workshop on Model Driven Development of Advanced User Interfaces (MDDAUI 2010) (2010)

14. Gwet, K.: Inter-rater reliability: dependency on trait prevalence and marginal homogeneity. Stat. Methods Inter-Rater Reliab. Assess. Series **2**(1), 9 (2002)

15. Fleiss, J.L., Levin, B., Paik, M.C.: Statistical Methods for Rates and Proportions. John Wiley & Sons (2013)

16. ISO, I., IEC 9126–1: Software engineering-product quality-part 1: Quality model, vol. **21**. International Organization for Standardization, Geneva, Switzerland (2001)

17. Wieringa, R., Maiden, N., Mead, N., Rolland, C.: Requirements engineering paper classification and evaluation criteria: a proposal and a discussion. Requirements Eng. **11**(1), 102–107 (2006). https://doi.org/10.1007/s00766-005-0021-6

18. Kitchenham, B., Brereton, O.P., Budgen, D., Turner, M., Bailey, J., Linkman, S.: Systematic literature reviews in software engineering – A systematic literature review. Inform. Softw. Technol. **51**(1), 7–15 (2009). https://doi.org/10.1016/j.infsof.2008.09.009

19. Brereton, P., Kitchenham, B.A., Budgen, D., Turner, M., Khalil, M.: Lessons from applying the systematic literature review process within the software engineering domain. J. Syst. Softw. **80**(4), 571–583 (2007). https://doi.org/10.1016/j.jss.2006.07.009

20. Sousa, K., Mendonça, H., Vanderdonckt, J.: Towards method engineering of model-driven user interface development. In: Winckler, M., Johnson, H., Palanque, P. (eds.) TAMODIA 2007. LNCS, vol. 4849, pp. 112–125. Springer, Heidelberg (2007). https://doi.org/10.1007/978-3-540-77222-4_10

21. Ding, X., Li, X.: Research of model-driven interactive automatic/semi-automatic form building. In: Smith, M.J., Salvendy, G. (eds.) Human Interface 2007. LNCS, vol. 4557, pp. 613–622. Springer, Heidelberg (2007). https://doi.org/10.1007/978-3-540-73345-4_70

22. Heinrich, M., et al.: MDA applied: a task-model driven tool chain for multimodal applications. In: Winckler, M., Johnson, H., Palanque, P. (eds.) TAMODIA 2007. LNCS, vol. 4849, pp. 15–27. Springer, Heidelberg (2007). https://doi.org/10.1007/978-3-540-77222-4_3

23. Di Santo, G., Zimeo, E.: Reversing GUIs to XIML descriptions for the adaptation to heterogeneous devices. In: Proceedings of the 2007 ACM symposium on Applied computing. ACM (2007). https://doi.org/10.1145/1244002.1244314

24. Witt, H., Nicolai, T., Kenn, H.: The WUI-Toolkit: A model-driven UI development framework for wearable user interfaces. In: 27th International Conference on Distributed Computing Systems Workshops. IEEE (2007). https://doi.org/10.1109/ICDCSW.2007.80

25. Link, S., et al.: Focusing graphical user interfaces in model-driven software development. In: First International Conference on Advances in Computer-Human Interaction. IEEE (2008). https://doi.org/10.1109/ACHI.2008.16

26. Adam, S., Breiner, K., Mukasa, K.S., Trapp, M.: Challenges to the model-driven generation of user interfaces at runtime for ambient intelligent systems. In: Mühlhäuser, M., Ferscha, A., Aitenbichler, E. (eds.) AmI 2007. CCIS, vol. 11, pp. 147–155. Springer, Heidelberg (2008). https://doi.org/10.1007/978-3-540-85379-4_18

27. García, J.G., Lemaigre, C., Vanderdonckt, J., Calleros, J.M.G.: Model-driven engineering of workflow user interfaces. In: Jaquero, V.L., Simarro, F.M., Masso, J.P.M., Vanderdonckt, J. (eds.) Computer-Aided Design of User Interfaces VI, pp. 9–22. Springer London, London (2009). https://doi.org/10.1007/978-1-84882-206-1_2

28. Funk, M., Hoyer, P., Link, S.: Model-driven instrumentation of graphical user interfaces. In: 2009 Second International Conferences on Advances in Computer-Human Interactions (2009). IEEE. https://doi.org/10.1109/ACHI.2009.16

29. Schramm, A., Preußner, A., Heinrich, M., Vogel, L.: Rapid UI development for enterprise applications: combining manual and model-driven techniques. In: Petriu, D.C., Rouquette,

N., Haugen, Ø. (eds.) MODELS 2010. LNCS, vol. 6394, pp. 271–285. Springer, Heidelberg (2010). https://doi.org/10.1007/978-3-642-16145-2_19

30. Hennig, S., Van den Bergh, J., Luyten, K., Braune, A.: User driven evolution of user interface models – The FLEPR approach. In: Campos, P., Graham, N., Jorge, J., Nunes, N., Palanque, P., Winckler, M. (eds.) INTERACT 2011. LNCS, vol. 6948, pp. 610–627. Springer, Heidelberg (2011). https://doi.org/10.1007/978-3-642-23765-2_41

31. López-Jaquero, V., Montero, F., González, P.: T:XML: a tool supporting user interface model transformation. In: Hussmann, H., Meixner, G., Zuehlke, D. (eds.) Model-Driven Development of Advanced User Interfaces, pp. 241–256. Springer Berlin Heidelberg, Berlin, Heidelberg (2011). https://doi.org/10.1007/978-3-642-14562-9_12

32. Cano, J., Vanderdonckt, J.: Towards Methodological Guidance for User Interface Development Life Cycle. In: 2nd Int. Workshop on User Interface Extensible Markup Language UsiXML'2011 (2011). http://hdl.handle.net/2078/118174

33. Breiner, K., Bizik, K., Rauch, T., Seissler, M., Meixner, G., Diebold, P.: Automatic adaptation of user workflows within model-based user interface generation during runtime on the example of the SmartMote. In: Jacko, J.A. (ed.) HCI 2011. LNCS, vol. 6761, pp. 165–174. Springer, Heidelberg (2011). https://doi.org/10.1007/978-3-642-21602-2_19

34. Breiner, K., Meixner, G., Rombach, D., Seissler, M., Zühlke, D.: Efficient generation of ambient intelligent user interfaces. In: König, A., Dengel, A., Hinkelmann, K., Kise, K., Howlett, R.J., Jain, L.C. (eds.) KES 2011. LNCS (LNAI), vol. 6884, pp. 136–145. Springer, Heidelberg (2011). https://doi.org/10.1007/978-3-642-23866-6_15

35. Basin, D., et al.: Model-driven development of security-aware GUIs for data-centric applications. In: Aldini, A., Gorrieri, R. (eds.) FOSAD 2011. LNCS, vol. 6858, pp. 101–124. Springer, Heidelberg (2011). https://doi.org/10.1007/978-3-642-23082-0_4

36. Figueroa-Martinez, J., López-Jaquero, V., Vela, F.L.G., González, P.: Enriching UsiXML language to support awareness requirements. Sci. Comput. Programm. 78(11), 2259–2267 (2013). https://doi.org/10.1016/j.scico.2012.09.020

37. Molina, A.I., Giraldo, W.J., Gallardo, J., Redondo, M.A., Ortega, M., García, G.: CIAT-GUI: A MDE-compliant environment for developing Graphical User Interfaces of information systems. Adv. Eng. Softw. 52, 10–29 (2012). https://doi.org/10.1016/j.advengsoft.2012.06.002

38. Wu, H., Hua, Q.: A model-driven interactive system. In: Yang, Y., Ma, M., Liu, B. (eds.) ICICA 2013. CCIS, vol. 392, pp. 430–439. Springer, Heidelberg (2013). https://doi.org/10.1007/978-3-642-53703-5_44

39. Kis, F., Bogdan, C.: Lightweight low-level query-centric user interface modeling. In: 2013 46th Hawaii International Conference on System Sciences/ IEEE (2013). https://doi.org/10.1109/HICSS.2013.384

40. Pleuss, A., Wollny, S., Botterweck, G.: Model-driven development and evolution of customized user interfaces. In: 5th ACM SIGCHI symposium on Engineering interactive computing systems. ACM (2013). https://doi.org/10.1145/2494603.2480298

41. Nguyen, V.-T., Tran, M.-T., Duong, A.-D.: Picture-driven user interface development for applications on multi-platforms. In: Kurosu, M. (ed.) HCI 2014. LNCS, vol. 8510, pp. 350–360. Springer, Cham (2014). https://doi.org/10.1007/978-3-319-07233-3_33

42. da Silva, L., et al.: Model-driven gui generation and navigation for android bis apps. In: 2nd International Conference on Model-Driven Engineering and Software Development (2014)

43. Basin, D., Clavel, M., Egea, M., de Dios, M.A.G., Dania, C.: A model-driven methodology for developing secure data-management applications. IEEE Trans. Softw. Eng. 40(4), 324–337 (2014). https://doi.org/10.1109/TSE.2013.2297116

44. Zeferino, N.V., Vilain, P.: A model-driven approach for generating interfaces from user interaction diagrams. In: Proceedings of the 16th International Conference on Information

Integration and Web-based Applications & Services. ACM (2014). https://doi.org/10.1145/2684200.2684326

45. Acerbis, R., Bongio, A., Brambilla, M., Butti, S.: Model-driven development based on OMG's IFML with WebRatio web and mobile platform. In: Cimiano, P., Frasincar, F., Houben, G.-J., Schwabe, D. (eds.) ICWE 2015. LNCS, vol. 9114, pp. 605–608. Springer, Cham (2015). https://doi.org/10.1007/978-3-319-19890-3_39

46. Seffah, A.: HCI design patterns as a building block in model-driven engineering. In: Patterns of HCI Design and HCI Design of Patterns. HIS, pp. 35–58. Springer, Cham (2015). https://doi.org/10.1007/978-3-319-15687-3_3

47. Roubi, S., Erramdani, M., Mbarki, S.: A model driven approach to generate graphical user interfaces for Rich Internet Applications using Interaction Flow Modeling Language. In: 15th International Conference on Intelligent Systems Design and Applications (ISDA). IEEE (2015) https://doi.org/10.1109/ISDA.2015.7489237

48. Ruiz, J., Sedrakyan, G., Snoeck, M.: Generating User Interface from Conceptual, Presentation and User models with JMermaid in a learning approach. In: Proceedings of the XVI International Conference on Human Computer Interaction. ACM (2015). https://doi.org/10.1145/2829875.2829893

49. Fischer, H., Yigitbas, E., Sauer, S.: Integrating Human-Centered and Model-Driven Methods in Agile UI Development. In: INTERACT 2015 Adjunct Proceedings: 15th IFIP TC. 13 International Conference on Human-Computer Interaction, University of Bamberg Press, Bamberg, Germany, 14–18 Sept 2015

50. Engel, J., Märtin, C., Forbrig, P.: A concerted model-driven and pattern-based framework for developing user interfaces of interactive ubiquitous applications. In: LMIS@ EICS (2015)

51. Khaddam, I., Mezhoudi, N., Vanderdonckt, J.: Adapt-first: A MDE transformation approach for supporting user interface adaptation. In: 2nd World Symposium on Web Applications and Networking (2015). https://doi.org/10.1109/WSWAN.2015.7209080

52. Yigitbas, E., Sauer, S., Engels, G.: A model-based framework for multi-adaptive migratory user interfaces. In: Kurosu, M. (ed.) HCI 2015. LNCS, vol. 9170, pp. 563–572. Springer, Cham (2015). https://doi.org/10.1007/978-3-319-20916-6_52

53. Frey, A., Sottet, J., Vagner, A.: A multi-viewpoint approach to support collaborative user interface generation. In: 19th International Conference on Computer Supported Cooperative Work in Design (CSCWD). IEEE (2015). https://doi.org/10.1109/CSCWD.2015.7230997

54. Basso, F.P., Pillat, R.M., Frantz, F.R., Frantz, R.Z.: Combining MDE and scrum on the rapid prototyping of web information systems. Int. J. Web Eng. Technol. **10**(3), 214 (2015). https://doi.org/10.1504/IJWET.2015.072347

55. Laaz, N., Mbarki, S.: A model-driven approach for generating RIA interfaces using IFML and ontologies. In: 2016 4th IEEE International Colloquium on Information Science and Technology (CiSt). IEEE (2016). https://doi.org/10.1109/CIST.2016.7805005

56. Yigitbas, E., Sauer, S.: Engineering context-adaptive UIs for task-continuous cross-channel applications. In: Bogdan, C., et al. (eds.) HCSE/HESSD -2016. LNCS, vol. 9856, pp. 281–300. Springer, Cham (2016). https://doi.org/10.1007/978-3-319-44902-9_18

57. Bocanegra García, J.J., Mariscal, J.A.P., Carrillo Ramos, A.C.: Towards a domain-specific language to design adaptive software: the DMLAS approach. Ingenieria y Universidad **20**(2), 335 (2016). https://doi.org/10.11144/Javeriana.iyu20-2.tdsl

58. Thanh, N., Vanderdonckt, J., Seffah, A.: UIPLML: Pattern-based engineering of user interfaces of multi-platform systems. In: International Conference on Research Challenges in Information Science. IEEE (2016). https://doi.org/10.1109/RCIS.2016.7549348

59. Fadhlillah, H.S., Adianto, D., Azurat, A., Sakinah, S.I.: Generating adaptable user interface in SPLE: using delta-oriented programming and interaction flow modeling language. In:

Proceedings of the 22nd International Systems and Software Product Line Conference – vol. 2 (SPLC'18). Association for Computing Machinery, New York, NY, USA, pp. 52–55 (2018). https://doi.org/10.1145/3236405.3237199

60. Rehman, S., et al.: Development of user interface for multi-platform applications using the model driven software engineering techniques. In: 2018 IEEE 9th Annual Information Technology, Electronics and Mobile Communication Conference (IEMCON). IEEE (2018). https://doi.org/10.1109/IEMCON.2018.8615013

61. Ostroff, J.S., Wang, C.-W.: Modelling and Testing Requirements via Executable Abstract State Machines. In: 2018 IEEE 8th International Model-Driven Requirements Engineering Workshop (MoDRE). IEEE (2018). https://doi.org/10.1109/MoDRE.2018.00007

62. Bouraoui, A., Gharbi, I.: Model driven engineering of accessible and multi-platform graphical user interfaces by parameterized model transformations. Sci. Comput. Program. **172**, 63–101 (2019). https://doi.org/10.1016/j.scico.2018.11.002

63. Ben Ammar, L., Mahfoudhi, A.: An empirical evaluation of a usability measurement method in a model driven framework. In: Holzinger, A., Ziefle, M., Hitz, M., Debevc, M. (eds.) SouthCHI 2013. LNCS, vol. 7946, pp. 157–173. Springer, Heidelberg (2013). https://doi.org/10.1007/978-3-642-39062-3_10

64. Dimbisoa, W., et al.: Automatically generate a specific human computer interaction from an interface diagram model. In: 2018 4th International Conference on Computer and Technology Applications. IEEE (2018). https://doi.org/10.1109/CATA.2018.8398671

65. Hussain, J., et al.: Model-based adaptive user interface based on context and user experience evaluation. J. Multimodal User Interfaces **12**(1), 1–16 (2018). https://doi.org/10.1007/s12193-018-0258-2

66. Parra, O., España, S., Panach, J.I., Pastor, O.: An empirical comparative evaluation of gestUI to include gesture-based interaction in user interfaces. Sci. Comput. Programm. **172**, 232–263 (2019). https://doi.org/10.1016/j.scico.2018.12.001

67. Daun, M., Weyer, T., Pohl, K.: Improving manual reviews in function-centered engineering of embedded systems using a dedicated review model. Softw. Syst. Model. **18**(6), 3421–3459 (2019). https://doi.org/10.1007/s10270-019-00723-2

68. Yigitbas, E., Anjorin, A., Jovanovikj, I., Kern, T., Sauer, S., Engels, G.: Usability evaluation of model-driven cross-device web user interfaces. In: Bogdan, C., Kuusinen, K., Lárusdóttir, M.K., Palanque, P., Winckler, M. (eds.) HCSE 2018. LNCS, vol. 11262, pp. 231–247. Springer, Cham (2019). https://doi.org/10.1007/978-3-030-05909-5_14

69. Ziegler, D., Peissner, M.: Modelling of polymorphic user interfaces at the appropriate level of abstraction. In: Ahram, T.Z. (ed.) AHFE 2018. AISC, vol. 787, pp. 45–56. Springer, Cham (2019). https://doi.org/10.1007/978-3-319-94229-2_5

70. Limbourg, Q., Vanderdonckt, J., Michotte, B., Bouillon, L., López-Jaquero, V.: USIXML: a language supporting multi-path development of user interfaces. In: Bastide, R., Palanque, P., Roth, J. (eds.) DSV-IS 2004. LNCS, vol. 3425, pp. 200–220. Springer, Heidelberg (2005). https://doi.org/10.1007/11431879_12

71. Vanderdonckt, J.: A MDA-compliant environment for developing user interfaces of information systems. In: Pastor, O., Falcão e Cunha, J. (eds.) CAiSE 2005. LNCS, vol. 3520, pp. 16–31. Springer, Heidelberg (2005). https://doi.org/10.1007/11431855_2

72. Puerta, A., Micheletti, M., Mak, A.: The UI pilot: a model-based tool to guide early interface design. In: Proceedings of the 10th international conference on Intelligent user interfaces. ACM (2005). https://doi.org/10.1145/1040830.1040877

73. Wolff, A., Forbrig, P.: Model based reengineering of user interfaces. In: MDDAUI (2005)

74. Trapp, M., Schmettow, M.: Consistency in use through model based user interface development. In: Workshop at CHI (2006)

75. Kavaldjian, S.: A model-driven approach to generating user interfaces. In: 6th joint meeting of the European software engineering conference and the ACM SIGSOFT symposium on The foundations of software engineering (2007). https://doi.org/10.1145/1287624.1287721
76. Abrahão, S., Iborra, E., Vanderdonckt, J.: Usability evaluation of user interfaces generated with a model-driven architecture tool. In: Law, E.-C., Hvannberg, E.T., Cockton, G. (eds.) Maturing Usability. HIS, pp. 3–32. Springer, London (2008). https://doi.org/10.1007/978-1-84628-941-5_1
77. Sottet, J.-S., Calvary, G., Coutaz, J., Favre, J.-M.: A model-driven engineering approach for the usability of plastic user interfaces. In: Gulliksen, J., Harning, M.B., Palanque, P., van der Veer, G.C., Wesson, J. (eds.) DSV-IS/EHCI/HCSE -2007. LNCS, vol. 4940, pp. 140–157. Springer, Heidelberg (2008). https://doi.org/10.1007/978-3-540-92698-6_9
78. Feuerstack, S., et al.: Automated Usability Evaluation during Model-Based Interactive System Development. In: Forbrig, P., Paternò, F. (eds.) HCSE/TAMODIA -2008. LNCS, vol. 5247, pp. 134–141. Springer, Heidelberg (2008). https://doi.org/10.1007/978-3-540-85992-5_12
79. Aquino, N., Vanderdonckt, J., Valverde, F., Pastor, O.: Using profiles to support model transformations in the model-driven development of user interfaces. In: Jaquero, V.L., Simarro, F.M., Masso, J.P.M., Vanderdonckt, J. (eds.) Computer-Aided Design of User Interfaces VI, pp. 35–46. Springer London, London (2009). https://doi.org/10.1007/978-1-84882-206-1_4
80. Sukaviriya, N., Mani, S., Sinha, V.: Reflection of a year long model-driven business and ui modeling development project. In: Gross, T., et al. (eds.) INTERACT 2009. LNCS, vol. 5727, pp. 749–762. Springer, Heidelberg (2009). https://doi.org/10.1007/978-3-642-03658-3_80
81. Sottet, J.-S., Calvary, G., Favre, J.-M., Coutaz, J.: Megamodeling and metamodel-driven engineering for plastic user interfaces: mega-ui. In: Seffah, A., Vanderdonckt, J., Desmarais, M.C. (eds.) Human-Centered Software Engineering: Software Engineering Models, Patterns and Architectures for HCI, pp. 173–200. Springer London, London (2009). https://doi.org/10.1007/978-1-84800-907-3_8
82. Kavaldjian, S., et al.: Semi-automatic user interface generation considering pointing granularity. In: 2009 IEEE International Conference on Systems, Man and Cybernetics. IEEE (2009). https://doi.org/10.1109/ICSMC.2009.5346356
83. Vanderdonckt, J., Simarro, F.M.: Generative pattern-based design of user interfaces. In: Proceedings of the 1st International Workshop on Pattern-Driven Engineering of Interactive Computing Systems. ACM (2010). https://doi.org/10.1145/1824749.1824753
84. Aquino, N., Vanderdonckt, J., Pastor, O.: Transformation templates: adding flexibility to model-driven engineering of user interfaces. In: Proceedings of the 2010 ACM Symposium on Applied Computing. ACM (2010). https://doi.org/10.1145/1774088.1774340
85. Raneburger, D.: Interactive model driven graphical user interface generation. In: Proceedings of the 2nd ACM SIGCHI symposium on Engineering interactive computing systems. ACM (2010). https://doi.org/10.1145/1822018.1822071
86. Van den Bergh, J., Sahni, D., Coninx, K.: Task models for safe software evolution and adaptation. In: England, D., Palanque, P., Vanderdonckt, J., Wild, P.J. (eds.) TAMODIA 2009. LNCS, vol. 5963, pp. 72–77. Springer, Heidelberg (2010). https://doi.org/10.1007/978-3-642-11797-8_6
87. de_Almeida Monte-Mor, J., et al.: Applying MDA approach to create graphical user interfaces. In: 2011 Eighth International Conference on Information Technology: New Generations. IEEE (2011), https://doi.org/10.1109/ITNG.2011.206
88. Raneburger, D., et al.: Automated WIMP-UI behavior generation: Parallelism and granularity of communication units. In: 2011 IEEE International Conference on Systems, Man, and Cybernetics. IEEE (2011). https://doi.org/10.1109/ICSMC.2011.6084099.

89. Mejía, A., et al.: Implementing adaptive interfaces: a user model for the development of usability in interactive systems. In: Proceedings of the CUBE International Information Technology Conference. ACM (2012). https://doi.org/10.1145/2381716.2381831

90. Molina, A.I., Gallardo, J., Redondo, M.A., Ortega, M., Giraldo, W.J.: Metamodel-driven definition of a visual modeling language for specifying interactive groupware applications: An empirical study. J. Syst. Softw. **86**(7), 1772–1789 (2013). https://doi.org/10.1016/j.jss.2012.07.049

91. Van Hees, K., Engelen, J.: Equivalent representations of multimodal user interfaces. Univ. Access Inf. Soc. **12**(4), 339–368 (2012). https://doi.org/10.1007/s10209-012-0282-z

92. Raneburger, D., et al.: A case study in automated gui generation for multiple devices. In: 2013 Africon. IEEE (2013). https://doi.org/10.1109/AFRCON.2013.6757645

93. Montero, F., López-Jaquero, V., González, P.: User-Centered Reverse Engineering. Technical Report. University of Castilla-La Mancha (2013)

94. Ammar, L.B., Trabelsi, A., Mahfoudhi, A.: Dealing with usability in model-driven development method. In: Hammoudi, S., Cordeiro, J., Maciaszek, L.A., Filipe, J. (eds.) ICEIS 2013. LNBIP, vol. 190, pp. 405–420. Springer, Cham (2014). https://doi.org/10.1007/978-3-319-09492-2_24

95. Zappia, I., et al.: Model and framework for multimodal and adaptive user interfaces generation in the context of business processes development. PhD Thesis, Faculty of Engineering, Department of Information Engineering (2014)

96. da Costa, S., Neto, V., de Oliveira, J.: A user interface stereotype to build web portals. In: 9th Latin American Web Congress. IEEE (2014). https://doi.org/10.1109/LAWeb.2014.8

97. Yigitbas, E., Mohrmann, B., Sauer, S.: Model-driven UI development integrating HCI patterns. LMIS@EICS **2015**, 42–46 (2015)

98. Yigitbas, E., Sauer, S.: Customized UI Development Through Context-Sensitive GUI Patterns. In: Mensch und Computer 2016–Workshopband (2016)

99. Yigitbas, E., Stahl, H., Sauer, S., Engels, G.: Self-adaptive UIs: integrated model-driven development of UIs and their adaptations. In: Anjorin, A., Espinoza, H. (eds.) ECMFA 2017. LNCS, vol. 10376, pp. 126–141. Springer, Cham (2017). https://doi.org/10.1007/978-3-319-61482-3_8

100. Hitz, M., Kessel, T., Pfisterer, D.: Automatic UI generation for aggregated linked data applications by using sharable application ontologies. In: Pires, L.F., Hammoudi, S., Selic, B. (eds.) MODELSWARD 2017. CCIS, vol. 880, pp. 328–353. Springer, Cham (2018). https://doi.org/10.1007/978-3-319-94764-8_14

101. Ruiz, J., Serral Asensio, E., Snoeck, M.: A fully implemented didactic tool for the teaching of interactive software systems. In: 6th International Conference on Model-Driven Engineering and Software Development (2018). https://doi.org/10.5220/0006579600950105

102. Jaouadi, I., Ben Djemaa, R., Ben-Abdallah, H.: A model-driven development approach for context-aware systems. Softw. Syst. Model. **17**(4), 1169–1195 (2016). https://doi.org/10.1007/s10270-016-0550-0

103. Ruíz, A., Giraldo, W.J., Geerts, D., Arciniegas, J.L.: A roadmap for user interface design of interactive systems: an approach based on a triad of patterns. In: Marcus, A., Wang, W. (eds.) DUXU 2018. LNCS, vol. 10918, pp. 223–240. Springer, Cham (2018). https://doi.org/10.1007/978-3-319-91797-9_16

104. Gaouar, L., et al.: HCIDL: Human-computer interface description language for multi-target, multimodal, plastic user interfaces. Future Computing and Informatics Journal **3**(1), 110–130 (2018). https://doi.org/10.1016/j.fcij.2018.02.001

105. Yigitbas, E., Jovanovikj, I., Biermeier, K., Sauer, S., Engels, G.: Integrated model-driven development of self-adaptive user interfaces. Softw. Syst. Model. **19**(5), 1057–1081 (2020). https://doi.org/10.1007/s10270-020-00777-7

106. Tanaka, S., et al., *Development Support of User Interfaces Adaptive to Use Environment*, in *ICSCA '19*. 2019, ACM. p. 223–228. https://doi.org/10.1145/3316615.3316663
107. Ruiz, J., Serral, E., Snoeck, M.: Technology Enhanced Support for Learning Interactive Software Systems. In: Hammoudi, S., Pires, L.F., Selic, B. (eds.) MODELSWARD 2018. CCIS, vol. 991, pp. 185–210. Springer, Cham (2019). https://doi.org/10.1007/978-3-030-11030-7_9
108. Trætteberg, H., Krogstie, J.: Enhancing the Usability of BPM-Solutions by Combining Process and User-Interface Modelling. In: Stirna, J., Persson, A. (eds.) PoEM 2008. LNBIP, vol. 15, pp. 86–97. Springer, Heidelberg (2008). https://doi.org/10.1007/978-3-540-89218-2_7
109. Tietz, V., et al. *Towards task-based development of enterprise mashups*. in *Proceedings of the 13th International Conference on Information Integration and Web-based Applications and Services*. 2011. ACM. https://doi.org/10.1145/2095536.2095594
110. Tesoriero, R., Bourimi, M., Karatas, F., Barth, T., Villanueva, P.G., Schwarte, P.: Model-Driven Privacy and Security in Multi-modal Social Media UIs. In: Atzmueller, M., Chin, A., Helic, D., Hotho, A. (eds.) MSM/MUSE -2011. LNCS (LNAI), vol. 7472, pp. 158–181. Springer, Heidelberg (2012). https://doi.org/10.1007/978-3-642-33684-3_9
111. Lachgar, M. and A. Abdali. *Generating Android graphical user interfaces using an MDA approach*. in *2014 Third IEEE International Colloquium in Information Science and Technology (CIST)*. 2014. IEEE. https://doi.org/10.1109/CIST.2014.7016598
112. Agt-Rickauer, H., Kutsche, R.-D., Sack, H.: Automated Recommendation of Related Model Elements for Domain Models. In: Hammoudi, S., Pires, L.F., Selic, B. (eds.) MODELSWARD 2018. CCIS, vol. 991, pp. 134–158. Springer, Cham (2019). https://doi.org/10.1007/978-3-030-11030-7_7
113. Faily, S.: A Conceptual Model for Usable Secure Requirements Engineering. In: Designing Usable and Secure Software with IRIS and CAIRIS, pp. 55–71. Springer, Cham (2018). https://doi.org/10.1007/978-3-319-75493-2_3
114. Molina, J., et al. *Towards virtualization of user interfaces based on UsiXML*. in *International conference on 3D Web technology*. 2005. ACM. https://doi.org/10.1145/1050491.1050516
115. Botterweck, G.: A Model-Driven Approach to the Engineering of Multiple User Interfaces. In: Kühne, T. (ed.) MODELS 2006. LNCS, vol. 4364, pp. 106–115. Springer, Heidelberg (2007). https://doi.org/10.1007/978-3-540-69489-2_14
116. Sousa, K., et al. *User interface derivation from business processes: a model-driven approach for organizational engineering*. in *Proceedings of the 2008 ACM symposium on Applied computing*. 2008. ACM. https://doi.org/10.1145/1363686.1363821
117. Sousa, K., H. Mendonça, and J. Vanderdonckt, *User Interface Development Life Cycle for Business-Driven Enterprise Applications*, in *Computer-Aided Design of User Interfaces VI*. 2009, Springer. p. 23–34. https://doi.org/10.1007/978-1-84882-206-1_3
118. López., et al. *Designing user interface adaptation rules with T: XML*. in *14th international conference on Intelligent user interfaces*. 2009. https://doi.org/10.1145/1502650.1502705
119. Wolff, A. and P. Forbrig, *Deriving user interfaces from task models*. Proc. of MDDAUI, 2012
120. García Frey, A., J.-S. Sottet, and A. Vagner. *Ame: an adaptive modelling environment as a collaborative modelling tool*. in *ACM SIGCHI symposium on Engineering interactive computing systems*. 2014. ACM. https://doi.org/10.1145/2607023.2611450
121. Krainz, E., Feiner, J., Fruhmann, M.: Accelerated Development for Accessible Apps – Model Driven Development of Transportation Apps for Visually Impaired People. In: Bogdan, C., et al. (eds.) HCSE/HESSD -2016. LNCS, vol. 9856, pp. 374–381. Springer, Cham (2016). https://doi.org/10.1007/978-3-319-44902-9_25
122. López-Jaquero, V., et al., *UML2App: Towards the automatic generation of user interfaces for mobile devices*, in *XX International Conference on Human Computer Interaction (Interacción 2019)*. 2019, ACM: Spain. https://doi.org/10.1145/3335595.3335617

123. Khaddam, I., H. Barakat, and J. Vanderdonckt. *Enactment of User Interface Development Methods in Software Life Cycles.* in *RoCHI.* 2016

124. Gallardo, J., et al.: A model-driven and task-oriented method for the development of collaborative systems. J. Netw. Comput. Appl. **36**(6), 1551–1565 (2013). https://doi.org/10.1016/j.jnca.2013.03.016

125. Valverde, F., I. Panach, and O. Pastor. *An abstract interaction model for a MDA software production method.* in *Tutorials, posters, panels and industrial contributions at the 26th international conference on Conceptual modeling.* 2007. Australian Computer Society, Inc.

126. Anjorin, A., et al. *On the development of consistent user interfaces.* in *Conference Companion of the 2nd International Conference on Art, Science, and Engineering of Programming.* 2018. ACM. https://doi.org/10.1145/3191697.3191716

Multi-label Search Model for Open Educational Resources Based on Learning Purpose

Klinge Villalba-Condori[1] ⓘ, Lushianna Tejada-Ortega[1] ⓘ, Julio Vera-Sancho[1] ⓘ,
Jorge Mamani-Calcina[2] ⓘ, Cesar Vera-Vasquez[3] ⓘ, and Héctor Cardona-Reyes[4(✉)] ⓘ

[1] Universidad Católica de Santa María, Arequipa, Peru
{kvillalba,ltejada,jveras}@ucsm.edu.pe
[2] Universidad Tecnológica del Peru, Lima, Peru
e16187@utp.edu.pe
[3] Universidad Continental, Arequipa, Peru
cverav@continental.edu.pe
[4] CONACYT-CIMAT, Zacatecas, Mexico
hector.cardona@cimat.mx

Abstract. The Open Educational Resources (OER) repositories store a large quantity and variety of data from multiple sources, and that present relevant and useful information for the student training process, improving student performance thanks to more up-to-date and didactic educational content, this generates the need for a more specialized Learning Objects (LO) search system. In this research work, a multi-label search platform is proposed based on the learning purpose that unifies the information from different OER in a single platform, using an information extraction process based on Web Scraping techniques and generating a selection of one of them. Or multiple tags, based on the SOLO taxonomy, using an MLP-based multi-tag classifier. As a result, we obtained the improvement of the most specialized search and content according to what teachers really need, up to 85% accuracy of the resources they needed and approval of the use of the platform up to 78.57%.

Keywords: Open educational resources · Machine learning · Scrapy

1 Introduction

Currently, the Internet has managed to interconnect all people in the world through social networks, blogs, repositories, etc. with which a large amount of information has been generated, applying the term BIG DATA, which includes data such as videos, images, audio, and unstructured texts [1]. Where the real challenge is to analyze and give value to all possible data or where the field of study is focused.

All the information available on the Internet can help improve academic performance, for this has been investigated and found several educational repositories such as ProComun, Commons, Inevery Crea, etc. with enough educational material accessible to all, but there are different points of storage without a platform to help streamline

V. Agredo-Delgado et al. (Eds.): HCI-COLLAB 2022, CCIS 1707, pp. 130–145, 2022.
https://doi.org/10.1007/978-3-031-24709-5_10

searches, in addition to not being able to find results-oriented to the purpose of learning. And a great consequence of not using these resources is the creation of poor and outdated content, as is the case in Peruvian education, where the educational level of students has not been improved and it is necessary to make changes to what has been proposed until today. An area in data mining that can help us to obtain and unify this information is the Web Scraping techniques that help to collect any type of information from web pages, besides helping to filter the necessary information.

For Multi-Label Classification, Machine Learning (ML) is a great help and the technique used for classification is the Multi-Layer Perceptron (MLP) which assigns one or several labels to each educational resource to make more effective searches. Throughout this proposal, the searches will be developed and validated, and a comparison will be made with other search engines to compare the effectiveness of the platform, in addition to achieving searches based on learning purposes.

2 Background

2.1 Open Educational Resources

Open educational resources (OER) are found as open content shared in public repositories which we can make use of, but going deeper we can say that OER itself is sharing the result of a design process (instructional), in which the knowledge and experience of a designer (teacher) are applied to produce a given resource [2], describing more precisely what is the process and how the content shown in the OER is obtained, in which in a certain way the content is improved, which is improved or specialized day by day, thanks to the feedback that is generated.

OER can be called a digital object or digital learning object, which serves to provide information and/or knowledge, also how it can help the generation of knowledge, skills, and attitudes according to what the person needs [3]. These learning objects when properly planned and implemented under the work structure of a teacher can be very useful for teaching according to studies conducted in an evaluation of students [4].

2.2 Learning Outcomes

When we talk about learning purpose, it is based on the pedagogical intentionality of the teacher who is responsible for the design of his class. Constructive Alignment is very efficient pedagogically speaking and is based on the S.O.L.O. (Structure of Observed Learning Outcome) taxonomy [5] that distinguishes between surface learning and deep learning. As students learn, their learning outcomes show first quantitative and then similar qualitative phases of increasing structural complexity [6].

It is under this taxonomy that we find levels of understanding and recurring actions that are important for learning and each level of understanding is linked to actions as shown below in Table 1.

Table 1. Levels of understanding and recurring actions. Source [6].

Levels of understanding	Recurring actions
Expanded Abstract	Theorize, Hypothesize, Generate, Reflect
Relational	Apply, Integrate, Analyze, Explain
Multistructural	Classify, Describe, Make a list
Unistructural	Memorize, Identify, Recognize, Recognize

The S.O.L.O. taxonomy is an excellent way to classify expected learning from the most concrete to the most abstract and complex levels. This ensures that we have learning that goes from the most superficial to the most profound.

2.3 Web Scraping and Web Crawling

Web Scraping is a form of unstructured data mining that is known to extract data from different web pages in a fast, efficient, and automated way, offering as results data that is easy to use or manipulate [7].

It extracts data from HTML pages through the use of programs, which perform searches of the URLs within the web page to obtain all the information within it so that they can be stored in a database or some storage method. The programs that interact with the web pages can be built in APIs to extract data from all subsequent pages from clicking on a single web page, and this automation can allow the extraction of data from the user to specify search terms so that searches can be performed on those terms [7].

Web Crawling is the automated browsing of different web pages and Web Scraping is the automated processing and transforming of semi-structured data into structured data. Web Crawling uses one or more references (URL) to start navigation, and its purpose is to find content associated with those references. In contrast, the job of web Scraping is to process all the content, looking for the most relevant and important data to be explored and processed. As a result, there is a recursive connection between Web Crawling and Web Scraping [8].

2.4 TF-IDF

It is an abbreviation of the Inverse Document Frequency formula whose purpose is to define the importance of a keyword or phrase in a document [9]. To be able to process documents or texts, it is necessary to make a mathematical representation of the text, for which we use this algorithm. The frequency of a term in a document is simply the number of times the term appears in that document. The value is usually normalized to prevent long documents from acquiring an unusual advantage. Thus, the importance of the term ti in the document dj is given by:

$$TF_{i,j} = \frac{n_{i,j}}{\sum_k n_{k,j}} \tag{1}$$

where n, j is the number of occurrences of the considered term in document dj and the denominator is the number of occurrences of all terms in document dj. The inverse frequency of the document is calculated with:

$$IDF_i = log \frac{|D|}{left|\{d_j : t_i \in d_j\}|}$$ (2)

where we define the numerator as the total number of documents, and the denominator as the number of documents where the term ti appears (i.e., nij 0), and this is where the TF-IDF calculation for the term ti in document dj comes out.

$$TF - IDF_{i,j} = TF_{i,j} x IDF_i$$ (3)

2.5 Multilayer Perceptron

Multilayer Perceptron (MLP) is one of the simplest neural networks and is based on a neural network that is Perceptron, and its architecture of MLP is characterized because it has its neurons grouped into layers of different levels and each of the layers can be formed by a set of neurons and three different types of layers are distinguished which are: input layer, hidden layers, and output layer [10].

Each neuron can be like a multi-label classifier, and MLP by handling several output neurons can be understood that these are represented with a possible label, moreover it is also easy and fast to handle [11]. It also has that the multi-label Perceptron classifier is one of the most feasible or preferred uses for large content classification [12].

3   Materials and Methods

3.1 Population and Sample

The population to be analyzed are three repositories of open educational resources, being around 40000 resources of different educational topics that were classified according to the verbs of S.O.L.O. For our sample, we will consider those resources that are in English language and have at least one tag.

The data collection was based on three repositories of open educational resources Commons, ProComun, and Inevery Crea. All the information obtained is directed to different educational topics for different educational levels (primary, secondary and higher education). The repositories were selected according to the language, the number of learning objects they have, and the accessibility to obtain the information.

Since all the information was accessible, there were no problems in downloading the necessary data from each repository, it was not necessary to have permission from the creators of the repositories and there was no copyright infringement.

For the selection of the required data, the different fields of the learning objects were analyzed to select those that provide more information about the resource and are useful for the corresponding analysis.

3.2 Data Extraction with Scrapy

The different data such as Link, Title, Overview, MaterialType, Subject, Author, and Level were obtained through Web Scraping techniques, where the Scrapy Framework will be used within the Python programming language, in which a script (spider) was generated to help automate searches on each page and obtain the information for each field that is being required.

For the development of the script, different analyses of the different web pages of the educational repositories had to be carried out to have a clear idea of each field it is composed of and the information it shows.

Second, after obtaining the link of each educational object, it is necessary to enter to obtain the information of the fields that were previously selected.

When the spider enters the URL that was sent as a parameter, it is already feasible to obtain the other fields within the item: The title of the resource that goes in the Title variable, the description of the resource that will be stored in the overview variable, depending on each repository the MaterialType variable of different fields of the web page will be stored.

3.3 Data Pre-processing

Data pre-processing seeks to improve the quality of the data set, through techniques or a series of steps that help to obtain more and better information, achieving quality data that will help us to improve the analysis of these data.

Data Cleaning. Data cleaning will help us to ensure data quality. In this step, all data will be placed in lowercase, so that there is no duplicity of data when applying TF-IDF or in the classification algorithms, then the elimination of different tags, special characters, and digits will be performed, to only have real data and these will be replaced by blanks. Also, the elimination of words in the text that are very repetitive or words that do not bring a special meaning to the text (e.g., from, after, before, he, they, etc.) will be called Stopwords, which will be eliminated from the data to have real data that has value and reduce the amount of data for better processing.

Assigning Value to Data with TF-IDF. The Term Frequency – Inverse Document Frequency procedure will help us to define the importance of a keyword or phrase in a document by assigning a weight that will help us to understand the meaning of each document. By means of the Scikit-learn Python library, the TF-IDF algorithm will be applied through the TfidfVectorizer class that will help to obtain the weights of each word for each document through an array. To then obtain an array of documents by keywords that will contain the weights within the array using the Pandas library.

3.4 Multi-label Classification

The main objective of multi-label classification is to achieve that, learn objects, and be able to assign a label that best describes them [13]. Because a single label to describe a group of documents is not enough, as they may contain more than one topic, and is a solution to several machine learning problems [14].

For this assignment are considered generic verbs that accommodate different taxonomies including the S.O.L.O. taxonomy, also these verbs contain cognitive processes that have similarities between them, so for the classification will be taken the verbs that were stored in the database, and in the platform will also appear the verbs that will help teachers better understand what they want to select and with which they are going to work [15]. For the assignments, we worked with prefixes of generic verbs and prefixes of synonymous verbs that help to better group each learning object.

Each verb is composed of several cognitive processes that will help the teacher to better understand the meaning of each verb.

3.5 Tool Implementation

Once we have the data in the tool, we look for the concatenation of the fields title, overview, materialType and subject in a single field called commentText that will be our documents, to simplify the work to a single field.

Once the data is clean, the next step is the classification of the data from the suffixes of the verbs where a list is given that will help to determine to which verb belongs each learning object and the results will be stored in a new Dataframe that will have as columns all the labels (Verbs), to later eliminate those that were not assigned any label. After determining which are our resulting documents, we will apply the TF-IDF algorithm to determine the keywords of all documents and assign a weight to each word for each document to have a format that helps the use of Machine Learning techniques with MLP.

To begin with, a vocabulary of all the words in the documents must be made, but we must also eliminate all those words found in our Stopwords file that are words that do not give relevant meaning to the documents, and that contain words in Spanish and English and complicate the obtaining of the keywords, as shown in Table 2.

Table 2. StopWords example.

English	Spanish
Your, yours, yourself, yourselves, you, yond, yonder, us, username, uponed, upons, uponing, upon, ups, upping, upped, up, unto, until, unless, unlike, unliker, unlikest, under, underneath, use, used, etc.	Al, algo, algunas, algunos, ante, antes, como, con, contra, cual, cuando, de, del, desde, donde, durante, e, el, ella, ellas, ellos, en, entre, era, erais, eran, han, has, hasta, hay, haya, hayamos, etc.

After eliminating all those words that are not useful for our work, we create a vocabulary and a counter for each word in all documents. Once we have the vocabulary and the word counter, we can generate the TF IDF weight matrix. The results that will be shown is a table that shows in descending order which are the words with the highest weight in all documents, as shown in Table 3.

Table 3. Words with greater weight.

#	Term	Weight
8138	Science	0.034605
7567	Reading	0.031466
5438	Life	0.031026
8818	Students	0.024082
113	Activity	0.021953

The final array is composed of the set of documents called doc as an index, the vocabulary created from the documents that are stored in the variable cv that will be the columns of the array and as the content, we will have the final array created called weights array, as shown in Table 4.

Table 4. Final TF-IDF weights matrix.

#	Word 1	Word 2	...	Word n
Document 1	0.0258	0.0014	...	0.0014
Document 2	0.0000	0.0254	...	0.0000
Document 3	0.0074	0.0052	...	0.0025
...	...	...	...	...
Document n	0.0147	0.0000	...	0.0000

The results of the matrix show fields where the value is zero, which indicates that the word does not belong to that document, but if the word does belong to the document, it shows the TF-IDF weight. Once the matrix and the data are sorted, the data are separated into two groups: Test and Train, where Train will be the trained data, and Test the data that will be used to make the predictions and corroborate that the training has been correct. X is assigned the weights obtained from TF-IDF and Y is assigned the fields containing the labels (Verbs).

First, Label binarization is performed for the data in Y, so that labels can be replaced with classes (0, 1, 2, etc.) to have better control when generating tables or graphs, and a counter of the total number of classes is generated for future use.

Before starting the actual training of the data, the data must first be normalized so that they have zero mean and standard deviation, for this purpose the StandardScaler function is used, which allows unifying the weighting of the variables, to perform the classification correctly. After applying the standardization to the data in X-train and X-test, we continue with the application of the MLP algorithm where MLPClassifier is selected, having around 50000 learning objects, training was performed with two hidden layers of 200 neurons each and a maximum of 1000 iterations.

4 Results

This section presents the results obtained from specialized searches and contents according to the needs of teachers. Table 5 presents the precision report.

Table 5. Precision report - recall - f1score

#	Precision	Recall	F1-Score	Support
0	0.86	0.77	0.81	1833
1	0.79	0.76	0.77	2017
2	0.87	0.79	0.83	1781
3	0.81	0.8	0.8	1528
4	0.85	0.7	0.77	1219
5	0.89	0.89	0.89	4384
6	0.81	0.81	0.81	1321
7	0.82	0.78	0.8	1453
8	0.9	0.86	0.88	4848
9	0.81	0.58	0.68	361
10	0.78	0.76	0.77	3971
11	0.87	0.88	0.87	4344
Micro avg	0.85	0.82	0.83	29060
Macro avg	0.84	0.78	0.81	29060
Weighted avg	0.85	0.82	0.83	29060
Samples avg	0.79	0.77	0.76	29060

- Precision: The ratio of correct predictions to total predictions. In other words, the accuracy indicates how good the model is at whatever it predicted.
- Recall: The ratio of correct predictions to the total number of correct elements in the ensemble.
- F1-Score: It is defined as the harmonic mean between accuracy and recall. It is used as a statistical measure to score performance. In other words, an F1-Score (from 0 to 9 where 0 is the lowest and 9 is the highest) is an average of individual performance, based on two factors (precision and recall).

Figure 1 shows that an average precision of up to 85% and recall of up to 82% is achieved.

A confusion matrix is a table often used to describe the performance of a classification model (or "classifier") of an algorithm used in supervised learning, given a set of test data for which the true values are known.

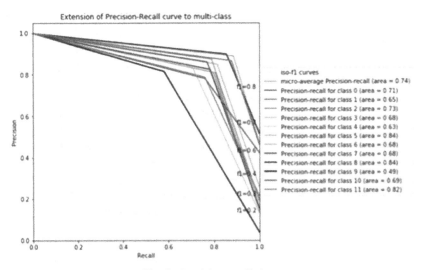

Fig. 1. Precision-recall chart.

Each column represents the number of predictions for each class, while each row represents the instances in the actual class. The main benefit of this matrix is to easily visualize how the algorithm is classifying the classes, so it is seen when it confuses its classification and where it places it according to its learning. Table 6 will show the confusion matrix. The page where the searches are performed will be shown and the results will be displayed to validate the requirements, design, and implementation.

Table 6. Confusion matrix.

	PC0	PC1	PC2	PC3	PC4	PC5	PC6	PC7	PC8	PC9	PC10	PC11
Class 0	1922	142	66	50	27	127	8	8	53	0	53	35
Class 1	94	1057	74	54	20	84	3	5	32	0	16	10
Class 2	54	58	504	27	13	39	9	2	13	1	11	10
Class 3	32	43	20	416	14	30	4	3	25	1	13	6
Class 4	18	22	8	24	216	36	5	2	16	0	7	7
Class 5	68	74	22	39	10	1147	11	9	36	4	21	24
Class 6	14	2	1	2	1	14	60	2	6	0	2	4
Class 7	12	5	1	2	0	11	1	162	15	0	1	4
Class 8	65	33	6	21	7	60	3	5	1101	1	42	17
Class 9	5	1	0	0	1	1	0	0	2	5	1	0
Class 10	61	12	5	6	3	30	2	1	22	0	202	19
Class 11	13	7	0	2	2	18	2	2	14	0	26	136

4.1   Web Application

Search Page. The page is composed of the part where you enter the search values (term, tags, and educational level) depending on what you want to search for, and the other part is the search results that show all the matching educational resources, as shown in Fig. 2.

Recurso Educativo Abierto

Plataforma de Recursos Educativos Abiertos

El propósito de este proyecto es el desarrollo de una plataforma de búsqueda multi-etiqueta basado en el propósito de aprendizaje para unificar la información de diferentes Recursos Educativos Abiertos en una sola plataforma, donde el proceso de extracción de información se basa en técnicas de Web Scraping y así a través de una selección de una o varias etiquetas, basadas en la taxonomía S.O.L.O., se use un clasificador multi-etiqueta basado en MLP, que ayudará a realizar una búsqueda más especializada y de acuerdo a que los profesores realmente necesitan.
Este trabajo contribuye a mejorar el proceso de aprendizaje de estudiante de los diferentes niveles educativos y lograr mejores resultados a través de una enseñanza no convencional.

Búsqueda

| Contenido | Etiquetas: Select | Niveles educativos: Select | BUSCAR |

Total de resultados   0   No se encontraron resultados

Etiquetas

Fig. 2. Multi-label search platform website.

Search Results (Example). The results are all those educational resources that match the values match the values entered in the search engine part, as shown in Fig. 3 and Fig. 4.

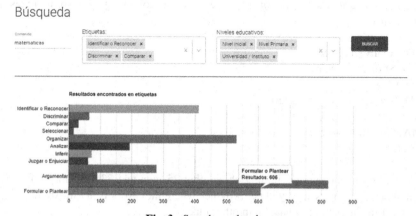

Fig. 3. Search results chart.

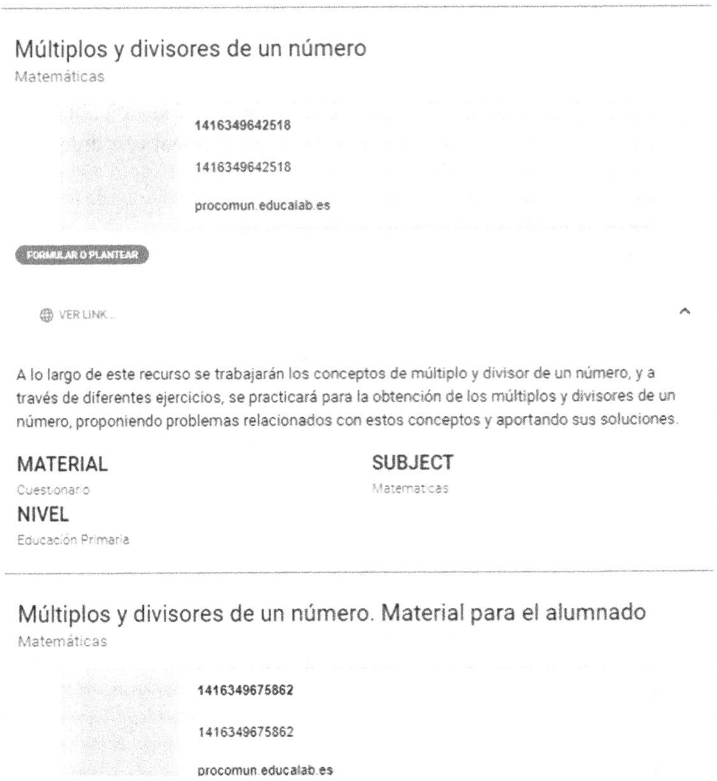

Fig. 4. Results on the Web page multi-label search platform.

The evaluation was carried out anonymously on 98 teachers from different educational levels to evaluate the use of the system and the following table summarizes the results, where:

- TD: Totally disagree
- MD: Strongly disagree
- ED: Disagree
- AD: Neither agree nor disagree
- DA: Agree
- MA: Very much agree
- TA: Strongly agree

According to the survey, Table 7 shows that 25 men and 73 women participated. The number of teachers surveyed per province where they work is: 87 in Arequipa, 1 in Camaná, 1 in Caravelí, 2 in Islay, 7 in other places.

In Fig. 5 (a), the number of respondents by years of experience is as follows: 85 teachers with 0 to 5 years, 4 teachers with 6 to 10 years of experience, 8 teachers with 11 to 20 years of experience, and 1 teacher with more than 21 years of experience.

Table 7. Usability evaluation.

Question Statement	1	2	3	4	5	6	7
System quality							
1. Overall, I am satisfied with how easy it is to use the platform	0	0	4	17	29	27	21
2. It was easy to use the platform	0	0	3	18	26	29	22
3. I was able to complete tasks and scenarios quickly using the platform	0	0	1	19	27	31	20
4. I feel comfortable using the platform	0	0	1	15	26	31	25
5. It was easy to learn how to use the platform	0	0	3	14	23	35	23
6. I think I could be productive using the platform	0	0	1	17	16	31	33
7. My interaction with the search platform is clear and understandable	0	0	3	15	25	30	25
8. I am satisfied with the speed of the search platform	0	0	1	12	23	31	31
9. I am satisfied with the reliability of the search platform	0	0	5	14	15	38	26
Information quality							
10. The platform displayed error messages that clearly stated how to fix the problem	1	3	3	20	30	19	22
11. Every time I made a mistake using the platform, I could recover easily and quickly	0	2	4	18	26	28	20
12. The information (e.g., online help, on-screen message, and other documentation) provided by the platform was clear	2	0	5	14	25	33	19

(*continued*)

Table 7. (*continued*)

Question							
Statement	1	2	3	4	5	6	7
13. It was easy to find the information I needed	1	3	2	14	27	27	24
14. The information was effective in helping me complete the tasks and scenarios	1	2	3	14	24	29	25
Interface quality							
15. The organization of the information on the platform screens was clear	0	1	1	17	21	32	26
16. The system interface was pleasant	0	1	1	17	27	27	25
17. I like using the platform interface	0	2	3	15	25	29	24
18. The platform has all the functions and capabilities I expected it to have	0	1	3	11	33	30	20
Perceived income							
19. The search platform helps me to complement my sessions/classes with more information	0	1	2	16	20	38	21
20. The search platform improves my performance as a teacher	0	0	3	12	25	36	22
Intention to use							
21. I plan to use the educational resources platform in the future	0	1	2	14	21	32	28
22. I plan to use the search platform frequently in the future	0	1	2	15	28	25	27
23. I will try to use the search platform as much as possible in the future	0	2	2	10	31	28	25

(*continued*)

Table 7. (*continued*)

Question							
Statement	1	2	3	4	5	6	7
24. I will talk about the positive aspects of the search platform to my colleagues	0	1	1	12	27	34	23
25. I will recommend using the search platform to my future colleagues	1	1	0	12	24	37	23
Overall							
Overall, I am satisfied with the silver-form	0	0	3	12	20	44	19

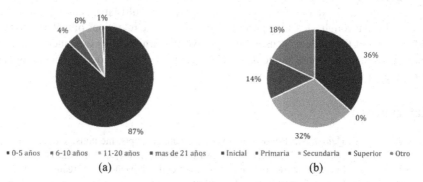

Fig. 5. (a) Number of Teachers Surveyed by years of experience. (b) Number of Teachers Surveyed by years of experience.

In Fig. 5 (b), according to the survey, the number of teachers by educational level is 32 in Initial, 10 in Primary, 28 in Secondary, 12 in Higher Education, and 16 in other educational levels.

5 Discussion

The work presented shows that processing the different educational resources gives us a favorable result, and when compared with the other research topics where it is applied in different ways.

It is proved that Web Scrapy can be integrated with different data processing methodologies such as the use of Naïve Bayes classification algorithm for the improvement of job search. This shows an average of 71. 87% [16], while the use of the MLP algorithm in the present work shows an average of over 80%. It should also be strongly noted that data mining is done legally and securely [17], so the repositories used are freely accessible to anyone, so no illegal activity is being committed.

In the same way that the impact of the use of Web Scrapy for the improvement of information presentation and reduction of problems that have been given for the information consultation system of phytosanitary products in Chile [18], it has also provided a great impact on the area of education providing educational resources required by the teacher helping to improve the quality of students in Peru.

6 Conclusions

In recent years the development of specialized search systems has grown significantly, being widely used in different fields, but particularly in education. In this research work, a multi-label search platform has been developed under the S.O.L.O. taxonomy approach, which is oriented to the use of verbs proposed for learning. These verbs contain cognitive processes or learning processes that serve a classification of categories and allow for more specialized OER searches. In addition, a complete model is shown from the extraction from different repositories to the conformation of an own repository composed of classified external resources. In this way, the multi-label search platform can be articulated through a learning purpose, considering the intentions of teachers to teach and the need of the student focused on cognitive or learning processes, mentioning that the proposal achieves on average up to 85% accuracy of the resources needed by each teacher and platform approval of up to 78.57%.

References

1. Gandomi, A., Haider, M.: Beyond the hype: big data concepts, methods, and analytics. Int. J. Inf. Manage. **35**(2), 137–144 (2015). https://doi.org/10.1016/j.ijinfomgt.2014.10.007
2. Sicilia, M.Á.: Más allá de los contenidos: compartiendo el diseño de los recursos educativos abiertos. Rev. U. Soc. Conocimiento **4**, 26 (2007)
3. Águila, J.V.B., Burgos, V.: Distribución de conocimiento y acceso libre a la información con Recursos Educativos Abiertos (REA). La educación (2010)
4. Villalba-Condori, K.O., et al.: Learning objects to strengthen learning. experience in regular basic education in Perú. In: 2018 XIII Latin American Conference on Learning Technologies (LACLO), pp. 499–504 (2018). https://doi.org/10.1109/LACLO.2018.00088
5. Díaz-Levicoy, D., Sepúlveda, A., Vásquez, C., Opazo, M..: Organización de las respuestas sobre tablas estadísticas por futuras maestras de educación infantil desde la taxonomía solo. Revista Didasc@lia: Didáctica y Educación **8**, 193–212, 06 (2017)
6. Villalba, K., Cuba, S.C., Deco, C., Bender, C., García-Peñalvo, F.J.: A recommender system of open educational resources based on the purpose of learning. In: 2017 Twelfth Latin American Conference on Learning Technologies (LACLO), pp. 1–4 (2017). https://doi.org/10.1109/LACLO.2017.8120899
7. Haddaway, N.R., et al.: The use of web-scraping software in searching for grey literature. Grey J. **11**(3), 186–190 (2015)
8. Massimino, B.: Accessing online data: web-crawling and information-scraping techniques to automate the assembly of research data. J. Bus. Logist. **37**(1), 34–42 (2016). https://doi.org/10.1111/jbl.12120
9. Dadgar, S.M.H., Araghi, M.S., Farahani, M.M.: A novel text mining approach based on tf-idf and support vector machine for news classification. In: 2016 IEEE International Conference on Engineering and Technology (ICETECH), pp. 112–116 (2016). https://doi.org/10.1109/ICETECH.2016.7569223

10. Bishop, C.M., Nasrabadi, N.M.: Pattern Recognition and Machine Learning, vol. 4(4), p. 738. Springer, New York (2006)
11. Cerri, R., Barros, R.C., de Carvalho, A.C.: Hierarchical multi-label classification using local neural networks. J. Comput. Syst. Sci. **80**(1), 39–56 (2014). https://doi.org/10.1016/j.jcss.2013.03.007
12. Zhang, L., Towsey, M., Xie, J., Zhang, J., Roe, P.: Using multi-label classification for acoustic pattern detection and assisting bird species surveys. Appl. Acoust. **110**, 91–98 (2016). https://doi.org/10.1016/j.apacoust.2016.03.027
13. Luaces, O., Díez, J., Barranquero, J., del Coz, J.J., Bahamonde, A.: Binary relevance efficacy for multilabel classification. Prog. Artif. Intell. **1**(4), 303–313 (2012). https://doi.org/10.1007/s13748-012-0030-x
14. Heß, A., Dopichaj, P., Maaß, C.: Multi-value classification of very short texts. In: Dengel, A.R., Berns, K., Breuel, T.M., Bomarius, F., Roth-Berghofer, T.R. (eds.) KI 2008. LNCS (LNAI), vol. 5243, pp. 70–77. Springer, Heidelberg (2008). https://doi.org/10.1007/978-3-540-85845-4_9
15. Villalba-Condori, K.O., et al.: A methodology to assign educational resources with metadata based on the purpose of learning. In: 2019 XIV Latin American Conference on Learning Technologies (LACLO), pp. 221–225, IEEE (2019). https://doi.org/10.1109/LACLO49268.2019.00045
16. Slamet, C., Andrian, R., Maylawati, D.S., Suhendar, Darmalaksana, W., Ramdhani, M.A.: Web scraping and naïve bayes classification for job search engine. IOP Conf. Ser.: Mater. Sci. Eng. **288**, 012038 (2018). https://doi.org/10.1088/1757-899X/288/1/012038
17. Mehak, S., Zafar, R., Aslam, S., Bhatti, S.M.:. Exploiting filtering approach with web scrapping for smart online shopping: penny wise: a wise tool for online shopping. In: 2019 2nd International Conference on Computing, Mathematics and Engineering Technologies (iCoMET), pp. 1–5. IEEE (2019). https://doi.org/10.1109/ICOMET.2019.8673399
18. Ahumada-García, R., Moller-Acuña, P., Reyes-Súarez, J.A.: An expert system for handling phytosanitary products in Chile an export fruit. In: 2017 CHILEAN Conference on Electrical, Electronics Engineering, Information and Communication Technologies (CHILECON), pp. 1–4, IEEE (2017). https://doi.org/10.1109/CHILECON.2017.8229596

Psychological Models and Instruments Employed to Identify Personality Traits of Software Developers: A Systematic Mapping Study

Juan David Delgado Jojoa[✉] ⬡, Oscar Revelo Sánchez ⬡,
and Sandra Vallejo Chamorro ⬡

University of Nariño, San Juan de Pasto, Colombia
{juan.delgado,orevelo,sandravallejo}@udenar.edu.co

Abstract. Over the years, a significant amount of research has been done to discover links and/or effects of human personality in the field of software engineering (SI). It has been shown that personality has a positive influence on the different tasks and/or processes in this field. Related studies helped to identify a suitable personality type for each profile in the SI. However, contradictions have also been found in the results that question their validity, therefore, generalizing and applying these results may be misleading. This is because one of the key and complex factors is evaluating the personality of engineers or software developers from a psychological point of view. Through a systematic mapping study, an attempt was made to characterize the most widely used, reliable and valid psychological instruments/models. However, most of the articles considered for this study were based solely on the data available in the literature; making purely conceptual comparisons. A more exhaustive comparative analysis between said instruments/models was expected. Despite this, it was possible to identify that MBTI is the most popular to examine the personality of software developers. However, the Big Five and its psychometric instruments such as BFI and NEO-FFI have gained more prominence in SI research in recent years. It is necessary to highlight and call on the scientific community to carry out this type of research in a more rigorous way and that it be supported and guided by specialized areas in human behavior, which allows for minimizing contradictions for future research.

Keywords: Human aspects · Software developers · Software engineering · Psychometric instruments · Psychological models · Personality

1 Introduction

From the beginning, the field of Software Engineering (SI) recognized that the human factor also had to be considered in software development since they have a very strong impact on the success of development efforts [1–5]. Software projects are generally always team efforts, and successful projects involve well-formed and composed teams. Studies have revealed that personality contributes to the effective composition of the team and, therefore, to the success of the project [6–9]. For this reason, personality in the field of SI is a growing research area that has been recognized as important over time [10, 11]. Considering that personality is generally a dynamic organization within the person, of psychophysical systems that create patterns of behavior, thoughts, and feelings characteristic of the person [12]. Researchers have explored and shown that the personalities of software developers can affect the different tasks and/or activities of SI [8, 13–18]. However, these results must be recognized and considered more generally, since there are numerous contradictions and ambiguities for professionals who intend to put them into practice in the field of SI [10–12, 15, 19, 20]. Demonstrating that it is an immature research field with many opportunities to be explored.

A systematic mapping study (SMS) by Cruz et al. [12], found contradictions in related studies on the influence of personality on academic performance, pair programming (XP), team efficiency, software process mapping, among others. For example, in [21] they evaluated personality with MBTI, in [22] they evaluated personality with Thurstone Temperament Schedule (TTS), and in [23] they evaluated personality with various instruments. These studies showed that individual personality increases or helps predict academic performance. However, in [24–27] they evaluated personality with BMTI, in [28] they evaluated personality with an instrument developed by the author, and finally, in [29] they evaluated personality with 16PF; showing that personality traits were not a significant factor in predicting academic success. On the other hand, Barroso et al. [30] mention that the higher the neuroticism score the greater the chances that the developer will control anxiety, self-awareness and anger. So you will hardly have signs of depression and will be less vulnerable to sudden mood swings. Therefore, these qualities can help the developer or improve the quality of the software, at least with CK (Chidamber & Kemerer) metrics such as Cyclomatic Complexity (CC), Coupling Between Objects (CBO), and Inheritance Tree Depth (DIT). However, other authors mention that neuroticism is considered the least important personality trait to influence software quality and team productivity [31–33].

Undoubtedly, it can be seen that one of the primary factors of contradiction in this type of research is the reliability and validity of psychological instruments/models to assess personality [2, 6, 12, 14]. Also, the interpretation of the results of personality tests and their practical work implications are not easy and require duly trained professionals [12, 34]. And it is not for less, since personality is one of the most complex constructs in the social sciences and personality analysis one of the most difficult tasks in psychology [35].

A significant number of studies have used different instruments/models to measure personality in SI [6, 17, 36–38], this may lead to each of these having differences both in the part of the psychological construct and in the tests of evaluation, generating contradictory and/or ambiguous results as demonstrated above. Therefore, the present work aimed to investigate the current state of studies that emphasize the detailed comparison of psychological instruments/models to assess the personality traits of software developers (both for the academy and the software industry).

To our knowledge, this is the first attempt to address an overview of the body of work where in-depth comparisons are made between psychological instruments/models to assess personality. We believe that with this study we contribute to researchers considering it as a reference to having a global vision about reliable and valid instruments/models to assess personality, minimizing contradictions for future work. In addition, to establish a base to continue exploring and consolidating a more enriching body of knowledge in this field.

To present this SMS, the following structure was defined: in Sect. 2, the mapping planning was defined; in Sect. 3, the results obtained are presented; in Sect. 4, the discussion is presented; and in Sect. 5, the conclusions are presented; finally, the corresponding references are listed.

2 Planning of the Systematic Mapping of Literature

An SMS is a process by which information on a specific topic can be collected in an orderly, methodical and replicable manner to provide an overview to the reader [39]. For the present study, the systematic mapping guide protocol was proposed by Petersen et al. [40]. This research is developed in five stages as shown in Fig. 1. Each of the stages produces a result that is used as input for the following stages.

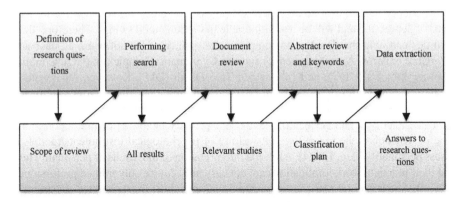

Fig. 1. Systematic mapping process proposed by Petersen et al. [40].

2.1 Definition of Research Questions

The first step in a SMS is to define the research questions to be answered by the studies. Table 1 presents each of the questions and their motivation.

Table 1. Research questions used for systematic mapping.

Research question	Motivation
What are the most used psychological instruments/models to assess the personality traits of software developers?	Check which psychological instruments/models are trending and most used in the SI field to assess the personality traits of software developers
What are the reliable and valid psychological instruments/models to assess the personality traits of software developers?	Identify which psychological instrument/model is reliable and valid to apply in the field of SI. Enabling researchers to safely assess the personality traits of software developers
What is the publication frequency of research that makes a comparative analysis between psychological instruments/models to assess the personality traits of software developers?	Check how often studies are being carried out that involve the evaluation and comparison of psychological instruments/models to identify more objectively the personality traits of software developers, in addition to observing if the trend line is positive and, therefore, if it is a current topic

2.2 Search Strategy

Defining a thorough and unbiased search process in a review will allow as many primary studies related to the research question as possible to be found [41]. As a first element, the bibliographic databases used were: ACM Digital Library, IEEE Digital Library and Scopus, which, for Dybå et al. [42] are considered one of the most relevant for the search for scientific articles. In addition, the search in the bibliographic databases includes all studies up to December 2021 without a restrictive time window; this is because a search range of 5 years (2016–2021) was initially established. However, a limited amount of information was obtained. In addition, secondary 'snowball' searches of references from primary studies were performed.

As a second element, a search string composed of keywords and phrases was established that served to systematically obtain relevant information in the bibliographic databases. This chain was built from expression prototypes and Boolean operators that were tested in SCOPUS. These tasks were executed iteratively, and as a final result the following search string was obtained: **(model OR method OR metrics OR measurement OR evaluation OR comparison OR instruments OR study OR comparative OR relationship) AND ("personality models" OR "personality traits" OR "personality types") AND (programming OR "computer programming" OR "software development" OR "software construction" OR "software engineering" OR "software build" OR "software development").**

2.3 Review of Relevant Documents

Table 2 summarizes the inclusion (I) and exclusion (E) criteria defined to add or eliminate relevant/irrelevant papers to the analysis.

Table 2. Research inclusion and exclusion criteria.

Inclusion	Exclusion
I1: Studies presented in English that take into account the personality and/or human aspects of software developers in the field of IS	E1: Studies that do not mention personality and/or human aspects in the SI field
I2: Primary studies that compare and/or mention more than one psychological instrument/model to assess personality in the field of SI	E2: Studies that do not discuss and/or do not make any type of comparison between psychological instruments/models used in the field of SI
I3: Secondary studies that compare and/or mention more than one psychological instrument/model to assess personality in the field of SI	E3: Studies not accessible in full text
	E4: Duplicate publications of the same authors

2.4 Abstract Review and Keywords

Once the inclusion and exclusion criteria have been established, the next stage is to find relevant articles through abstracts and keyword research. For this stage, the process is defined by Petersen et al. [40]. The titles and abstracts (in some cases the introduction and conclusions) were read to identify those considered irrelevant to the topics studied. After applying these criteria, a careful final selection of papers was made where the data was extracted and analyzed.

2.5 Data Extraction Strategy

The data extraction strategy focused on the extraction of relevant information to answer the questions of interest and on the synthesis of the results obtained. Using a series of possible answers and in this way ensure the application of the same criteria for all the work.

The articles were analyzed and classified according to categories created to separate the research contributions of each article (results section). The data extracted from the articles were stored and subjected to qualitative and quantitative analysis.

To organize the findings and document the data extraction process, a spreadsheet was used, which also allowed for other statistical analyses, such as determining the number of publications by year and by type of publication.

3 Results

It is important to note that there are limitations that must be taken into account. Firstly, it should be considered that this review may have missed some relevant work. The quality of the studies used in this analysis was not homogeneous, it was enough for them to compare and/or mention more than one psychological instrument/model to assess the personality of the software developments. This behavior may limit the conclusions drawn from the published results.

That said, a bubble graph was chosen to inform the frequencies as shown in Fig. 2. In it, you can see the total number of articles categorized by each of the databases used in this work.

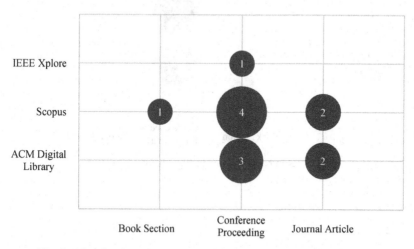

Fig. 2. Visualization of the number of jobs obtained by type of database.

In phase 1, the search string was applied to each of the 3 bibliographic databases, obtaining a total of 495 results. Subsequently, the inclusion and exclusion criteria were used on the abstract, keywords and the title of each of the articles, as well as the elimination of duplicate investigations. Resulting in a total of 13 results, called "candidates for primary studies". Later, in phase 2, the same process of applying selection criteria was carried out, but in this case on the complete article, having as a final result a total of 5 articles, called "primary articles". Finally, in phase 3, the data extraction, the characterization of the studies and the answers to the proposed research questions were carried out.

Figure 3 shows the number of articles by type of publication: Journal Article, Conference and Book Chapter, versus the bibliographic database from which they were extracted. In this sense, it is observed that the articles finally selected come from conferences for a total of 5 documents.

This result highlights the importance of the conferences for the dissemination of research on the subject of psychological instruments/models to assess personality traits in the field of SI.

Figure 4 shows a low frequency in terms of publications corresponding to comparative analyzes between psychological instruments/models to assess the personality traits of software developers. This paucity may indicate that the relationship between SI and personality styles is too complex to investigate [43].

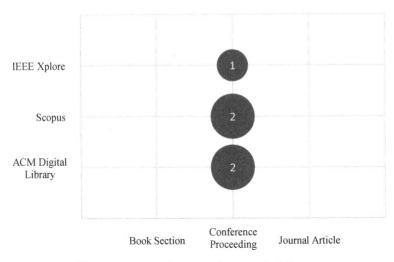

Fig. 3. Number of documents by type of publication.

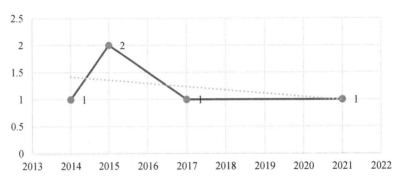

Fig. 4. Number of documents by year of publication.

Next, the research questions posed above are answered.

3.1 RQ1: What are the Most Used Psychological Instruments/Models to Assess the Personality Traits of Software Developers?

Human factors are of paramount importance when focusing on the qualities of a software engineer, as they can help predict various industry trends and improve the performance of the process as a whole [44]. Consequently, measuring the personality of software engineers is a challenge, due to the number of available psychological instruments/models and the possibility of using different theories, scales and classifications [14].

Table 3 lists the most significant instruments/models and/or used to assess personality in the SI field according to the selected articles. In addition, Fig. 5 shows the frequency of articles that cite them.

Table 3. Psychological instruments/models used to identify personality traits in the field of SI.

Models/Instruments	Papers
Myers-Briggs Type Indicator (MBTI)	[10, 14, 43–45]
Big Five	[10, 14, 43–45]
Big Five Inventory (BFI)	[14]
16 Personality Factors (16PF)	[14, 45]
NEO Personality Inventory (NEO-PI-R)	[14]
Context Cards (CC)	[14]
Five-Factor Model (FFM)	[10, 44, 45]
International Personality Item Pool (IPIP)	[14]
Temperament Classification Keirsey (KTS)	[10, 43, 44]
Job Diagnostic Survey (JDS)	[10, 45]
Personal Style Inventory (PSI)	[10, 45]

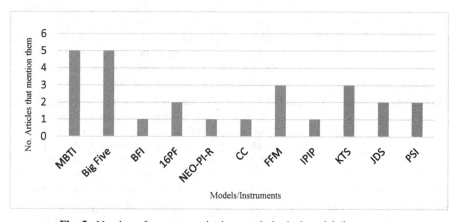

Fig. 5. Number of papers mentioning psychological models/instruments.

3.2 RQ2: What are the Reliable and Valid Psychological Instruments/models Used by the Scientific Community to Identify the Personality Traits of Software Developers?

The instruments/models presented in Table 3 have been applied in a significant amount of research to understand the links and/or effects of personality in the field of SI [8, 20, 30, 46–48]. However, it should be noted that if the psychometric instruments or their use are invalid, all the resulting conclusions are also invalid [14]. McDonald et al. [34] mention the misuse of personality tests in SI, questioning that the inappropriate use of psychological tests and fundamental misunderstandings of personality theory has produced a lack of progress in this field.

Table 4 lists the psychological instruments/models that, despite not finding articles where they are analyzed or compared in depth, are elementary so far to assess the personality of software developers.

Table 4. Most significant instruments/models to assess the personality of software developers.

Model/Instruments	Paper	Year	Summary
BFI, 16PF y CC	[14]	2021	The authors carried out a comparative and empirical study between these instruments, collecting data from software developers and analyzing the correlation between the responses of the instruments. Their results showed a moderate correlation between 16PF and BFI, a weak correlation between 16PF and CC, and BFI and CC Although this analysis was not to show which is the best instrument to assess personality, these three instruments were identified as the most important and used in the field of SI. Some of their reasons were the following: studies in the SI use them recurrently, they are in the public domain or easily accessible to researchers, they are clear to use in the SI, and their data analysis has a vocabulary that is simple to understand and do not have a large number of items, which facilitates their execution and interpretation
MBTI, FFM, Big Five	[10]	2017	They identified that MBTI is most popular for analyzing the personalities of software developers. However, the studies differ in their use of experimental projects. In addition, research on software developer personality should distinguish more carefully between the Big 5 and FFM models, since they differ in certain characteristics such as theoretical basis, causality, and measurement
FMM	[43]	2015	After making a comparison between Big Five (according to the authors also known as FFM), MBTI and KTS based on their content, measurement method and existing applications, they show that the applicability of FFM is better than that of MBTI and KTS. First, from a content point of view, FFM provides a richer and more complete description of the human personality. Second, the FFM measurement method is more acceptable and accurate for assessing personality type. In addition, it is the most used by researchers. They recommend FFM as an assessment tool to explore human personality types, especially in the field of SI

(*continued*)

Table 4. (*continued*)

Model/Instruments	Paper	Year	Summary
MBTI y FFM	[44]	2015	They show that MBTI and FFM concentrate the largest number of articles associated with them. MBTI is the most popular personality test. However, it requires prior certification. Also, FFM covers the freely available IPIP test, which may be the reason behind its popularity
MBTI, Big Five	[45]	2014	MBTI is the most popular to examine the personalities of software developers. However, psychological research has recognized that the MBTI is inconclusive and may bias conclusions drawn from the results. MBTI operationalizes Jungian psychodynamic type theory insufficiently in terms of construct validity and reliability Big Five has gained prominence in software engineering research in recent years. The model has been applied at both individual and team levels. The Big Five has been used primarily to determine the effect of a developer's personality on programming effectiveness

As a result and to the best of our knowledge, most of the selected articles compare psychological instruments/models based solely on the data available in the literature; they made purely conceptual comparisons that lack evidence on how psychometric instruments compare in the context of SI. The only study that analyzed and evaluated the correlation between three psychometric instruments (BFI, 16PF and CC) was by Guimarães et al. [14].

Despite these findings, the authors agree that MBTI and Big Five over the years have been the most used and main ones to assess personality in the field of SI [14, 18, 35, 39, 42]. Although MBTI was the most popular and applied in personality research as shown in Table 4; Big Five, along with its measurement instruments such as BFI, 16PF and NEO-FFI. They have acquired greater prominence and greater acceptance by researchers to assess the personality of software developers [10, 32, 41, 45]. The time it takes to answer these tests and the number of questions is less, which is advantageous from the perspective of the subject who is going to take the test. Its data analysis vocabulary is easy to understand and people generally do not want to fill out a long questionnaire because it can lead to distractions and frustration [14, 43]. As for the type of option of each answer, MBTI and others like KTS, it is a forced choice; the participants have to choose one of the two alternatives (A/B or YES/NO). In contrast, with the 5-point Likert-type scale of the Big Five model instruments, it is easy for subjects to accept so that they can carefully consider and select the correct response [14, 43], allowing a greater advantage for the measurement method.

However, these statements are not sufficient or solid to determine which instrument/model is reliable and valid, more studies are needed where more serious and exhaustive comparisons are made, at least between Big Five and MBTI, since they are the most used in the SI field according to the studies analyzed.

3.3 RQ3: What is the Frequency of Publication of Research Comparing and Analyzing Psychological Instruments/Models to Assess the Personality Traits of Software Developers?

Although research on personality in SI has been promoted for many years [18, 45, 49], Fig. 4 shows a low frequency of publications on the comparison and analysis of psychological instruments/models for assessing the personality traits of software developers. As a consequence, it can be inferred that the lack of this type of research has been one of the important factors to show contradictory and inconclusive study results between personality and SI [12, 18].

Lastly, it is possible that the low frequency of publications does not mean a negative trend line or that it is not a current theme. This may be because the relationship between SI and personality is too complex to investigate [14, 43]. In addition, this type of research must be carried out in conjunction with other areas related to human behavior such as psychology and/or social sciences and not only from the field of SI [12].

4 Discussion

The objective of this mapping was to draw an overview of the body of work on comparative analyzes between psychological instruments/models to identify which one(s) are reliable and valid to assess the personality of software developers. In this section, the results and implications for research and practice in SI are also discussed.

4.1 Implications for Research and Practice

Many researchers studied and mentioned the psychological instruments/models that have been applied over the years in the field of SI. Highlighting MBTI and Big Five as the most popular and primary to assess the personality of software engineers. However, the reliability and validity of these and other psychological instruments/models to be applied in this field have not been rigorously evidenced. Although it is a very interesting and important topic, no significant correlations or comparisons between these instruments/models were demonstrated. These comparisons were purely based on conceptual elements of the existing literature; revealing its reliability and validity. One of the implications of these findings for the academic community is that this research area has opened up many research opportunities [12, 15, 47]. On the other hand, and as mentioned above, these investigations that involve human behavior must be carried out in conjunction with areas such as sociology and/or psychology if they want to consolidate a consistent body of knowledge that can guide future research and influence practice of the SI.

In terms of practical uses for researchers who require these elements to assess the personality of software developers, the direct application of the results presented in this study must be done with care. The evidence of which psychological instruments/models are reliable or valid is purely conceptual. Therefore, it can be said that the research field is not mature and if the corresponding measures are not taken in this emerging area, it will continue to produce unwanted and contradictory effects in personality research in SI.

4.2 Limitations of This Review

Without a doubt, the main limitation in this mapping may exist as the possible biases introduced in the selection process and inaccuracies in the data extraction. The research protocol was based on established guidelines that incorporated measures to prevent selection bias. Another common mapping limitation is the difficulty in finding all the relevant articles. The combination of an automatic search in the different bibliographic databases, a manual search of relevant publications and a secondary "snowball" search of the references of the primary studies improves the coverage of the selection process, reducing possible biases. A multi-stage selection process was used and reasons for the inclusion and exclusion of studies at each stage were recorded as recommended by Petersen et al. [40]. On the other hand, an important limitation is that the evaluation and selection of the articles were carried out only by the researcher of the present study.

It should be noted that the studies analyzed mention psychometric instruments to measure personality, but do not relate it to any theory or psychological construct; especially with those that are less common in this field. Finally, mention that, without knowledge or expertise about human behavior, misconceptions or misconceptions can be given, and consequently undesirable results.

5 Conclusions

The present study evidenced the existence of numerous psychological instruments/models that are applied in the field of SI to assess the personality of software developers (see Table 3). Unfortunately, it was not possible to identify with certainty which ones are valid and reliable to assess personality, so the uncertainty of choosing between one or the other is not easy at all. However, important findings can be rescued that can be used for further research. For example, most of the selected articles share that MBTI, Big Five and FFM are significantly used to assess personality in the field of SI. It is highlighted that Big Five and its measurement instruments (NEO-FFI and BFI) have taken on greater prominence and importance to assess the personality of software developers [14, 43, 45]. However, they mention the importance of evaluating the differences between Big Five and FFM, since for some authors these models are similar [43] and for others, there are differences in certain characteristics such as theoretical basis, causality and measurement [10]. It would be interesting for future work to take into account these outstanding instruments/models to carry out a deeper and more detailed comparison. That in addition to evaluating the theoretical part of the personality, comparisons are also made empirically.

Finally, mention that this study has shown the need for more studies and attention in this area. And that these studies are supported and guided by specialized areas in human behavior. Having a better theoretical and practical understanding of psychological instruments/models could notably help to improve the personality assessment of software developers, and consequently improve the results of future research on personality in SI.

References

1. Turley, R.T., Bieman, J.M.: Competencies of exceptional and nonexceptional software engineers. J. Syst. Softw. **28**(1), 19–38 (1995). https://doi.org/10.1016/0164-1212(94)000 78-2
2. Weinberg, G.M.: The Psychology of Computer Programming. Van Nostrand Reinhold Co., USA (1988)
3. John, M., Maurer, F., Tessem, B.: Human and social factors of software engineering: workshop summary. ACM SIGSOFT Softw. Eng. Notes **30**, 1–6 (2005). https://doi.org/10.1145/108 2983.1083000
4. Acuña, S., Juristo, N.: Assigning people to roles in software projects. Pr. Exper. **34**, 675–696 (2004). https://doi.org/10.1002/spe.586
5. Wynekoop, J., Walz, D.: Traits of top performing software developers. IT People **13**, 186–195 (2000). https://doi.org/10.1108/09593840010377626
6. Weilemann, E.: A winning team-what personality has to do with software engineering. In: Proceedings - 2019 IEEE/ACM 41st International Conference on Software Engineering: Companion, ICSE-Companion 2019, pp. 252–253 (2019). https://doi.org/10.1109/ICSE-Companion.2019.00100
7. Yilmaz, M., O'Connor, R.V., Colomo-Palacios, R., Clarke, P.: An examination of personality traits and how they impact on software development teams. Inf. Softw. Technol. **86**, 101–122 (2017). https://doi.org/10.1016/j.infsof.2017.01.005
8. Iqbal, M.A., Ammar, F.A., Aldaihani, A.R., Khan, T.K.U., Shah, A.: Predicting most effective software development teams by mapping MBTI personality traits with software lifecycle activities. In: 2019 IEEE 6th International Conference on Engineering Technologies and Applied Sciences (ICETAS), pp. 1–5 (2019). https://doi.org/10.1109/ICETAS48360.2019.9117370
9. Casado-Rivas, A., Archidona, M.M.: The influence of personality traits on software engineering and its applications (2017)
10. Barroso, A., Madureira, J., Soares, M., Nascimento, R.: Influence of human personality in software engineering - a systematic literature review (2017)
11. Lenberg, P., Feldt, R., Wallgren, L.: Behavioral software engineering: a definition and systematic literature review. J. Syst. Softw. **107**, 15–37 (2015). https://doi.org/10.1016/j.jss.2015.04.084
12. Cruz, S., da Silva, F.Q.B., Capretz, L.F.: Forty years of research on personality in software engineering: a mapping study. Comput. Hum. Behav. **46**, 94–113 (2015). https://doi.org/10.1016/j.chb.2014.12.008
13. Capretz, L.F., Varona, D., Raza, A.: Influence of personality types in software tasks choices. Comput. Human Behav. **52**, 373–378 (2015). https://doi.org/10.1016/j.chb.2015.05.050
14. Guimarães, G., et al.: A comparative study of psychometric instruments in software engineering. In: Proceedings of the International Conference on Software Engineering and Knowledge Engineering, SEKE, vol. 2021-July, pp. 229–234 (2021). https://doi.org/10.18293/SEKE2021-108
15. Weilemann, E., Brune, P.: The influence of personality on software quality – a systematic literature review. In: Rocha, Á., Adeli, H., Reis, L., Costanzo, S., Orovic, I., Moreira, F. (eds.) WorldCIST 2020. AISC, vol. 1159, pp. 766–777. Springer, Cham (2020). https://doi.org/10.1007/978-3-030-45688-7_75
16. Acuña, S.T., Gómez, M., Juristo, N.: How do personality, team processes and task characteristics relate to job satisfaction and software quality? Inf. Softw. Technol. **51**(3), 627–639 (2009). https://doi.org/10.1016/j.infsof.2008.08.006

17. Doungsa-ard, C., Chaiwon, V.: The software engineering position mapping from personality traits. In: 2020 Joint International Conference on Digital Arts, Media and Technology with ECTI Northern Section Conference on Electrical, Electronics, Computer and Telecommunications Engineering (ECTI DAMT & NCON), pp. 194–199 (2020). https://doi.org/10.1109/ECTIDAMTNCON48261.2020.9090730

18. Cruz, S.S.J.O., da Silva, F.Q.B., Monteiro, C.V.F., Santos, P., Rossilei, I., dos Santos, M.T.: Personality in software engineering: Preliminary findings from a systematic literature review. In: 15th Annual Conference on Evaluation Assessment in Software Engineering (EASE 2011), pp. 1–10 (2011). https://doi.org/10.1049/ic.2011.0001

19. Gilal, A.R., Jaafar, J., Abro, A., Omar, M., Basri, S., Saleem, M.Q.: Effective personality preferences of software programmer: a systematic review. J. Inf. Sci. Eng. **33**(6), 1399–1416 (2017). https://doi.org/10.6688/JISE.2017.33.6.1

20. Baumgart, R., Holten, R., Hummel, M.: Personality traits of scrum roles in agile software development teams - a qualitative analysis. In: 23rd European Conference on Information Systems, ECIS 2015, vol. 2015-May (2015). https://www.scopus.com/inward/record.uri?eid=2-s2.0-85007518506&partnerID=40&md5=2b9c92d69f343dc0aff2f8c0f4580368

21. Layman, L.: Changing students' perceptions: an analysis of the supplementary benefits of collaborative software development. In: Proceedings of the Software Engineering Education Conference, vol. 2006, pp. 159–166 (2006). https://doi.org/10.1109/CSEET.2006.10

22. Alspaugh, C.A.: Identification of some components of computer programming aptitude. J. Res. Math. Educ. 3(2), 89–98 (1972). http://www.jstor.org/stable/748667. Accessed 07 Aug 2022

23. Kagan, D.M., Douthat, J.M.: Personality and learning FORTRAN. Int. J. Man. Mach. Stud. **22**(4), 395–402 (1985). https://doi.org/10.1016/S0020-7373(85)80046-8

24. Golding, P., Facey-Shaw, L., Tennant, V.: Effects of peer tutoring, attitude and personality on academic performance of first year introductory programming students. In: Proceedings of the 36th Annual Conference on Frontiers in Education, pp. 7–12 (2006). https://doi.org/10.1109/FIE.2006.322662

25. Werth, L.H.: Predicting student performance in a beginning computer science class. In: Proceedings of the Seventeenth SIGCSE Technical Symposium on Computer Science Education, pp. 138–143 (1986). https://doi.org/10.1145/5600.5701

26. Corman, L.S.: Cognitive style, personality type, and learning ability as factors in predicting the success of the beginning programming student. SIGCSE Bull. **18**(4), 80–89 (1986). https://doi.org/10.1145/15003.15020

27. Whipkey, K.L.: Identifying predictors of programming skill. SIGCSE Bull. **16**(4), 36–42 (1984). https://doi.org/10.1145/382200.382544

28. Lutes, K.D., Harriger, A., Purdum, J.: Do Introverts perform better in computer programming courses (2009)

29. Hostetler, T.R.: Predicting student success in an introductory programming course. SIGCSE Bull. **15**(3), 40–43 (1983). https://doi.org/10.1145/382188.382571

30. Barroso, A., Madureira, J., Souza, T., Cezario, B., Soares, M., Nascimento, R.: Relationship between Personality traits and software quality - big five model vs. object-oriented software metrics, pp. 63–74 (2017). https://doi.org/10.5220/0006292800630074

31. Rehman, M., Safdar, S., Mahmood, A.K., Amin, A., Salleh, R.: Personality traits and knowledge sharing behavior of software engineers. In: 2017 8th International Conference on Information Technology (ICIT), pp. 6–11 (2017). https://doi.org/10.1109/ICITECH.2017.8079908

32. Qamar, N., Malik, A.A.: Determining the relative importance of personality traits in influencing software quality and team productivity. Comput. Inform. **39**(5), 994–1021 (2021). https://doi.org/10.31577/CAI_2020_5_994

33. Kosti, M.V., Feldt, R., Angelis, L.: Archetypal personalities of software engineers and their work preferences: a new perspective for empirical studies. Empir. Softw. Eng. **21**(4), 1509–1532 (2015). https://doi.org/10.1007/s10664-015-9395-3
34. McDonald, S., Edwards, H.M.: Who should test whom? Commun. ACM **50**(1), 66–71 (2007). https://doi.org/10.1145/1188913.1188919
35. Costa, P.T., McCrae, R.R.: The five-factor model of personality and its relevance to personality disorders. J. Pers. Disord. **6**(4), 343–359 (1992). https://doi.org/10.1521/pedi.1992.6.4.343
36. Acuña, S.T., Gómez, M.N., Hannay, J.E., Juristo, N., Pfahl, D.: Are team personality and climate related to satisfaction and software quality? Aggregating results from a twice replicated experiment. Inf. Softw. Technol. **57**, 141–156 (2015). https://doi.org/10.1016/j.infsof.2014.09.002
37. Pieterse, V., Leeu, M., van Eekelen, M.: How personality diversity influences team performance in student software engineering teams. In: 2018 Conference on Information Communications Technology and Society (ICTAS), pp. 1–6 (2018). https://doi.org/10.1109/ICTAS.2018.8368749
38. Rutherfoord, R.H.: Using personality inventories to form teams for class projects - a case study. In: Proceedings of the 7th ACM SIG-Information Technology Education Conference, SIGITE 2006, vol. 2006, pp. 9–13 (2006). https://doi.org/10.1145/1168812.1168817
39. Kitchenham, B., Pearl Brereton, O., Budgen, D., Turner, M., Bailey, J., Linkman, S.: Systematic literature reviews in software engineering – a systematic literature review. Inf. Softw. Technol. **51**(1), 7–15 (2009). https://doi.org/10.1016/j.infsof.2008.09.009
40. Petersen, K., Feldt, R., Mujtaba, S., Mattsson, M.: Systematic mapping studies in software engineering. In: Proceedings of the 12th International Conference on Evaluation and Assessment in Software Engineering, vol. 17 (2008)
41. Kitchenham, B.A., Charters, S.: Guidelines for performing systematic literature reviews in software engineering (2007). https://www.elsevier.com/__data/promis_misc/525444systematicreviewsguide.pdf
42. Dybå, T., Dingsøyr, T., Hanssen, G.: Applying systematic reviews to diverse study types: an experience report. In: Proceedings - 1st International Symposium on Empirical Software Engineering and Measurement, ESEM 2007, pp. 225–234 (2007). https://doi.org/10.1109/ESEM.2007.59
43. Jia, J., Zhang, P., Zhang, R.: A comparative study of three personality assessment models in software engineering field. In: 2015 6th IEEE International Conference on Software Engineering and Service Science (ICSESS), pp. 7–10 (2015). https://doi.org/10.1109/ICSESS.2015.7338995
44. Gulati, J., Bhardwaj, P., Suri, B.: Comparative study of personality models in software engineering. In: Proceedings of the Third International Symposium on Women in Computing and Informatics, pp. 209–216 (2015). https://doi.org/10.1145/2791405.2791445
45. Wiesche, M., Krcmar, H.: The relationship of personality models and development tasks in software engineering. In: SIGMIS-CPR 2014 - Proceedings of the 2014 Conference on Computers and People Research, pp. 149–161 (2014). https://doi.org/10.1145/2599990.2600012
46. Aqeel Iqbal, M., Shah, A.: A novel RE teams selection process for user-centric requirements elicitation frameworks based on big-five personality assessment model. In: 2020 IEEE 15th International Conference on Industrial and Information Systems, ICIIS 2020 - Proceedings, pp. 522–527 (2020). https://doi.org/10.1109/ICIIS51140.2020.9342649
47. Du, J., Shi, R., Zhen, Y., Lu, W.: An analysis of influence factors for academic performance about personality traits and thinking styles of students: use a C programming language course in college as an example. In: 2017 12th International Conference on Computer Science and Education (ICCSE), pp. 167–171 (2017). https://doi.org/10.1109/ICCSE.2017.8085483

48. Toala-Sanchez, G., Cachero, C., Melia, S.: Evaluating the impact of the personality traits in the perception of model-driven engineering. In: 2018 13th Iberian Conference on Information Systems and Technologies (CISTI), pp. 1–6 (2018). https://doi.org/10.23919/CISTI.2018.8399170

49. Goldberg, L., et al.: The international personality item pool and the future of public-domain personality measures. J. Res. Pers. **40**, 84–96 (2006). https://doi.org/10.1016/j.jrp.2005.08.007

Social Interventions to Encourage Co-located Collaboration: An Experimental Study

Alessandra Reyes-Flores[1] , Carmen Mezura-Godoy[1]([⊠]) ,
Edgard Benítez-Guerrero[1] , and Juan Manuel González Calleros[2]

[1] Universidad Veracruzana, 91020 Xalapa-Enríquez, Veracruz, Mexico
{itreyes,cmezura,edbenitez}@uv.mx
[2] Benemérita Universidad Autónoma de Puebla, 72592 Puebla, Puebla, Mexico
juan.gonzalez@cs.buap.mx

Abstract. Technologies that support co-located collaboration must not only provide a shared workspace, but also support collaboration. We are interested in supporting co-located collaboration through computer systems that encourage group interaction, that is, systems that observe and analyze the interaction of collaborators, identify when there is a problem in the collaboration and execute social interventions to improve collaboration while they try to complete their activity. In order to validate whether the effectiveness of the group would improve when they receive social interventions on their group performance, an experimental study was executed. The study consisted of observing co-located student groups collaborating to design a web interface prototype, comparing teams that received social interventions from external human facilitator and those that did not. With this experimental study, results were obtained that help to characterize groups of students working in a co-located environment, and that could be considered in a system that encourages collaboration.

Keywords: Co-located collaboration · Encourage collaboration · Experimental study · Social interventions · Effective collaboration

1 Introduction

Collaboration is essential in all areas of human activity, such as science, art, technology, or business, and even in everyday life, in family life, at school, in the workplace and in business. Collaboration means that two or more people work together to complete a task or achieve a common goal [1]. Considering the taxonomy of Ellis et al. [2] collaboration can take different forms: 1) Co-located (same time/same place), 2) Distributed (same time/different place), 3) Asynchronous (different time/same place), and 4) Distributed asynchronous (different time/place different).

Col-ocated collaboration focuses on scenarios where, people interact face-to-face in close physical proximity [3]. In particular, this kind of collaboration provides certain benefits, for example, there are natural channels for continuous and multimodal communication; nonverbal cues; and potential for higher productivity in performing tasks

V. Agredo-Delgado et al. (Eds.): HCI-COLLAB 2022, CCIS 1707, pp. 162–175, 2022.
https://doi.org/10.1007/978-3-031-24709-5_12

[4]. However, in co-located collaboration, as in any collaboration scenario, people in order to achieve effective and efficient collaboration conflict situations can also arise, for instance, some persons participate less than others, do not respected assigned roles, tasks, deadlines, etc.

In order to support people to achieve effective collaboration, technological tools have been built under the Computer Supported Collaborative Work (CSCW) approach, which is responsible for developing new theories and technologies to support people who work together. In technological development, there are interactive systems in which the collaboration of groups of people in the same place is inherently allowed. Such is the case of Tabletops, Interactive Whiteboards, Tangible User Interfaces, among others. However, the effort that has been put into these CSCW technologies to support co-located collaboration has attracted less interest than technologies for distributed interaction. The role that technology has played is conventionally limited to passively mediating or enabling interaction between co-located people, serving only as catalysts for collaboration [3].

So, a research question has been opened about how a group of people could receive computational support to achieve effective co-located collaboration. A possible hypothesis to answer this question is that co-located collaboration could be supported by a system that observe and analyze the interaction of collaborators, identify when there is a problem in the collaboration and execute social interventions, that is, suggestions, help and/or comments that help improve collaboration while they try to complete their activity. To research this, it is necessary to observe groups of people working on a co-located activity, to validate whether the effectiveness of the group improves when they receive the support of an external facilitator through social interventions on group performance.

In this paper, an experimental study is presented. The objective of the study was to compare the effectiveness of the collaboration of groups of people who do or do not receive support from an external facilitator. The external facilitator was a human who simulated the social interventions that the computer system would make. Groups of people collaborating on the design of a web interface were observed in a co-located manner. In addition, the results of the experimental study helped to characterize groups of people who collaborate in the design of interface prototypes, which could be considered in a system that encourage collaboration.

2 Background

Collaboration means that two or more people work together to complete a task or achieve a common goal [1]. In a co-located collaborative activity, participants work face to face synchronously in the same physical space. There are several group performance variables that influence the effectiveness of a collaborative activity, for example, group size, group cohesion, similarity, interdependence, entitativity, social identity, leadership, social presence [5], and so on. There are also several variables to measure the effectively achieved of the activities, such as: percentage of achievement, activity time, effort of each group member, and so on. In the CSCW literature, to calculate the value of these variables, it has been done through the analysis of Interactions, actions executed by each participant in a shared workspace [6], since they are the most relevant element in a collaborative activity and through its analysis the behavior of the participants can be known.

For Olsson et al. [3], computer systems can assume four roles to support collaboration interactions: enabling, facilitating, inviting, and encouraging interaction. Enabling interaction refers to the role of a technological tool in enabling or allowing interaction to take place. Facilitating interaction refers to facilitating users' communication and coordination, relieving tension, and minimizing negative experiences, and generally helping to make the best of a social situation. Inviting interaction refers to providing additional information to users about their current social situation, so that they freely decide whether to act based on the additional information provided and social cues or not. And finally, encouraging interaction consists of motivating or persuading people to start interacting or maintain an ongoing interaction. For this, hardware and software must be used to stimulate people to act during collaboration, for instance, software system could make a social intervention when a person does not dare to say something to another person, or it could encourage two persons to collaborate on something in which they seem to have a common interest.

In the literature, works have been found on how co-located collaboration has been supported, and they have been classified according to the roles of technology proposed by Olsson et al. [3], as shown in Table 1.

In the case of the enabling technology for interaction, a wide range of examples of interactive systems such as Tabletops and Tangible User Interfaces have been found, however, they are only catalysts for collaboration and do not support collaboration. Some research works have focused on facilitating communication and coordination, considering usability issues in the design of these tools. And other works have focused on inviting user interaction by showing them information on some interaction indicators, such as the number of participations per user or graphic representations of which participant has collaborated the most, so that users can make decisions that benefit their collaboration process. To date, few studies have been found on how to encourage collaboration and those are limited just to analyzing the interaction, but not how to execute a social intervention or what impact the interventions have on the effectiveness of the collaboration.

Although related works have made important contributions to supporting collaboration in the same place, we believe that support for co-located collaboration could be broader. The works where collaboration is invited through group awareness tools have helped to show users their current situation in the activity so that they decide how to act accordingly, however, our goal is that decisions about collaboration do not fall only in the people, because sometimes they do not know how to collaborate effectively. Instead of that, users could receive well-planned interventions that suggest a change in their behavior to improve their collaboration effectiveness.

Table 1. Role of technology in supporting co-located collaboration

Role technology	Collaborative design objective	Related works
Enable	Enabling or allowing interaction to take place	Schneider et al., 2012 [7]; Hamidi et al., 2012 [8]; Sylla, 2013 [9]; Antle et al., 201 [10]; Leversund et al., 2014 [11]; Waje et al., 2016 [12]; Baranauskas and Posada, 2017 [13]; Wallbaum et al., 2017 [14]; Melcer and Isbister, 2018 [15]
Facilitate	Support users' communication and coordination, relieving tension and minimizing negative experiences, and generally helping to make the best of a social situation	Nacenta et al., 2010 [16]; Doeweling et al., 2013 [17]; Antle et al., 2013 [10]; Xambó et al., 2013 [18]; Cherek et al., 2018 [19]; Huber et al., 2019 [20]; Koushik et al., 2019 [21]
Invite	Providing additional information to users about their current social situation, so that they freely decide whether to act based on the additional information provided and social cues or not	Morris et al., [22]; ter Beek et al., 2005 [23]; Kim et al., 2008 [24]; Cherek et al., 2018 [19]
Encourage	Motivating or persuading people to start interacting or improve their interactions	Martinez-Maldonado et al., 2019 [4]; Praharaj, 2019 [15]

3 Study Methodology

To understand the effects of social interventions on co-located collaboration, we designed an experimental study. To this end, we have the following hypotheses:

H_0. There is no difference in effectiveness of a group in their co-located collaborative activity when they receive social interventions on their group performance and when they do not receive any intervention.

H_1. The effectiveness of a group in their collocated collaborative activity improves when they receive social interventions on their group performance than when they do not receive any intervention.

So, the independent variable is the social intervention on group performance during the co-located collaborative activity. While the dependent variable is the effectiveness based on 1) balance of the members' interactions, 2) efficacy, considering the achievement activity, and 3) efficiency, considering the activity time. Variables on which the external facilitator's interventions were based.

We used a between-group design, which consisted of the analysis of 2 study groups, a control group, and an experimental group. The control group were teams that executed collaborative activities to design a web pages interfaces without facilitator interventions, while the experimental group were teams that executed the activity supported by facilitator interventions. The participants, procedure and data analyzed are presented below.

3.1 Participants

In the study, 24 undergraduate students participated as study objects (6 female, 18 male). They were from two Mexican universities: "Benemérita Universidad Autónoma de Puebla" and "Universidad Veracruzana" (called for this study University 1 and University 2, respectively). Ages ranged from 20 to 30 years old ($\overline{X} = 22.37$, SD = 2.16). The semester of study is between 6 to 10 ($\overline{X} = 7.6$, SD = 2.1). In both universities, 12 students were divided into 2 groups, one control and one experimental group.

In the control group of the University 1, 6 students participated (1 female, 5 male) from the programs of Computer Science Engineering (2 out of 6), Information Technology Engineering (1 out of 6), Engineering Environmental (1 out of 6) and Automotive Systems (1 out of 6). And other 6 students (4 female, 2 male) participated in the experimental group, all of them from the program of Management of Smart Cities and Technological Transitions.

At the University 2, all participants were students of the program of Computational Technologies. 6 students participated on control group (1 female, 5 male) and other 6 students participated on experimental group (6 male). Participants were recruited from class groups from different programs. The groups were randomly assigned and therefore the participants knew each other to different degrees: some were friends, classmates, others did not know each other at all. Figure 1 shows experimental study participants distribution.

Fig. 1. Experimental study participants. (a) Control group university 1; (b) Experimental group university 1; (c) Control group university 2; (d) Experimental group university 2.

Most participants have worked on interface design (22 out of 2) and have used desktop software tools (13 out of 24), web software (20 out of 24), pencil and paper (11 out of 24), but no one had performed this type of activity using paper objects.

In addition, the experiment involved 5 different observers who took notes on the behavior of the students and 1 moderator who worked as organizer of the experiment and external facilitator in the case of the experimental groups (Teacher, PhD student, Interface Design Expert, age 29 years old).

3.2 Procedure

Experimental study was executed in 2 different places (University 1 and University 2). In both, sessions were in PhD classrooms with a waiting room space and an observation space. Each group of students was observed on a different day, in sessions of approximately 2 h. At the beginning of each session, 6 students concentrated in the waiting room were welcomed; the dynamics of the experimental study were explained to them, they were asked to fill out a form with participant data and a consent form approving their participation in the experiment, as well as the use of video cameras. In addition, to distinguish each student, they were assigned a different color, from which they were provided with a badge and two bracelets for each hand.

In order to capture the largest number of collaboration scenarios, participants from control and experimental groups performed 3 different activities, working in teams of 2, 3, and 6 students. This originated 24 study teams in total. That is, from the 6 participants in each group, 3 teams of 2 students, 2 teams of 3 students and 1 team of 6 students were formed. All teams were randomly assigned. Table 2 shows the distribution of the participants by university, group, and team. In University 1 the students began their participation in teams of 2, then 3 and finally 6 participants. While in University 2, the students began their participation in teams of 6, then 3 and finally 2 participants. This was to prevent the result from being affected, since in the second and third activities the participants were already more familiar with it (see Table 2).

In the observation space, there was a table with the activity materials and two video cameras (top and side) to record student interactions. When each team of students entered the observation space, they received instructions on the activity. Activity consisted of designing a web interface on the shared space (white cardboard), placing paper objects that represented web user interface elements, such as: icons, images, videos, text input, labels, text paragraph, buttons, menus, etc. This can be seen in Fig. 2.

Fig. 2. Experimental study materials.

Table 2. Participants distribution

Group	Team	# Participants	Participants distribution
		University 1	
Control	1	2	◐●
	2	2	●●
	3	2	●●
	4	3	◐●●
	5	3	◐●●
	6	6	◐●●◐●●
Experimental	7	2	◐●
	8	2	◐●
	9	2	◐●
	10	3	◐●●
	11	3	●●●
	12	6	◐●●●●●
		University 2	
Control	13	6	◐●●●●●
	14	3	●●●
	15	3	◐●●
	16	2	◐●
	17	2	◐●
	18	2	◐●
Experimental	19	6	◐●●●●●
	20	3	◐●●
	21	3	●●●
	22	2	◐●
	23	2	●●
	24	2	●●

Since each participant worked in 3 different teams, a different activity was assigned, with the same level of complexity, as described in Table 3. Time for each activity was 10 min, asking the participants to stop the activity if they completed the design before.

Table 3. Activities assigned to teams

Team size	Activity
2 students	Design of the main page of a software development company
3 students	Design of the main page of a grocery store
6 students	Design of the main page of a Publicity and Marketing company

Control groups did not receive any social intervention on their activity. While the experimental groups received two types of social interventions: 1) interaction balance, and 2) activity time. Facilitator executed the social interventions depending on the conditions described in Table 4.

Table 4. Social interventions description.

Social intervention	Description	Condition	Intention
Interaction balance	Facilitator said to students: "Remember that everyone must interact equally"	When one or more participants are executing fewer interactions than the rest	Improve the balance of interactions
Activity time	Facilitator said to students: "You have worked 5 min on the activity" or "You have worked 7 min on the activity"	When 5 or 7 min have elapsed in the activity	Improve the efficacy and efficiency activity

To determine the number of interactions of each student, facilitator counted them and noted on a sheet. The considered interactions are described in Table 5. Likewise, a stopwatch was used to count the activity time.

Table 5. Identified interactions description.

Interaction	Description
Put an object	Place an object directly on the shared design space
Put an object with someone's intermediation	Place an object in the shared design space through the intermediation of another participant
Move an object	Change the position of an object directly in the shared design space
Move an object with someone's intermediation	Change the position of an object in the shared design space through the intermediation of another participant
Remove an object	Remove an object directly from the shared design space
Remove an object with someone's intermediation	Remove an object from the shared design space through the intermediary of another participant
Send message one to one	Send a message directly to another participant
Send message one to all	Send a message to all other participants

Each team activity was recorded for later analysis. At the end of each activity, the participants were asked to wait in the waiting room until they were called back.

3.3 Data Collection an Analysis

The design of the experimental study involved the collection of quantitative data. To collect data, videos of each team activity were captured and replayed for analysis (as an example, see Fig. 3).

Fig. 3. Example of analyzed experimental study videos.

The analysis of these videos allowed to count: the number of interactions executed by each participant, the number of interactions dispersion between students, the activity time and the number of social interventions executed by the facilitator.

Table 6. Team results

Group	Team	# Students	# Interactions	Interaction dispersion	Time (minutes)	% Completion	# Social interventions
Control	1	2	55	16.97	10:00	60	0
	2	2	79	0.00	10:00	100	0
	3	2	99	4.24	10:00	100	0
	4	3	99	18.36	10:00	90	0
	5	3	103	8.02	10:00	90	0
	6	6	116	18.76	10:00	80	0
Experimental	7	2	103	5.66	10:00	90	3
	8	2	122	9.90	9:43	100	2
	9	2	95	6.36	8:25	100	2
	10	3	107	7.81	6:18	100	1
	11	3	129	7.37	10:00	100	3
	12	6	150	1.47	8:10	100	3
Control	13	6	174	32.23	10:00	70	0
	14	3	146	22.03	10:00	90	0
	15	3	143	19.67	6:30	100	0
	16	2	98	18.38	7:06	100	0

(*continued*)

Table 6. (*continued*)

Group	Team	# Students	# Interactions	Interaction dispersion	Time (minutes)	% Completion	# Social interventions
	17	2	96	3.54	8:30	100	0
	18	2	101	0.00	8:04	100	0
Experimental	19	6	129	7.07	8:14	100	3
	20	3	143	14.00	7:56	100	3
	21	3	96	4.36	6:04	100	2
	22	2	124	6.36	6:30	100	1
	23	2	71	2.83	6:28	100	1
	24	2	64	2.83	4:48	100	0

Table 6 shows the data collected from the videos of 24 teams. It shows the number of team participants, the number of interactions that all the students executed, the dispersion of the interactions between the students, the time in minutes that it took to complete the activity and the percentage of completion of the activity, as well as the number of social interventions that were executed by facilitator to support team collaboration.

For example, the first control team had 2 students who executed a total of 55 interactions with an interaction dispersion of 16.97, the activity time was 10:00 min, and they only completed 60% of the prototype; being a control group, they did not receive any social intervention. And the experimental team number 10 had 3 students who executed 107 interactions with an interaction dispersion of 7.81, the activity time was 6:18 min, the activity was 100% completed and they received 1 intervention.

Our results address a research question: "What is the difference between control groups and experimental groups in their balance of interactions, activity time, and percentage of activity completion?". We first report our specific findings on each team, and then we report the overall results distinguishing those of the control and experimental groups.

Table 7 reports the interaction balance, activity time, and activity completion data for each control and experimental group by university. These data are calculated by the mean of the results of the teams of each control and experimental group.

Table 7. Group results

Group	Interaction dispersion	Activity time	Activity completion
University 1			
Control	10.29	10	86.67
Experimental	6.43	8:46	98.33
University 2			
Control	15.98	8:21	93.33
Experimental	6.24	6:40	100

At University 1 the control groups had a mean interaction dispersion of 10.29, mean activity time was 10 min, and mean percent completion was 86.67, while the experimental groups had a mean interaction dispersion of 6.43, mean activity time was 8:46 min, and mean percent completion was 98.33. And University 2 the control groups had a mean interaction dispersion of 15.98, mean activity time was 8:21 min, and mean percent completion was 93.33, while the experimental groups had a mean interaction dispersion of 6.24, mean activity time was 6:40 min, and mean percent completion was 100.

4 Discussion

From the results of the exploratory study, it can be concluded that social interventions impact the effectiveness of collaboration. In the results it is visible that in the experimental groups, where social interventions were executed, the dispersion of the interactions between the students is less than in the control groups (University 1: 6.43 < 10.29; University 2: 6.24 < 15.98). This may be due to the fact that some of the social interventions executed were focused on specifically improving this aspect. Even, according to the notes of the experiment observers and videos, in most cases it was evident that the students who had executed fewer interactions began to interact more after receiving the social intervention in this regard (4 out of 5 teams: 7, 12, 19, 21).

Also, time and completion activity improved. Time was shorter (University 1: 8:46 < 10:00; University 2: 6:40 < 8:21) and percentage of completion was higher (University 1: 98.33 > 86.67; University 2: 100 > 93.33) in the experimental groups than in the control groups, probably also due to the social interventions that were executed over the time that had elapsed (11 out of 12 teams: 7–12, 19–23).

Thus, the hypothesis that is accepted from this experimental study is the alternative hypothesis, since effectiveness of a group in their co-located collaborative activity improves when they receive social interventions on their group performance than when they do not receive any intervention.

However, it was notorious that the effectiveness of team collaboration is not only conditioned by the social interventions, but also that some characteristics of the team have an influence. For example, it was observed that the group size also impacts the interactions dispersion of the students, since in two of the four groups, it was greater in the teams of 6 students (Team 6 = 18.76 and Team 13 = 32.23). In addition, in the videos it was noted that in all the teams there was at least one student who stayed away from the activity, only visualizing what the rest of the team was doing.

Another variable that could have affected the time and completion activity, was the number of times the student had previously worked on a similar activity, since in some teams the students replicated the work that they had done in previous activities.

Based on these results, it is possible to consider the development of a computer system that encourages collaboration through interventions, since it seems that the effectiveness of collaboration would improve. For example, it would be useful to develop a coaching system that identifies the interactions of collaborators through a camera, counts the number of interactions of each one and executes a social intervention when it is reasoned that a collaborator is not actively participating. This type of system would be useful for co-located work environments, for example, when people are collaborating at a table or even in an interactive system with a shared space, such as digital whiteboards, tabletops, or tangible user interfaces, among others.

Something that must be considered is that people may not have the same level of acceptance when receiving social interventions executed by a computerized system. Other experimental studies would be necessary in which the behavior of teams collaborating in a co-located activity that receive interventions from a computer system is observed and evaluated. It would be necessary to compare the results of the teams that receive interventions from a human facilitator, against the results of the teams that receive interventions from a computer system to identify if the effectiveness of the team improves or not.

5 Conclusion

We are interested in supporting co-located collaboration through computer systems that encourage group interaction through social interventions. In this paper, we present the results of an exploratory study that compared the collaborative effectiveness of experimental groups receiving support for their co-located collaborative activity, versus control groups receiving no support at all. This was done in order to explore the impact that social interventions executed from computer systems would generate to support co-located collaboration and evaluate the possibility of developing it, since few studies have been found in the literature that support co-located collaboration in this way.

We provide information on how people interact in collaborative activities on the design of prototypes of web interfaces. Our specific findings include that the dispersion of team member interactions is lower when there are interventions, the activity time is lower, and the percentage of completion is higher. This article also presents valuable information about characterizing groups of collaborators working on interface design, and that could be considered in a system that encourage collaboration.

References

1. Schuman, S.: Creating a Culture of Collaboration: The International Association of Facilitators handbook, vol. 4. Wiley, Hoboken (2006)
2. Ellis, C.A., Gibbs, S.J., Rein, G.: Groupware: some issues and experiences. Commun. ACM **34**(1), 39–58 (1991). https://doi.org/10.1145/99977.99987
3. Olsson, T., Jarusriboonchai, P., Woźniak, P., Paasovaara, S., Väänänen, K., Lucero, A.: Technologies for enhancing collocated social interaction: review of design solutions and approaches. Comput. Supported Cooper. Work (CSCW) **29**(1–2), 29–83 (2019). https://doi.org/10.1007/s10606-019-09345-0
4. Martinez-Maldonado, R., Kay, J., Buckingham Shum, S., Yacef, K.: Collocated collaboration analytics: principles and dilemmas for mining multimodal interaction data. Hum.-Comput. Interact. **34**(1), 1–50 (2019). https://doi.org/10.1080/07370024.2017.1338956
5. Montane-Jimenez, L.G., Benitez-Guerrero, E., Mezura-Godoy, C.: A context-aware architecture for improving collaboration of users in groupware systems. In: 9th IEEE International Conference on Collaborative Computing: Networking, Applications and Worksharing, pp. 70–76. IEEE (2013). https://doi.org/10.4108/icst.collaboratecom.2013.254185

6. Mezura-Godoy, C., Riveill, M., Talbot, S.: MARS: modelling arenas to regulate collaborative spaces. In: Favela, J., Decouchant, D. (eds.) CRIWG 2003. LNCS, vol. 2806, pp. 10–25. Springer, Heidelberg (2003). https://doi.org/10.1007/978-3-540-39850-9_2

7. Schneider, B., Blikstein, P., Mackay, W.: Combinatorix: a tangible user interface that supports collaborative learning of probabilities. In: Proceedings of the 2012 ACM International Conference on Interactive Tabletops and Surfaces (2012). https://doi.org/10.1145/2396636.2396656

8. Hamidi, F., Baljko, M., Moakler, A., Gadot, A.: Synchrum: a tangible interface for rhythmic collaboration. In: Adjunct proceedings of the 25th Annual ACM Symposium on User Interface Software and Technology (2012). https://doi.org/10.1145/2380296.2380323

9. Sylla, C.: Designing a tangible interface for collaborative storytelling to access' embodiment' and meaning making. In: Proceedings of the 12th International Conference on Interaction Design and Children (2013). https://doi.org/10.1145/2485760.2485881

10. Antle, A.N., et al.: Youtopia: a collaborative, tangible, multi-touch, sustainability learning activity. In: Proceedings of the 12th International Conference on Interaction Design and Children (2013). https://doi.org/10.1145/2485760.2485866

11. Leversund, A.H., Krzywinski, A., Chen, W.: Children's collaborative storytelling on a tangible multitouch tabletop. In: Streitz, N., Markopoulos, P. (eds.) DAPI 2014. LNCS, vol. 8530, pp. 142–153. Springer, Cham (2014). https://doi.org/10.1007/978-3-319-07788-8_14

12. Waje, A., Tearo, K., Sampangi, R.V., Reilly, D.: Grab this, swipe that: Combining tangible and gestural interaction in multiple display collaborative gameplay. In: Proceedings of the 2016 ACM International Conference on Interactive Surfaces and Spaces (2016). https://doi.org/10.1145/2992154.2996794

13. Baranauskas, M.C.C., Posada, J.E.G.: Tangible and shared storytelling: Searching for the social dimension of constructionism. In: Proceedings of the 2017 Conference on Interaction Design and Children (2017). https://doi.org/10.1145/3078072.3079743

14. Wallbaum, T., Ananthanarayan, S., Borojeni, S.S., Heuten, W., Boll, S.: Towards a tangible storytelling kit for exploring emotions with children. In: Proceedings of the on Thematic Workshops of ACM Multimedia (2017). https://doi.org/10.1145/3126686.3126702

15. Melcer, E.F., Isbister, K.: Bots & (Main) frames: exploring the impact of tangible blocks and collaborative play in an educational programming game. In: Proceedings of the 2018 CHI Conference on Human Factors in Computing Systems (2018). https://doi.org/10.1145/3173574.3173840

16. Nacenta, M. A., Pinelle, D., Gutwin, C., Mandryk, R.: Individual and group support in tabletop interaction techniques. In: Müller-Tomfelde, C. (ed.) Tabletops - Horizontal Interactive Displays. Human-Computer Interaction Series, pp. 303–333. Springer, London (2010). https://doi.org/10.1007/978-1-84996-113-4_13

17. Doeweling, S., Tahiri, T., Sowinski, P., Schmidt, B., Khalilbeigi, M.: Support for collaborative situation analysis and planning in crisis management teams using interactive tabletops. In: Proceedings of the 2013 ACM International Conference on Interactive Tabletops and Surfaces (2013). https://doi.org/10.1145/2512349.2512823

18. Xambó, A., Hornecker, E., Marshall, P., Jordà, S., Dobbyn, C., Laney, R.: Let's jam the reactable: peer learning during musical improvisation with a tabletop tangible interface. ACM Trans. Comput.-Hum. Interact. (TOCHI) 20(6), 1–34 (2013). https://doi.org/10.1145/2530541

19. Cherek, C., Brocker, A., Voelker, S., Borchers, J.: Tangible awareness: how tangibles on tabletops influence awareness of each other's actions. In: Proceedings of the 2018 CHI Conference on Human Factors in Computing Systems (2018). https://doi.org/10.1145/3173574.3173872

20. Huber, S., Berner, R., Uhlig, M., Klein, P., Hurtienne, J.: Tangible objects for reminiscing in dementia care. In: Proceedings of the Thirteenth International Conference on Tangible, Embedded, and Embodied Interaction (2019). https://doi.org/10.1145/3294109.3295632

21. Koushik, V., Guinness, D., Kane, S.K.: StoryBlocks: a tangible programming game to create accessible audio stories. In: Proceedings of the 2019 CHI Conference on Human Factors in Computing Systems (2019). https://doi.org/10.1145/3290605.3300722

22. Morris, M.R., Cassanego, A., Paepcke, A., Winograd, T., Piper, A.M., Huang, A.: Mediating group dynamics through tabletop interface design. IEEE Comput. Graphics Appl. **26**(5), 65–73 (2006). https://doi.org/10.1109/mcg.2006.114

23. ter Beek, M.H., Massink, M., Latella, D., Gnesi, S., Forghieri, A., Sebastianis, M.: A case study on the automated verification of groupware protocols. In: 2005Proceedings. 27th International Conference on Software Engineering, ICSE 2005. IEEE (2005). https://doi.org/10.1109/icse.2005.1553606

24. Kim, T., Chang, A., Holland, L., Pentland, A.S.: Meeting mediator: enhancing group collaboration using sociometric feedback. In: Proceedings of the 2008 ACM Conference on Computer Supported Cooperative Work (2008). https://doi.org/10.1145/1460563.1460636

Steps for Decreasing Noises in Interaction Process with Video Games

Omar Correa Madrigal[1]([⊠]) [iD], Yadira Ramírez Rodríguez[1] [iD],
and Vlada Kugurakova[2] [iD]

[1] Universidad de las Ciencias Informáticas, Havana, Cuba
{ocorrea,yramirezr}@uci.cu
[2] Federal University of Kazan, Kazan, Russia

Abstract. The Human-Computer Interaction can be modelled as Signals and Noises process. In this sense game-player interaction could be improved when this point of view is applied. Signals-Noises-Aiders (SNA) is presented as method with heuristics that help to reducing noises using power-ups as aiders. The results in Flappy Bird Mechanic showed the method's pertinence and its effectiveness in power-ups design. This work presents how to compute the rewards (e.g. power-ups) influences, contributing thus to HCI in games.

Keywords: HCI · Power-ups · Aider · Noises

1 Introduction

The innovation in video games is essential. More challengers and better interaction level, are needed in the current gamers context. The tendencies are related with new and more immersive interaction devises, realistic graphics, artificial intelligence and social mechanisms for increasing the interchanges and global gamer network. All of this are related with to search the new and upgrade gamers experiences, it is important the relationships between game and player, more in deep, it is important increasing the user performances/entertainment with improved game mechanisms or new mechanisms [1]. The human computer interaction (HCI) is a research discipline that helps to working on this goal and digital signal processing is a powerful tool for improve the interaction between game and player.

The good player experience is a multi-factors result. One of them is the articulation of formal elements in the game. Rules system should be oriented to articulate the goals with expected results and correct rewards taking into account the conflicts and game limits. On the other hand, the player wants challenges and feedbacks in a dramatics history or interesting context, this aims to relation between Challenge and Game-Player Feedbacks, this controls the interaction cycle [2].

Entertainment is the expected state for player and the Flow theory resume that it is possible when challenge and player skill are balance [3, 4]. Reach this goal is an important tasks for games developers and is possible with dynamic difficulty adjustment (DDA). Adjust dynamically the games contents, gameplay, taking into account the player actions is a solution and could be with passive or active DDA. Passive DDA approach is a full digital signal processing where the computer define the Flow Critical Path checking the player performances in real time while the active DDA make feeling a sensation of control over the game activity because bring different play options and adjust the contents taking into account the user decision. Both intervene in the Flow Critical Path and the current approaches work about challenge complexity [5, 6]. The researches work about adaptation scheme increasing and decreasing challenge complexity for better game experiences [7–9], the problems has been when to change the challenge and how do that for beginner and advanced players. First problem has been solved with controlling the players performances (track the successes) and emotion detections [6]. On the other hand how change the challenge depends content type to change, for improving the experiences. This are related with adaptation engine and is an open research area because have large amount of contents that could impact in the challenges complexity for instance: game worlds and its objects, gameplay mechanisms, non-player controller (NPC), game narratives, game scenarios and quest. In this work we contribute in game mechanisms system take into account the aider contents.

In learning and rehabilitations process is very common to assist. The points of views related with video games define the video games as aiders, it possible because immersive environments and the try-error context help learning new knowledge and acquiring abilities [10–13]. The video games are tutoring systems or virtual therapist for each learning and rehabilitation process respectively [14, 15] but what are the aiders in deep? What kind of content could be an aider? At the moment only the NPCs are identified as aider [11, 12] but can be others. This work aim to new point of view about aider content and its impact in casual games. The proposed method describes the interaction player-game context as signals and noises context and present some heuristics that computing *power-ups* influences for reducing the noises and contributing to player's experiences.

2   Method

HCI analyses the signals between human and computer for a better communication. This signals have interferences by different noises, these are related with human and computer factors (Fig. 1). In this sense the relation between player and games is more vulnerable because depends player engagement. Game Design concepts permit keeping the player engagement, but each player is different to others and contents need be adapted for keeping player's enjoying. That is possible if noises are identified and decreased in interaction process using special contents, aiders (Fig. 2).

For understand the proposal is important defining noise and aider concepts in player-game interaction (PGI).

- *Noise* is the interference in the process of PGI caused by player or game's factors that hinders the full enjoyment of the video game. Example: little hand-eye skill, knowledge of game mechanisms and game feedbacks low.
- *Aid* is content type graphic, sound or haptic effect that attenuates one or various noises in PGI.

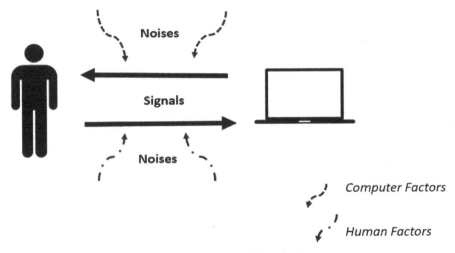

Fig. 1. HCI signals and related noises.

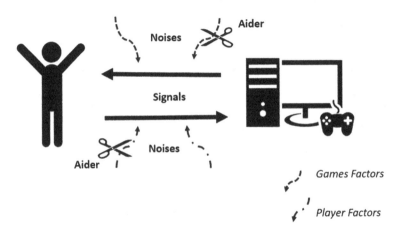

Fig. 2. Signals, noises and aiders (SNA), one approach for protecting the player's engagement.

Second aspect in this approach is how design aiders. Thinking about one to one reltionships between noise and aider is bad design because the PGI is multi-factorial and an aider could impacting in more than one noise for example: Shooter game an aider can reducing the contents speed, it impacts in noises like slow hand-eye ability (player factor) and NPCs complexity (game factor). In this sense for define aiders can taking two ways, the Table 1 summarize important game design elements to take into account.

Table 1. Game design elements for design aiders

Player engages by design [13]	Hooks [16]
Focused goals Challenging tasks	Action hooks
Protection from adverse consequences for initial failures	Resources hooks
Affirmation of performance	Tactical and strategic hooks
Affiliation with others	Time hooks
Choice	
Authenticity	

Both ways are relates and the hooks are the main elements [13]. The aiders are hooks that afford new actions and transform the interaction context. In this work we focus in resources hooks like power-ups. The power-ups are common rewards and have a short life time [17]. A power-up as star in Mario Bros, is perfect example for showing how much helps to the players engagement. Today the power-ups have different restrictions in game because these are rewards and lanced in different game's times. Empirical studies about power-ups in mobile games show these are activated by user's decision or outcome of game's advances [18], but player can needed it in other moments e.g. for protecting adverse consequences for initial failures. In this sense power-ups as aiders have special advantages and our experiences in games for health show this [19]. In this work was developed a space shooter game and the power-ups were activated automatically. In an order form, each aiders was applied and the result showed how after each application the successes increased with meaningfully differences between aiders (p < 0:05). Taking into account this study results, some heuristics was created for identifying better power-ups and to reduce the meaningful noises.

Successes have direct relation with challenges, a wined challenge is a success. The sum of successes (S) after applied an aider has a casuistry relation with each aiders. The aiders have an influence times (i.e. time where de player performance improve without help) after aider is applied. A first approximation to the influence time is the successes mean (SMean) [19] and the first heuristics for measuring an aider influences is:

$$P(S_i|H_i) = \frac{P(H_i)P(H_i|S_i)}{\sum_{i=1}^{m} P(H_i)P(H_i|S_i)} \quad \forall S_i \in N, S_i \geq SMean \tag{1}$$

where S_i is the successes mount of H_i (aider).

The interaction with an aider can have not success (S = 0), in this sense other heuristic is presented in Eq. 2:

$$\varepsilon_i = \frac{1}{m}(P(H_i|S_i) + P(H_i|C)) \quad \forall S_i \in N, S_i \geq SMean, C = 0 \tag{2}$$

where m is the number of aiders and $\varepsilon_i = P(H_i|S_i)$.

The before heuristics have as disadvantage, if $P(H_i|C) > P(H_i|S_i)$ then the decision for select the better power-up could be affected. This condition is important because the more relevant aspect of aider's influence is $P(H_i|S_i)$ Moreover this conditions allows identifying problems in the designed aiders because shows how an aider has more failures than successes. The before heuristic could be developed for improving the compute of aiders influence, it is possible with other and deeper variable e.g. reaction time (RT), a second influence's level ε_{2th}. This variable is related with S and maximizes the influence's value; ε_{2th} could be calculated as the proportion $\frac{RTBefore}{RTAfter}$ where RTBefore and RTAfter are the means before and after that an aider was applied respectively. The last heuristic in the approach's evolution is:

$$\varepsilon_i = \frac{1}{m}(\varepsilon_{2th}P(H_i|S_i) + P(H_i|C)) \quad \forall S_i \in N, S_i \geq SMean, C = 0 \tag{3}$$

2.1 Game for Computing the Aiders Influence

For exploring the before approach was created a platform game with Flappy Bird mechanic [20]. This kind of game have two important factors that affects the interaction process, one of them is the game speed, obstacles show up rapidly and then second factor (human factor) appear, the low eye-hand coordination. The designed aiders as power-ups work about these noises and increasing the player's performances (Fig. 3).

- Slow Time impacts in the game speed decreasing it and helping to a better eye-hand coordination.
- Psychic removes the obstacles some time with open door effect. This aider remove de main noise, obstacles.
- Shield protect the collisions between player and obstacles some time.

The lives' time for aiders was configured for finishing when the player passed three obstacles. The game counts the successes after applies an aider and resume the stats in table and graphics for each aider (Fig. 4). The games applies aiders ten times each one and these are presented in the third obstacle always. When to apply the aiders is important aspect for futures works, passed experience showed how increasing the player's performance when an aider was applied in low eye-hand ability [19]. Designed Game permits exploring the performances without identifying the low performances.

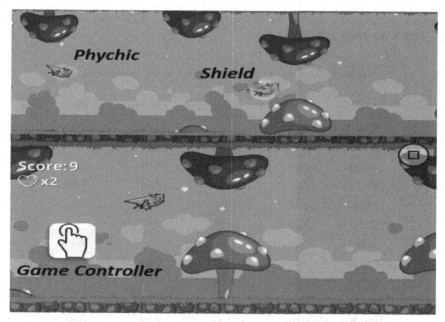

Fig. 3. Base gameplay and main power-ups

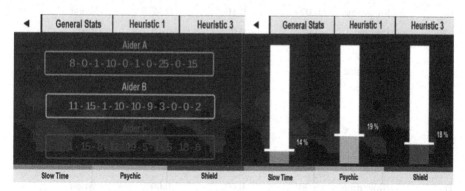

Fig. 4. General Stats and graphic of Heuristic 3 in the tested game

3 Experimental Results

The experiment was prepared for analyzing the developed heuristics for identifies power-ups influence and analysis the player's performance. Ten students were selected randomly in the Kazan Federal University from Russia, three had not previous experiences with Flappy Bird mechanic. The group played the games 30 times and interacted 10 times with each power-up. The successes were counted after expired power-ups and the influences value (ε) was computed with heuristics. The heuristic 3 was computing using $\varepsilon_{2th} = 1.9$ the worst RTBefore and RTAfter in the novice players (A, D, H). Moreover players answered which power-up was the best or worst in interaction processes. All data are resumed in the Table 2.

Table 2. Experiment results. Heuristics and players opinions.

Player id	Power-up	Heuristic 1	Heuristic 2	Heuristic 3	Player opinion
A	Slow time	0	0	0.07	Worst
	Psychic	0.02	0.04	0.06	
	Shield	0.03	0.07	0.09	Best
B	Slow time	0.03	0.10	0.14	Worst
	Psychic	0.08	0.09	0.15	Best
	Shield	0.09	0.09	0.17	
C	Slow time	0.01	0.07	0.07	Worst
	Psychic	0.07	0.07	0.13	Best
	Shield	0.08	0.08	0.15	
D	Slow time	0.01	0.08	0.09	
	Psychic	0.04	0.06	0.09	Best
	Shield	0.06	0.08	0.13	Worst
E	Slow time	0.02	0.10	0.12	Worst
	Psychic	0.08	0.09	0.16	Best
	Shield	0.03	0.03	0.06	
F	Slow time	0.01	0.10	0.11	Worst
	Psychic	0.07	0.07	0.13	Best
	Shield	0.03	0.04	0.07	
G	Slow time	0.06	0.07	0.014	Best
	Psychic	0.10	0.10	0.19	
	Shield	0.09	0.10	0.18	Worst
H	Slow time	0.00	0.09	0.09	Worst
	Psychic	0.06	0.07	0.13	Best
	Shield	0.07	0.09	0.16	
I	Slow time	0.03	0.11	0.13	Worst
	Psychic	0.10	0.10	0.19	Best
	Shield	0.08	0.09	0.16	
J	Slow time	0.01	0.10	0.11	Worst
	Psychic	0.08	0.08	0.15	Best
	Shield	0.08	0.09	0.16	

The worst power-up identified per each heuristics was Slow Time, it has correspondence with eight player's opinions. This power-up helps to player with low eye-hand skill because reduce the game speed, a human factor that affect the interaction process but it is no main noise in Flappy Bird mechanics. Psychic and Shield power-ups make decreasing the obstacles noises and the player can focuses in the eye-hand skill and to improve his skill after applied the power-ups. Both had special influences and relative balance when the heuristics results were analyzed (Table 3). The heuristics result were contrasted apply the Wilcoxon test (not parametric) using the SPSS 2 software. The results not showed significant difference between Psychic and Shield power-ups ($p > 0.05$; $p = 0.84$) while the analysis related with Slow Time-Psychic and Slow Time-Shield was gotten significant differences ($p = 0.0001$).These result reaffirm that heuristics could be used for selecting better power-ups and activating it for reducing de noises in the interaction process and improve player's performance.

Table 3. Sum of Positive (Best), Negative (Worst) and Similar (Same) results taking in to account compared player's experience with Psychic and Shield aiders.

Power-ups	Heuristic 1	Heuristic 2	Heuristic 3
Psychic-shield	Best - 5	Best - 3	Best - 3
	Worst - 4	Worst - 5	Worst - 5
	Same - 1	Same - 2	Same - 1

3.1 Player's Evolution Tracking the Successes Series

This part of the experiment helped to analyze player's performance after each applied power-up. The successes for beginner players were checked and each aider improved the player's performance generally. Player opinions were related with the Slow Time power-up as the worst. This power-up makes that one lose the control about the game because it decrease the tap frequency"; changing the normal to low speed not helped to beginner players in these studies cases.

Slow Time power-up have an incorrect application as aider in beginner players but when the player thinks in it as challenge his performances could be improved. Two study case were analyzed, one advances players and beginner player. Both improved the performance in the second test and the players' opinions were in the sense "I focused in Slow Time and thought it is a challenge". This work about power-ups like aids is just the first steps, a deeper analyses are necessary with the statistic studies.

4 Conclusions

The engagement between player and video games is the base for successful game. The Signal-Noise-Aiders (SNA) approach is a new point of view and permits modelling the interaction process in video games. Power-ups as aiders is a correct design decision for improving the performances in platform games. The created bayesian heuristics help to compute the power-ups influences and give a new way for dynamic difficulty adjustment through aiders. Power-ups can reducing or increasing noises, in both case help to better game experience. The future works will focus in exploring the SNA approach en other kinds of video games and analyzing the application of proposed heuristics when these are used for regulated the player's experience through dynamic difficulty adjustment [1].

References

1. Wesley, D., Barczak, G.: Innovation and Marketing in the Video Game Industry: Avoiding the Performance Trap. CRC Press, Boca Raton (2016)
2. Fullerton, T.: Game Design Workshop: A Playcentric Approach to Creating Innovative Games. CRC Press, Boca Raton (2014)
3. Chen, J.: Flow in games (and everything else). Commun. ACM **50**, 31–34 (2007)
4. Csikszentmihalyi, F.: The Psychology of Optimal Experience. Harper and Row, New York (1990)
5. Karpouzis, K., Yannakakis, G.N.: Emotion in Games: Theory and Praxis, vol. 4. Springer, Cham (2016). https://doi.org/10.1007/978-3-319-41316-7
6. Lopes, R., Bidarra, R.: Adaptivity challenges in games and simulations: a survey. IEEE Trans. Comput. Intell. AI Games **3**(2), 85–99 (2011)
7. Shaker, N., Togelius, J., Yannakakis, G.N.: The experience-driven perspective. In: Shaker, N., Togelius, J., Nelson, M.J. (eds.) Procedural Content Generation in Games. Computational Synthesis and Creative Systems, pp. 181–194. Springer, Cham (2016). https://doi.org/10.1007/978-3-319-42716-4_10
8. Rogers, K., Kamm, C., Weber, M.: Towards player-centric adaptivity: interactions of gameplay behaviour and player traits in a survival game. In: Proceedings of the 2016 Annual Symposium on Computer-Human Interaction 210 in Play Companion Extended Abstracts, CHI PLAY Companion 2016, pp. 269–276. ACM, New York (2016). https://doi.org/10.1145/2968120.2987725, http://doi.acm.org/10.1145/2968120.2987725
9. Farooq, S.S., Kim, K.-J.: Game player modeling. In: Encyclopedia of Computer Graphics and Games, pp. 1–15 (2016)
10. Lappegard, P.: The implementation of commercial video gaming in rehabilitation: a scoping review. Master's thesis, Department of Psychology, University of Oslo (2016). https://www.duo.uio.no/handle/10852/51008
11. Lohse, K., Shirzad, N., Verster, A., Hodges, N., Van der Loos, H.M.: Video 220 games and rehabilitation: using design principles to enhance engagement in physical therapy. J. Neurol. Phys. Ther. **37**(4), 166–175 (2013)
12. Heins, M.C.: Video games in education. Master's thesis, SUNY College at Brockport, New York (2016). http://digitalcommons.brockport.edu/ehd_theses/625/
13. Dickey, M.D.: Engaging by design: How engagement strategies in popular computer and video games can inform instructional design. Educ. Tech. Res. Dev. **53**(2), 67–83 (2005)
14. Connell, M., Stevens, D.: A computer-based tutoring system for visual-spatial skills: dynamically adapting to the users developmental range. In: 2002 Proceedings of the 2nd International Conference on Development and Learning, pp. 245–251 (2002)
15. Pirovano, M., Mainetti, R., Baud-Bovy, G., Lanzi, P.L., Borghese, N.A.: Selfadaptive games for rehabilitation at home. In: 2012 IEEE Conference on Computational Intelligence and Games (CIG), pp. 179–186 (2012)
16. Howland, G.: Balancing gameplay hooks. Game Design Perspect. 78–84 (2002)

17. Lewis, Z.H., Swartz, M.C., Lyons, E.J.: What's the point?: a review of reward systems implemented in gamification interventions. Games Health J. **5**(2), 93–99 (2016)
18. Cao, D.: Game design patterns in endless mobile minigames. Master's thesis, Faculty of Technology and Society, Malmo University (2016)
19. Correa, O., Cuervo, C., Perez, P.C., Arias, A.: A new approach for self adaptive video game for rehabilitation-experiences in the amblyopia treatment. In: 2014 IEEE 3rd International Conference on Serious Games and Applications for Health (SeGAH), pp. 1–5. IEEE (2014)

Usability and User Experience are not Enough: Gaps to Fill to Design for and Assess Well-Being and Engagement

Célia Martinie[1] (iD), Philippe Palanque[1 (✉)] (iD), and Marco Winckler[2] (iD)

[1] ICS-IRIT, Université Toulouse III – Paul Sabatier, Toulouse, France
`{martinie,palanque}@irit.fr`
[2] SPARKS-Wimmics Team, I3S, Université Côte d'Azur, Nice, France
`winckler@inria.fr`

Abstract. Well-being is a complex phenomenon that is deeply depends on the individuals themselves and includes subjective perception of the past, present and future experiences. Connecting with work adds a concrete dimension to that well-being that makes it possible to consider designing for well-being and assessing it. One key element related to well-being is engagement at work and gameful design is a mean to increase engagement. This position paper builds on the evolution of the field of HCI over the years to identify means of addressing well-being through engagement. We describe the concepts related to Usability and how they evolved towards User Experience to encompass more complex (related to self) elements. We show how previous work in the field has connected these two major properties (using tasks descriptions) and how it might be possible to extend further embracing human needs and motivation theory. A concrete example is given in the context of interaction with a digital clock. Even though this example is simple, it conveys the concerns and highlights possible directions towards solutions.

Keywords: Task models · Usability · User experience · Motivation · Human needs · Work · Operator

1 Introduction

The Human Factors community has been working on understanding the multiple internal states of operators (and more globally human beings) but also how to change this internal state to increase Subjective Well-Being (SBW) [1]. For instance, in [2], authors assess the connection between neurosis of adolescents and SWB. Foundations of human motivation and needs were made concrete with the seminal work of Maslow [3] and further studied to identify humans' motives [4]. Even though its validity was (and still is) highly criticized in the literature [5] evidences are shown that self-actualization (the top-level need in the Maslow's hierarchy) is not questioned. Concomitantly, Human-Computer Interaction community has been extending its research focus from Usability-centered design of services, systems and products to hedonic aspects covered by the User Experience property. Beyond, one contributing factor to well-being is engagement that connects to the

V. Agredo-Delgado et al. (Eds.): HCI-COLLAB 2022, CCIS 1707, pp. 186–200, 2022.
https://doi.org/10.1007/978-3-031-24709-5_14

stimulation dimension of User Experience [6]. In this paper, we propose to use gameful design and automation as two design options to increase engagement of users/operators while performing their activities. We use the task modelling notation HAMSTERS [7] to describe these activities and to assess their evolutions when automation and gameful design options are considered.

The paper is structured as follows. Next section introduces the contributions of Usability and User Experience on the design of interactive applications and interactions. This section also presents how task models can be used to represent usability and user experience related information. Section 3 extends Sect. 2 by adding two additional concepts: hierarchy of needs and engagement. Section 4 introduces a simple illustrative example to show how targeting engagement (using gameful design and automation) can stimulate operators and reduce their workload. Section 5 concludes the paper and highlights potential directions for future work.

2   Usability and User Experience Contributions

2.1   Usability

HCI community historically focused on the usability of interactive systems, in order to ensure that operators will achieve their tasks with the interactive systems. Usability standard (as defined in [8]) has deeply changed the design of interactive systems by decomposing usability for ensuring careful consideration of three contributing factors. Assessing usability can be done in multiple manners and, as argued in [9], in some research contributions without careful consideration of the correlation between them. These contributing factors are:

- **Effectiveness**: corresponds to the coverage of users tasks offered by the system functions. It describes the capability of users to reach their goals with a given system.
- **Efficiency**: corresponds to the performance of users to reach their goals. It includes objective measurable elements such as number of errors or execution time.
- **Satisfaction**: corresponds to the users perceived satisfaction while performing their work with a given system.

Figure 1 represents the schematic view of the field of HCI in terms of users performing a task. The Human Processor model proposed in [10] decomposes human activity into perceptive, cognitive and motor elementary tasks. This is close to the biological behavior of humans and remains far away from human affects and needs that is presented in models in the following sections.

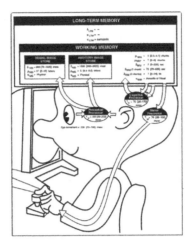

Fig. 1. The operator at work as depicted in the Human-Processor Model [10].

2.2 User Experience (UX)

User Experience property has been addressed more recently with methods supporting the design for User Experience [11, 12] with methods for the assessment of User Experience [13].

Fig. 2. The six contributing factors of User Experience as proposed in [14].

Various definitions have been proposed for User Experience including affects and emotions, aesthetics or values [6]. According to the work of [14] User Experience can be decomposed in the following 6 contributing factors (visually presented in Fig. 2):

- **Aesthetics**: The aesthetic level involves a product's capacity to delight one or more of our sensory modalities;
- **Emotion**: The emotional level involves those experiences that are typically considered in emotion psychology and in everyday language about emotions;

- **Identification**: A hedonic attribute group, which captures the product's ability to communicate important personal values to relevant others;
- **Stimulation**: The stimulation dimension describes to what extent a product can support the human need for innovative and interesting functions, interactions and contents
- **Meaning and Value**: The meaning level involves our ability to assign personality or other expressive characteristics and to assess the personal or symbolic significance of products;
- **Social-connectedness**: The social connectedness involves means to increase social pleasure offering means to interact and share information with others.

User experience goes beyond Usability and gets closer to feelings and emotions that are contributing to human motivation and human needs which are in return impacting well-being.

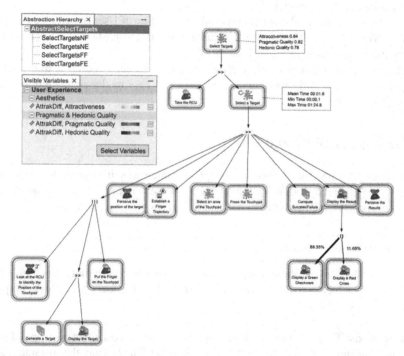

Fig. 3. Representation of user study result related to user experience in the HASMSTERS task model indicating variations in the UX dimensions using color panels and representing frequencies of choice (%) on the connecting arrows to support usability analysis (from [13]).

2.3   Connecting Usability and UX Through Task Models

User Experience is usually connected to entertaining activities such as media consumption, but recent work demonstrates that the concept is being used in work context [15] but also in the workplace [16]. Operators' work can be easily described using task models which decompose work in a set of goals each of them being refined by a set of tasks to reach the goal.

HAMSTERS [7] is a tool-supported graphical task modeling notation for representing human activities and work in a hierarchical and ordered manner. At the higher abstraction level, goals can be decomposed into sub-goals, which can in turn be decomposed into activities. The output of this decomposition is a graphical tree of nodes. Nodes can be tasks or temporal operators. Tasks can be of several types (Fig. 3) and contain information such as a name, information details, and criticality level. Only the single user high-level task types are presented here but HAMSTERS has a variety of further task types available and accounts for information, objects and knowledge involved in the performance of the work [17].

In [13], Bernhaupt et al. have proposed the integration of User Experience contributing factors including both hedonic and pragmatic qualities inside task models (addressing mainly the effectiveness factor of Usability).

The objective of that research work was to connect User Experience to the activity of operators in their daily work and activity (in that case media consumption using a remote-control unit (RCU)).

3   Beyond Usability and UX

This section presents two additional conceptual frameworks: the pyramid of needs from Maslow and Gameful design for Engagement. These frameworks go beyond classical Usability and even the more recent concept underlying User Experience.

3.1   Motivation and Needs

The work of Maslow on the hierarchy of human needs was early introduced in [3] and refined in [18] which revisits the concepts introduced by Maslow which are decomposed in three core concepts:

- **Basic needs**: They encompass physiological and safety needs that correspond to the immediate and short-term survival of the individual. They ensure the sustainability of the biological machinery that compose human beings.
- **Psychological needs**: Encompass relationship to others i.e., social aspects of human being as well as relationship with self, including prestige and subjective perception of accomplishment.
- **Self-fulfillment needs**: Correspond to the definition of self-actualization aiming at deploying the full potential of the individual.

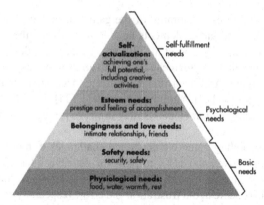

Fig. 4. The hierarchy of needs and motivation from [19] original work in [3]

Work is a transverse concept with respect to the hierarchy of needs presented in Fig. 4. Indeed, for each of the levels of the pyramid, work is:

- **Physiological needs**: E.g. work can contribute to provide food directly (farming) or indirectly (money);
- **Safety needs**: E.g. building fences or constructing protections may contribute to safety and security;
- **Belongingness and love needs**: E.g. earning resources via work might allow building a family;
- **Esteem needs**: E.g. building a career in a company might contribute to esteem via success;
- **Self-actualization need**: E.g. evolution in the work environment during the entire life might support the construction of the personality to become self-actualized.

3.2 Gameful Design and Engagement

Although gameful design and gamification techniques have not been studied evenly across application domains (most of the contributions come from the application domains of education and health), Seaborn and Fels [20] surveyed the literature and established that the results of gamification are mostly positive. They highlight that gameful design, including gamification, raise engagement and user performance. Indeed, a study on the gamification of the tutorial of the AutoCAD 3D objects modelling application [21] reported higher subjective engagement levels with the gamified application, and that users performed a set of testing tasks from 20% to 76% faster after using the tutorial with the gamified components. Gameful design can also encourage participation and collaboration with other users as demonstrated in the context of online learning [22]. These examples (and many other ones) show that the range of potential benefits of gameful design is quite wide if design choices are carefully elicited.

Gameful design requires fine-tuning of the game mechanics that are integrated in the interactive system, and game elements have to match what the user is able to perform in the context of use. Wilson et al. [22] argue that some design choices may be counterproductive and that engagement and motivation may vary a lot depending on the type of game element. Adding artificial challenge to a system supporting functional needs engenders frustration [23]. Moreover, Korn et al. [24] showed that in an industrial environment, some gamification elements may improve production speed but may also increase the error rate.

As stated above, adding game elements and challenges to motivate the user leads to add additional objectives and tasks to perform with the interactive system. These additional tasks interleave with work tasks, and have thus to integrate in a consistent manner with them in order to avoid frustration and errors (especially capture and interference ones). Moreover, the design of game elements also requires identifying automation opportunities (for these game elements), with the objective of increasing the overall usability of the system but also to make sure that proposed challenges are important and motivating experiences for the user [23].

Gameful design for interactive systems at work thus requires being able to describes exhaustively and systematically:

- User work tasks;
- User tasks while interacting with work automation;
- User tasks to reach game elements objectives.

Analyzing all these elements together is also critical in order to detect conflicting elements.

4   Illustrative Example: The Mackworth Clock

4.1   Introduction to the Example

The Mackworth clock is an interactive system designed and developed to study the performance of operators monitoring information on airborne radars [24]. The system was developed to build experiments to assess vigilance capabilities of human being while monitoring autonomous systems. The Mackworth autonomous system (presented in Fig. 5 a)) includes a green point, which moves in steps every second (like the second hand of a clock). In the experiment, at irregular time intervals, the green point moves the double of the usual distance (jumps one step). The operator has to detect this unexpected movement (representing a problem or a failure) and to press a button to prove that the malfunction has been detected.

Figure 5 b) presents a modified and digitalized version of the Mackworth clock. We chose to present it because it makes more explicit (as a symbolic representation) how the Mackworth autonomous system was functioning.

Fig. 5. a) Original Mackworth Clock [24] and b) Modified Mackworth Clock from [26].

The hypothesis behind this experiment was that human performance in detecting malfunctions would decrease over time. Indeed, the study of performance of operators monitoring this autonomous system confirmed the fact that attention and vigilance decrease over time. The main outcome of this study was to propose identify the best compromise between the duration of the monitoring period (the watch-time of the operator) and the errors. In the following sections, we discuss the opportunity to alter this experiment adding game elements to the monitoring task to assess the possible increase of attention and vigilance for longer monitoring tasks.

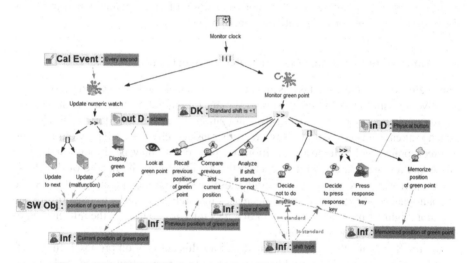

Fig. 6. HAMSTERS|XL task model describing the tasks to "Monitor clock"

Figure 6 presents the detailed description of the tasks the operator has to perform to monitor the clock. The main goal, represented at the top of the task model, is "Monitor clock". Under this main goal, the temporal ordering operator "|||" named concurrency has two branches that describe the tasks performing in parallel. On the left branch under the main goal, the system updates the clock every second (abstract system task "Update numeric watch" with an incoming arrow from the calendar event "Every second"). This task decomposes in a sequence (temporal ordering operator ">>") of a system task (a choice, indicated with the choice temporal ordering operator "[]", between the tasks "Update to next" and "Update (malfunction)") and the interactive output task "Display green point" which uses the output device "screen". The system tasks update the value of the software object "position of green point", which is required to perform the system output task "Display green point". In the right branch under the main goal "Monitor clock", the abstract iterative task "Monitor green point" decomposes in a sequence of user tasks. First, the user performs the perceptive task "Look at green point" using the output device "screen", which produces the information "current position of green point'. Then the user performs the cognitive task "Recall previous position of green point" using the information "Memorized position of green point" and producing the information "previous position of green point". Then the user performs the cognitive analysis task "Compare previous and current position" using both information "current position of green point" and "previous position of green point". This task produces the information "size of shift". Then, the user performs the cognitive analysis task "Analyze if shift is standard or not" using the information "size of shift" and the declarative knowledge "Standard shift is +1". Then from the result of this analysis task, the user makes a choice (described using the choice temporal ordering operator "[]" combined with the test arcs on the value of the information "shift type"). If the shift type is standard, the user decides not to do anything. If the shift type is different from standard, then the user decides to press the response key, and then presses the response key. At last, the user performs the cognitive task "Memorize position of green point" which produces the information "Memorized position of green point".

4.2   Automation as a Design Option to Reduce Workload

The main goal of the user task is to monitor the clock and the challenge of being attentive and staring at the clock should remain (as migrating it to automation raise similar challenges such as monitoring automation instead of monitoring the clock – which is already an automation). However, other tasks such as "Recall previous position of green point" and "Memorize position of green point" may be difficult and error-prone and are articulatory with respect to the monitoring of the handle of the clock. For these reasons, we propose to migrate those tasks from the operator to the system. The automation of these work tasks decreases the number of tasks to perform for the operator. Figure 7 presents a screenshot of a new interface to present the information of these migrated tasks to the operator.

Figure 8 presents the task model modified for this automation proposal. In the left main branch of the model, we added two system tasks: an output system task named "display previous position of green point", as well as a storing system task. We also added a new software object "stored position of green point" to describe that the system will be storing the value of the previous position instead of the user doing it. In the abstract iterative task "Monitor green point", we replaced the cognitive task "recall previous position of green point" with the perceptive task "Look at previous position of green point", and removed the cognitive task "Memorize position of green point", as well as the associated memorized information "Memorized position of green point".

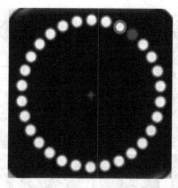

Fig. 7. Illustration of the design proposal for automating operator's work

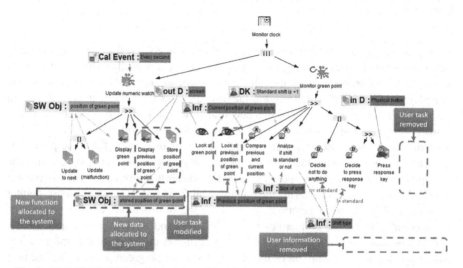

Fig. 8. HAMSTERS|XL task model modified for the work automation (Color figure online)

This proposal of work automation should decrease cognitive load but may lead operator to be less attentive. We thus propose to integrate a game element, focused on a continuous input from the operator, to increase immersion. The game element the continuous tracking of the green point using a mouse pointer. The operator has one hand on the mouse device and has to move the mouse pointer to the green point each time the green point shifts. Figure 9 presents three screenshots that illustrate this design proposal. At the bottom of the screens, a panel indicates the total time on the green point and the total time outside of the green point.

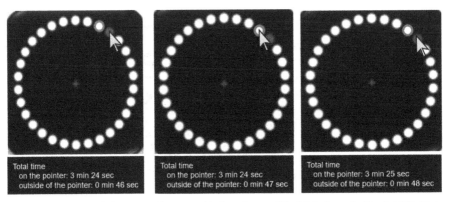

Fig. 9. Illustration of the game element added to the modified Mackworth Clock [25] (Color figure online)

Figure 10 presents the task model modified to include the tasks related to the game element "mouse pointer tracking using a mouse device", as well as the automation of work (explained previously). In the left main branch, we added the system output task "Display mouse pointer" which requires the software object "Mouse pointer position". In the right part of the model, we added a new branch which main task is "Monitor mouse pointer" and is iterative. This task interleaves with the two other sub-goals "Update numeric watch" and "Monitor green point". It decomposes using the same pattern as the green point monitoring task, but for the mouse pointer. The user first performs the perceptive task "Look at mouse pointer", which produces the information "mouse pointer position". The user then performs the cognitive analysis task "Compare mouse pointer position with green point position", using both the information "current position of green point" and "mouse pointer position". This task produces the information "mouse pointer position relative to green point". Depending on the value of this information, mouse pointer is on green point or mouse pointer is not on green point, either the user will perform the cognitive decision task "Decide not to do anything" or the cognitive decision task "Decide to move the mouse pointer" followed by the interactive input task "Move mouse pointer".

This task model helps to identify and understand the impact of the game element on the operator's tasks. We see that the new set of tasks that we introduced represents as many tasks as the set of tasks to monitor the green point and that this set of tasks interleaves with the work task, and share a common information to process for the tasks (Information "current position of green point" at the bottom in Fig. 10). This confirms that the design proposal should increase the operator's workload while helping the operator to focus on the main goal.

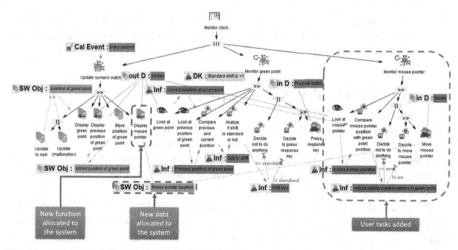

Fig. 10. HAMSTERS|XL task model modified to integrate both automation and game element (Color figure online)

By supporting the precise comparison of the original work tasks with the tasks altered by adding work automation and game elements, we argue that a task models-based approach enables to identify relevant automation and gamification opportunities. The level of precision of task descriptions enables to filter out tasks that should be migrated to the system and tasks for which gamification will benefit to user performance and engagement. In that way, it supports reaching an optimum level of workload as exemplified in Fig. 11.

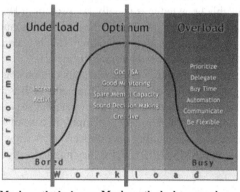

Mackworth clock   Mackworth clock+game element

Fig. 11. Using Yerkes-Dodson [27] curve as a mean to represent evolution of user engagement and performance when integration game elements are added to work tasks.

In this example, the gaming elements would support the self-actualization needs of human being as defined in [18]. More precisely, enjoyment and fun would be part of this journey to self-actualization. Other game elements could have been related to the work of other operators (for instance being able to share on a social media their success in accomplishing the work). In that case these game elements would be related to the "belongness and love" needs which are lower in Maslow's hierarchy of needs.

5   Conclusions and Perspectives

This paper has presented the potential benefits of using game elements interleaved with operators' work in order to increase user experience and engagement of operators. We argue that describing how these game elements transform the operators' work is critical in order to be able to assess the impact (positive and negative) of the activities added by the game elements on operators' work.

We have revisited the Mackworth clock experiment which is centered on the monitoring (by an operator) of an autonomous system. We took the position that degradation of the monitoring performance of the operators was related to a loss of engagement, and an increase of boredom and was due to the lack of active participation of the operator on the system.

To improve performance, we decided to integrate in the work tasks additional tasks related to game elements added to the system. We used the HAMSTERS|XL notation [7] to describe the original and the altered task models and used these models to demonstrate the higher engagement of operators when game elements are added. We have developed some tools [28] which would support the work of developers in ensuring that the application developed completely matches the work of operators described in task models.

One of the key difficulties with this approach lies in the quantity of required knowledge to integrate game elements inside an interactive application. Even though the work from [23] proposes "The lens intrinsic skill atoms", a five steps method to identify and design game elements, this knowledge is usually not present in HCI and UX designers background. It thus adds an additional burden to the design, evaluation and development work which is already very complex and demanding. This is even more complex when the needs are getting higher in Maslow's hierarchy of needs.

Future work will consolidate these research results demonstrated on a very simple case study by applying them to more complex environments such as safety critical control rooms where engagement is critical to ensure that operators are constantly monitoring the evolutions of the system and able to react promptly in case of failures. Beyond, we will consider tasks descriptions including operators errors as slips, lapses and mistakes (which can be described in HAMSTERS [29]) as they might deeply influence motivation and engagement.

References

1. Tay, L., Diener, E.: Needs and subjective well-being around the world. J. Pers. Soc. Psychol. **101**(2), 354–356 (2011)
2. Winzer, R., Vaez, M., Lindberg, L., et al.: Exploring associations between subjective well-being and personality over a time span of 15–18 months: a cohort study of adolescents in Sweden. BMC Psychol. **9**, 173 (2021). https://doi.org/10.1186/s40359-021-00673-9

3. Maslow, A.: A theory of human motivation. Psychol. Rev. **50**(4), 370–396 (1943)
4. Kenrick, D.T., Neuberg, S.L., Griskevicius, V., Becker, D.V., Schaller, M.: Goal-driven cognition and functional behavior: the fundamental-motives framework. Curr. Dir. Psychol. Sci. **19**(1), 63–67 (2010)
5. Wahba, M.A., Bridwell, L.G.: Maslow reconsidered: a review of research on the need hierarchy theory. Organ. Behav. Hum. Perform. **15**(2), 212–240 (1976)
6. Desmet, P.M.A., Hekkert, P.: Framework of product experience. Int. J. Des. **1**(1), 13–23 (2007)
7. Martinie, C., Palanque, P., Bouzekri, E., Cockburn, A., Canny, A., Barboni, E.: Analysing and demonstrating tool-supported customizable task notations. Proceedings of the ACM Human-Computer Interaction, vol. 3(EICS), Article 12, pp. 1–26 (2019)
8. Geneva, C.H.: International organization for standardization. Ergonomics of Human System Interaction-Part 210: Human-centred Design for Interactive Systems. ISO 9241–210 (2008)
9. Frøkjær, E., Hertzum, M., Hornbæk, K.: Measuring usability: are effectiveness, efficiency, and satisfaction really correlated?. In: Proceedings of the SIGCHI Conference on Human Factors in Computing Systems (CHI 2000), pp. 345–352. ACM (2000)
10. Card, S.K, Moran, T.P, Newell, A.: The model human processor: an engineering model of human performance. In: Handbook of Perception and Human Performance. Cognitive Processes and Performance, vol. 2, pp. 1–35 (1986)
11. Kaye, J., et al.: Designing for user experience: academia and industry. In: CHI 2011 Extended Abstracts (CHI EA 2011), pp. 219–222. ACM (2011). https://doi.org/10.1145/1979742.1979486
12. Law, E.L.C., Van Schaik, P., Roto, V.: Attitudes towards user experience (UX) measurement. Int. J. Human-Comput. Stud. **72**(6), 526–541 (2014)
13. Bernhaupt, R., Ardito, C., Sauer, S. (eds.): HCSE 2020. LNCS, vol. 12481. Springer, Cham (2020). https://doi.org/10.1007/978-3-030-64266-2
14. Pirker, M., Bernhaupt, R.: Measuring user experience in the living room: results from an ethnographically oriented field study indicating major evaluation factors. In: Proceedings of the 9th European Conference on Interactive TV and Video (EuroITV 2011), pp. 79–82. ACM (2011)
15. Roto, V., Palanque, P., Karvonen, H.: Engaging Automation at Work – A Literature Review. In: Barricelli, B.R., et al. (eds.) HWID 2018. IAICT, vol. 544, pp. 158–172. Springer, Cham (2019). https://doi.org/10.1007/978-3-030-05297-3_11
16. Baldauf, M., et al.: Automation experience at the workplace. In: Extended Abstracts of the 2021 CHI Conference on Human Factors in Computing Systems, pp. 1–6 (2021)
17. Martinie C., Palanque, P., Ragosta, M., Fahssi, R.: Extending procedural task models by systematic explicit integration of objects, knowledge and information. In: European Conference on Cognitive Ergonomics (ECCE 2013), Article 23, p. 10 (2013)
18. Maslow, A.: Motivation and personality, 3rd edn. Pearson Education, Delhi, India (1987)
19. The School of life. Retrieved 6 April 2022. https://www.theschooloflife.com/article/the-importance-of-maslows-pyramid-of-needs/
20. Seaborn, K., Fels, D.L.: Gamification in theory and action: a survey. Int. J. Human-Comput. Stud. **74**, pp. 14–31 (2015). ISSN 1071–5819
21. Li, W., Grossman, T., Fitzmaurice, G.: GamiCAD: a gamified tutorial system for first time autocad users. In: Proceedings of the ACM Symposium on UIST, ACM DL, pp. 103–112 (2012)
22. Wilson, D., Calongne, C., Henderson, S.: Gamification challenges and a case study in online learning Internet Learning, **4**(2), Article 8 (2016)
23. Deterding, S.: The lens of intrinsic skill atoms: a method for gameful design. Human-Comput. Interact. **30**(3–4), 294–335 (2015)

24. Korn, O., Funk, M., Schmidt, A.: Towards a gamification of industrial production: a comparative study in sheltered work environments. In: 7th ACM SIGCHI Symposium on Engineering Interactive Computing Systems (EICS 2015), pp. 84–93 (2015)
25. Mackworth, N.H.: The breakdown of vigilance during prolonged visual search. Q. J. Exp. Psychol. **1**, 6–21 (1948)
26. Martel, A., Dähne, S., Blankertz, B.: EEG predictors of covert vigilant attention. J. Neural Eng. **11**(3), 035009 (2014). Accessed 19 May 2014, PMID: 24835495
27. Yerkes, R.M., Dodson, J.D.: The relation of strength of stimulus to rapidity of habit-formation. J. Comp. Neurol. Psychol. **18**, 459–482 (1908)
28. Martinie, C., Navarre, D., Palanque, P., Fayollas, C.: A generic tool-supported framework for coupling task models and interactive applications. In: 7th ACM SIGCHI Symposium on Engineering Interactive Computing Systems (EICS 2015), pp. 244–253 (2015)
29. Fahssi, R., Martinie, C., Palanque, P.: Enhanced Task Modelling for Systematic Identification and Explicit Representation of Human Errors. In: Abascal, J., Barbosa, S., Fetter, M., Gross, T., Palanque, P., Winckler, M. (eds.) INTERACT 2015. LNCS, vol. 9299, pp. 192–212. Springer, Cham (2015). https://doi.org/10.1007/978-3-319-22723-8_16

Virtual Reality and Augmented Reality Applied to E-Commerce: A Literature Review

Jenny Morales[1]([✉]) [iD], Fabián Silva-Aravena[1] [iD], Yolanda Valdés[2] [iD],
and Sergio Baltierra[2] [iD]

[1] Facultad de Ciencias Sociales y Económicas, Universidad Católica del Maule,
Avda San Miguel 3605, Talca, Chile
{jmoralesb,fasilva}@ucm.cl
[2] Facultad de Ingeniería, Universidad Autónoma de Chile, Providencia, Chile
{yvaldesr,sergio.baltierra}@uautonoma.cl

Abstract. The massification of technologies, the implementation of 5G and the Internet of Things (IoT), allow implementing systems that contain virtual or augmented reality or implementation of both. In this sense, the covid 19 pandemic in the last years, has also affected people's behavior and leaned to shop without leaving their homes. VR, RA, and/or MR techniques are currently widely used for medicine, education, and entertainment, among others. In this study, we combine both elements to analyze the literature on e-commerce and the use of VR, AR, and/or RM. Searching and analyzing recent scientific articles were defined, and virtual reality is the most used, followed by the mixture of RV and RA, the above to improve the shopping experience, providing the customer with a more authentic and immersive environment. In future works, we will expect to expand this study, including how to evaluate the shopping experience and relate it to the customer experience.

Keywords: Literature review · E-commerce · Virtual reality · Augmented reality

1 Introduction

We have all noticed the massification of information and communication technologies, which has allowed more and more people to have mobile devices such as smartphones. In addition, the implementation of 5G and the Internet of Things, favor the implementation of systems that contain virtual or augmented reality. Other factors have also influenced the change in the way consumers purchase and observe the price of products and their features. Studies indicate that many people prefer not to leave home to make their purchases, thus avoiding contact with other people due to the pandemic [1]. Currently, VR, AR, and/or MR techniques are widely used for medicine [2], education [3], and entertainment, among others. We carried out a literature review study to identify aspects of the use of VR, AR, and/or RM in e-commerce sites, for this, we established 4 steps: research questions, data sources, selection of articles, and article classification and results. It was defined to search and analyze recent scientific articles. The results obtained show that

V. Agredo-Delgado et al. (Eds.): HCI-COLLAB 2022, CCIS 1707, pp. 201–213, 2022.
https://doi.org/10.1007/978-3-031-24709-5_15

virtual reality is the most used, followed by the mixture of VR and RA, the above to improve the shopping experience, focused on the client, providing a more immersive environment with a greater sense of reality.

This document is structured as follows: Sect. 2 presents the background and concepts related to the study, Sect. 3 details the work methodology, Sect. 4 shows the answers to the research questions, and, finally, Sect. 5 presents the conclusions and ideas for the future work.

2 Background

2.1 Customer eXperience

Companies seek to differentiate themselves from the rest by considering different ways of reaching customers or consumers. Globalization has made consumers make much more informed decisions due to the various means by which they can obtain information about a company and learn about its products or services and the associated prices.

The customer experience considers any contact that a customer has with a company, whether directly through the purchase or use of a product, system, or service, or indirectly through recommendations, suggestions, or advertising, among others, that the customer does not intend [4]. In turn, the concept of customer experience considers emotional and personal aspects inherent to the person. These emotions compose and influence an essential part of the decisions [5] and then affect the client's decision.

2.2 E-Commerce

Due to globalization and the penetration of information and communication technologies, there are open spaces that companies have been able to use, thus promoting the sale of products, systems, or services through the Internet. The concept of electronic commerce is not new. Jeffrey Rayport in 1999, defined electronic commerce as: "the practice of selling real products for real money through online channels" [6].

Nowadays, e-commerce has taken a relevant space within companies' sales, a situation exacerbated by the covid 19 pandemic because people avoid leaving their homes [7]. E-commerce can be implemented in various ways, considering whether the person who buys or sells is a client or a business or company, we have, business to business (B2B), business to consumer (B2C), consumer to consumer (C2C, consumer to consumer) and consumer to business (C2B) among others [8].

2.3 Virtual and Augmented Reality

Technologies such as Virtual Reality (VR) and augmented reality have been on the rise, although they are not new techniques, with the presentation of Mark Zuckerberg's metaverse in 2021 (Meta Platforms, Inc.) these technologies have emerged with greater force, and we all look forward to these environments more immersive and new associated experiences.

Authors indicate that the definition of virtual reality dates back to the mid-1970s [9]. With various definitions of Virtual Reality (VR), authors have given way to studies to unify their definition [10]. We can highlight that several authors agree on their definitions in the use of three-dimensional computing technology, which provides an interactive and immersive environment for users, through the use of several devices.

Augmented Reality (AR) for your part, is defined as follows: "a medium in which digital information is overlaid on the physical world that is in both spatial and temporal registration with the physical world and that is interactive in real time" [11].

Today, VR is widely used in various areas such as video games, education, and medicine. In the medical area, such as kinesiology, it has been used to treat movement problems due to pain and for the proper performance of exercises [12, 13]. Together, VR and AR have also been used for medical and educational purposes [3, 14]. In this sense, Mixed Reality (MR) is used in this work as that technology that implements virtual reality and augmented reality [15] in a combined way, not as a synonym of augmented reality or a more immersive augmented reality as other authors have proposed.

3 Methodology

The literature review consisted of four stages: research questions, data sources, selection of articles, article classification, and results.

3.1 Research Questions

We defined the research questions to obtain general concepts in such a way to collect works and get trends associated with the topics under study. The research questions that were defined were:

(1) Are there uses of augmented, virtual, or mixed reality in e-commerce?
(2) what is the purpose of the implementation VR, AR or MR in the articles found?
(3) What results does it have on the consumer experience?

3.2 Data Sources

To search for the articles, five databases were used, all related to the topics under study, hoping to find an adequate number of articles to analyze, these databases are Web of Science (WoS), ACM Digital Library, IEEE Xplore, Science Direct and Scopus.

The articles were searched using the search string detailed in Table 1, and considering the elements described in the research questions.

The search criteria in the databases were applied with the search by abstract option because all the databases consulted have this option, so we will carry out a more efficient search using the tools provided by the same data sources. The search for articles was carried out in May 2022.

Table 1. Search string.

Item	Description
Concepts	e-commerce, virtual reality, augmented reality, mixed reality, client, customer, consumer, satisfaction, experience
Group of terms	(e-commerce) ("virtual reality" or "augmented reality" or "mixed reality") (client or customer or consumer) (satisfaction or experience)
Search string	((e-commerce) AND ("virtual reality" OR "augmented reality" OR "mixed reality") AND ((client OR customer OR consumer) AND (satisfaction OR experience)))

3.3 Selection Articles

After searching the data sources, a total of 106 scientific articles were obtained (see Table 2). The results were limited to the last ten years from 2013 to 2022, obtained a total of 78 articles. The above is because we want to study new articles and discover current trends in using VR and AR in e-commerce.

In addition to the above, repeated articles were removed from the selection, as well as those already literature reviews, so that they do not influence or affect the current study. With this limitation of articles, the total number of papers selected for the first reading was 53.

In the process of abstract reading, articles were discarded for the following reasons:

(1) Articles that speak only of electronic commerce websites, without use in the use of VR, AR, MR.
(2) Articles that address VR, AR, and MR only as a tool, emphasizing the technology, not its use applied to electronic commerce.
(3) Articles that consider the customer experience not related to VR, AR, MR.

After the abstract reading, 28 articles were selected for full reading, of which 5 were not included in the study because we did not have access to them. Finally, the study was carried out with 23 scientific articles. See Fig. 1.

Table 2. Articles found.

Data source	Abstract selection	Limited 10 years
Web of Science	12	11
ACM Digital Library	17	8
IEEE Xplore	13	10
Science Direct	6	5
Scopus	58	44
Total	106	78

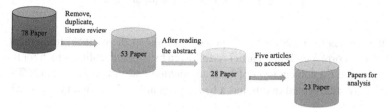

Fig. 1. Selection articles process.

3.4 Articles Classification and Results

Most of the articles under study were published in different journals (16 articles), representing 70%. In turn, conference articles represent 30% of the total analyzed, corresponding to 7 articles (see Fig. 2).

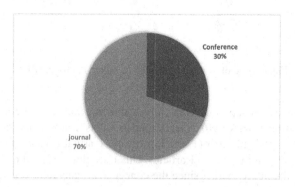

Fig. 2. Articles published in journals and conferences.

About the year of publication of the selected articles, there is a tendency to increase the number of items as the years progress. In Fig. 3 we can see the papers published by year, only in 2019 is there a drop. Concerning 2022, since the search ended in May, there will probably be more publications to add.

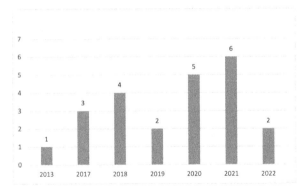

Fig. 3. Publication year of the articles.

In the articles reviewed, it can be noted that most of them (56%) implement virtual reality, which corresponds to 12 articles, followed by a mixed reality, which for this study is related to the implementation of both augmented and virtual realities (26%), with 6 items. Finally, augmented reality has a lower percentage (22%) with only 5 articles.

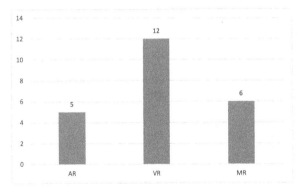

Fig. 4. Use of virtual augmented or mixed reality in articles.

Regarding the types of products that the e-commerce market, in the articles reviewed, they are aimed at supermarkets (6 papers), food products (2 articles), furniture (1 article), sunglasses (2 articles), tourism (1 article), travel (1 article), video games (1 article), clothing (1 article), and watches (1 article). Other articles analyzed do not specifically identify the product they market since the concepts are generally used for the product markets (7 articles). This information only represents a frequency of ideas. Then, it has no direct relationship with the number of papers. See Fig. 5.

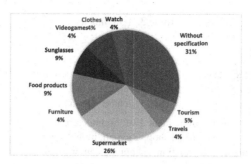

Fig. 5. Types of products found in electronic commerce.

The classification of the articles was carried out considering (i) articles that implement Virtual Reality (Table 3), (ii) articles that present the incorporation of both augmented reality and virtual reality (Table 4), and (iii) articles that implement Augmented Reality (Table 5).

Table 3. Articles of virtual reality.

Cite	Brief description
[16]	This paper uses VR to examine an offline showroom versus an online virtual reality web room linked with artificial intelligence to recommend products to customers. The results indicate that adopting AI will improve your return policies, maximize resale returns and reduce the risks of stock-outs and shortages
[17]	It uses VR with a haptic combination so the customer can realize the weight of the ordered item. This allows for greater customer immersion and improves customer satisfaction
[18]	Use VR to demonstrate a positive effect on customer loyalty to the brand considering the entire purchase process
[1]	This article uses VR to simulate social interaction in a virtual supermarket using avatars. It presents an improvement in the virtual shopping experience. Through social interaction with VR, consumers' enjoyment, immersion, and telepresence experience were significantly enhanced
[19]	The study proposes a framework to incorporate a set of virtual reality solutions that allow obtaining information about the consumer through the analysis of consumer interaction in a virtual reality store. This gives the consumer an immersive experience and provides a personalized experience that promotes the purchase of the product
[20]	The research focuses on defining UI and UX design criteria considering VR factors to meet the needs and user experience in an e-commerce environment. For this, it uses various questionnaires and methodologies that allow UI and UX design criteria for VR. Centered on five main themes: screen, operation and prompt, safety and experience of use, system functions, and transaction

(*continued*)

Table 3. (*continued*)

Cite	Brief description
[21]	Analyze the effectiveness of VR devices and VR content formats. Establishing that attractive virtual environments generate affection and a deep sense of presence improves commercial performance, impacting purchase intention
[22]	It uses VR to design and implement a VR architecture for product purchase, which consists of six modules: virtual shopping mall, item display, online payment, interaction, game, and advertising. Recreating a shopping center for electronic commerce
[23]	In this article, VR is used to create a new shopping experience considering the spatial placement of products in apartment settings
[24]	Uses VR to implement e-commerce that incorporates three-dimensional elements and intelligent sensors, thus integrating elements of industry 4.0 in retail created with virtual reality
[25]	Presents a theoretical study showing a typology of VR and a dual theoretical model of participation and use of VR to establish that immersive processes influence consumer responses through imagination, co-creation, and telepresence
[26]	Recreate a supermarket in areas of beer, water, and wine. It puts two virtual environments, one navigable 360 and another free 3D navigation. It states that although HMDs are more cumbersome than other devices, they provide better experiences and more excellent consumer responses. Furthermore, discomfort does not impact the sense of presence or brand recall. Improves purchase intention

Table 4. Articles of mixed reality.

Cite	Brief description
[27]	AR and VR use them to display various photos from different locations and angles. In addition, it features audio and video clips providing a broader range of physical store information. In other words, it is assimilated as if the customer were in person at the store—aspects of rescuing: use machine learning, specifically neural networks, to discover customer purchasing patterns
[28]	Use virtual and augmented reality to assess how information availability supports customer experience and decision-making, comparing traditional e-commerce to virtual commerce
[29]	They use an AR/VR-based clothing fitting system to validate how it positively contributes to the online shopping experience and provides consumers with positive experiences. They also carry out tests based on AR with personalized human movement to provide a more comfortable shopping experience Attractive and, therefore, increase their purchase intention

(*continued*)

Table 4. (*continued*)

Cite	Brief description
[30]	Analyze customer perception in virtual spaces compared to physical spaces, comparing what is offered on a website, 2D, versus what is provided by an AR or VR
[31]	This paper consider an e-commerce purchases within a game, a store to buy, with much more immersive virtual reality, with augmented reality with a virtual assistant or avatar
[32]	The use of a HoloLens mixed reality device is proposed to implement a holographic application that allows personalized recommendations to be made to customers of a store. This shopping experience is more pleasant, facilitates free mobility for the user, and encourages the purchase decision

Table 5. Articles of augmented reality.

Cite	Brief description
[33]	Evaluate the user experience when trying on lenses in an AR application. A mobile app with an AR feature needs to incorporate indicators of perceived ease of use, perceived usefulness, and hedonic benefits (perceived enjoyment and seamless experience) for consumers
[34]	Identify the key factors influencing e-commerce companies' intent to adopt AR. These are technological, organizational, and environmental, which affect the intention to adopt an AR by e-commerce companies
[35]	The realization of two studies focused on the effect of the functional mechanisms of interactivity and vividness of AR, which impact the presentation of products and customers' purchase intention
[36]	It exposes what other companies do, such as catalogs with RA and showing videos, among other things, which allows for more engaging experiences for customers
[37]	For retail sales, four AR applications in the retail and marketing markets. A proven model for measuring consumer/user acceptance of AR applications in marketing and retail. Considers aspects such as hedonic (enjoyment, pleasure, fun) and utilitarian (information)

4   Response to Research Questions

According to the articles reviewed, the following answers can be given to the research questions defined.

Are There Uses of Augmented, Virtual, or Mixed Reality in E-commerce? We found various articles that implement virtual, augmented, and mixed reality. In this sense, it is essential to note that of the selected studies, virtual reality has the highest frequency of use (12 articles, which represents 56%), as shown in Fig. 4. Next, in the second place, we found the use of both technologies complementary (found in 6 articles that represent 26%). Finally, augmented reality (found in 5 articles representing 22%). It is important to note that all the papers analyzed showed implementations of e-commerce that market several products. Interestingly, using both technologies together is more popular than the sole implementation of augmented reality. Finally, we found that there is an upward trend concerning the articles that analyze implementing these technologies in e-commerce.

What is the Purpose of the Implementation VR, AR or MR in the Articles Found? In the analyzed papers, several purposes are distinguished for the implementation of virtual, augmented, and mixed reality. One of the main elements is to improve the way of showing the product to the customer, bringing it as close as possible to a face-to-face purchase reality, adding information that is relevant to the product, to induce a purchase decision by the customer. On the other hand, we found elements to facilitate the purchase, and navigation, to generate greater immersion and customer enjoyment. In addition, an important element to highlight is the placement in real spaces of the product that has not yet been purchased, again facilitating the purchase decision for the customer.

What Results does it have on the Consumer Experience? The shopping experience improved or at least remained the same in all the scientific articles analyzed, even in those articles that, given the nature of the study, required hardware or devices such as a head-mounted display. Establishing that although they are necessary elements that could make the customer uncomfortable, they ultimately it does not affect the shopping experience. In this sense, it is essential to highlight that some articles show ways to evaluate the customer experience while shopping using VR, AR, and/or MR, mainly including elements such as post-use questionnaires and customer behavior analysis. However, each article proposes different factors to evaluate the shopping experience.

5 Conclusion and Future Work

We found several articles that use virtual, augmented, and mixed reality in e-commerce. In this case, virtual reality was placed as the most used technology among the articles analyzed, followed by both virtual and augmented reality. Also, we found a trend to increase the number of articles that analyze the implementation of these technologies in e-commerce. The use of VR, AR and/or MR targets to induce a purchase decision by the customer through an immersive experience in the shopping articles. In the scientific articles analyzed, using VR, AR and/or MR improves the shopping experience. We note that it is necessary to establish a guide to implement the evaluation of the shopping experience due to the articles found implementing different and personalized ways to carry out this evaluation.

Important elements can be identified to highlight in the analyzed studies. We identified the use of VR, AR and/MR, to establish more immersive realities, improving the shopping experience. We also noted that there are incorporations of AI algorithms, neural networks, to suggest customer preferences [16, 27], which incorporates new elements for the use of recommender systems.

Some aspects that could limit the shopping experience in the studies analyzed were related to the need for a good internet connection and the availability of specific hardware, such as smart phones, to obtain a better experience. However, given the incorporation of 5G technologies and the widespread use of mobile devices, these possible limitations could be reduced.

This work reviews specific articles related to VR, AR, and/or MR. In future work, we intend to extend this work, analyzing the customer shopping experience and evaluating the customer experience in e-commerce, which relates to VR, AR and/or MR.

References

1. Nasser, N., Makled, E., Sharaf, N., Abdennadher, S.: Social interaction in virtual shopping. In: 2021 IEEE International Symposium on Multimedia (ISM), pp. 204–205. IEEE (2021). https://doi.org/10.1109/ISM52913.2021.00040
2. Emmelkamp, P.M., Meyerbröker, K.: Virtual reality therapy in mental health. Annu. Rev. Clin. Psychol. 17, 495–519 (2021). https://doi.org/10.1146/annurev-clinpsy-081219-115923
3. Akçayır, M., Akçayır, G.: Advantages and challenges associated with augmented reality for education: a systematic review of the literature. Educ. Res. Rev. 20, 1–11 (2017). https://doi.org/10.1016/j.edurev.2016.11.002
4. Meyer, C., Schwager, A.: Understanding customer experience. Harv. Bus. Rev. 85(2), 116 (2007)
5. Alfaro, E., Velilla, J., Brunetta, H., Navarro, B., Molina, C.: Customer experience. Una vis. Multidimension. del market. de experiencias. La experiencia del cliente, un marco para el mark. del futuro, Libro colaborativo, 12–19 (2012)
6. Rayport, J.F.: The truth about Internet business models. Strategy Bus., 5–7 (1999)
7. Bhatti, A., Akram, H., Basit, H.M., Khan, A.U., Raza, S.M., Naqvi, M.B.: E-commerce trends during COVID-19 pandemic. Int. J. Future Gener. Commun. Netw. 13(2), 1449–1452 (2020)
8. Babenko, V., Kulczyk, Z., Perevosova, I., Syniavska, O., Davydova, O.: Factors of the development of international e-commerce under the conditions of globalization. In: SHS Web of Conferences, vol. 65, p. 04016. EDP Sciences (2019). https://doi.org/10.1051/shsconf/201 96504016
9. Machover, C., Tice, S.E.: Virtual reality. IEEE Comput. Graph. Appl. 14(1), 15–16 (1994). https://doi.org/10.1109/38.250913
10. Kardong-Edgren, S.S., Farra, S.L., Alinier, G., Young, H.M.: A call to unify definitions of virtual reality. Clin. Simul. Nurs. 31, 28–34 (2019). https://doi.org/10.1016/j.ecns.2019.02.006
11. Craig, A.B.: Understanding augmented reality: concepts and applications (2013)
12. Calbo, P.G.: Sistema de ayuda frente a la kinesiofobia mediante técnicas de Realidad Virtual (2021)
13. Khundam, C., Nöel, F.: A study of physical fitness and enjoyment on virtual running for exergames. Int. J. Comput. Games Technol. 2021, 1–16 (2021). https://doi.org/10.1155/2021/6668280
14. Yeung, A.W.K., et al.: Virtual and augmented reality applications in medicine: analysis of the scientific literature. J. Med. Internet Res. 23(2), e25499 (2021). https://doi.org/10.2196/25499
15. Bekele, M.K., Pierdicca, R., Frontoni, E., Malinverni, E.S., Gain, J.: A survey of augmented, virtual, and mixed reality for cultural heritage. J. Comput. Cult. Heritage (JOCCH) 11(2), 1–36 (2018). https://doi.org/10.1145/3145534
16. Yang, G., Ji, G., Tan, K.H.: Impact of artificial intelligence adoption on online returns policies. Ann. Oper. Res. 308(1–2), 703–726 (2020). https://doi.org/10.1007/s10479-020-03602-y
17. Farooq, A., Seyedmahmoudian, M., Horan, B., Mekhilef, S., Stojcevski, A.: Overview and exploitation of haptic tele-weight device in virtual shopping stores. Sustainability 13(13), 7253 (2021). https://doi.org/10.3390/su13137253

18. Xie, S., Yuan, Y.: An empirical study on the impact of online travel consumers' brand loyalty: the mediating effect of flow experience. In: E3S Web of Conferences, vol. 253, p. 03043. EDP Sciences (2021). https://doi.org/10.1051/e3sconf/202125303043

19. Elboudali, A., Aoussat, A., Mantelet, F., Bethomier, J., Leray, F.: A customised virtual reality shopping experience framework based on consumer behaviour: 3DR3CO. Int. J. Interact. Des. Manufact. (IJIDeM) **14**(2), 551–563 (2020). https://doi.org/10.1007/s12008-020-00645-0

20. Su, K.-W., Chen, S.-C., Lin, P.-H., Hsieh, C.-I.: Evaluating the user interface and experience of VR in the electronic commerce environment: a hybrid approach. Virtual Reality **24**(2), 241–254 (2019). https://doi.org/10.1007/s10055-019-00394-w

21. Alves, C., Luís Reis, J.: The intention to use e-commerce using augmented reality - the case of IKEA place. In: Rocha, Á., Ferrás, C., Montenegro Marin, C.E., Medina García, V.H. (eds.) ICITS 2020. AISC, vol. 1137, pp. 114–123. Springer, Cham (2020). https://doi.org/10.1007/978-3-030-40690-5_12

22. Zhao, Z., Luo, H., Chu, S.C., Shang, Y., Wu, X.: An immersive online shopping system based on virtual reality. J. Netw. Intel. **3**(4), 235–246 (2018)

23. Speicher, M., Hell, P., Daiber, F., Simeone, A., Krüger, A.: A virtual reality shopping experience using the apartment metaphor. In: Proceedings of the 2018 International Conference on Advanced Visual Interfaces, pp. 1–9 (2018). https://doi.org/10.1145/3206505.3206518

24. Benes, F., Svub, J., Stasa, P., Bohm, J., Rhee, J., Vojtech, L.: Novel approach to shopping experience. In: Proceedings of the 14th EAI International Conference on Mobile and Ubiquitous Systems: Computing, Networking and Services, pp. 525–526 (2017). https://doi.org/10.1145/3144457.3144516

25. Cowan, K., Ketron, S.: A dual model of product involvement for effective virtual reality: the roles of imagination, co-creation, telepresence, and interactivity. J. Bus. Res. **100**, 483–492 (2019). https://doi.org/10.1016/j.jbusres.2018.10.063

26. Rese, A., Baier, D., Geyer-Schulz, A., Schreiber, S.: How augmented reality apps are accepted by consumers: a comparative analysis using scales and opinions. Technol. Forecast. Soc. Chang. **124**, 306–319 (2017). https://doi.org/10.1016/j.techfore.2016.10.010

27. Billewar, S.R., et al.: The rise of 3D e-commerce: the online shopping gets real with virtual reality and augmented reality during COVID-19. World J. Eng. **19**(2), 244–253 (2022). https://doi.org/10.1108/WJE-06-2021-0338

28. Jang, Y.-T., Hsieh, P.-S.: Understanding consumer behavior in the multimedia context: incorporating gamification in VR-enhanced web system for tourism e-commerce. Multimed. Tools Appl. **80**(19), 29339–29365 (2021). https://doi.org/10.1007/s11042-021-11149-8

29. Liu, Y., Liu, Y., Xu, S., Cheng, K., Masuko, S., Tanaka, J.: Comparing vr-and ar-based try-on systems using personalized avatars. Electronics **9**(11), 1814 (2020). https://doi.org/10.3390/electronics9111814

30. Wölfel, M., Reinhardt, A.: Immersive shopping presentation of goods in virtual reality. In: CERC, pp. 119–130 (2019)

31. Billewar, S.R., Jadhav, K., Babu, D.H., Ghane, S.: E-commerce shopping gets real: the rise of interactive virtual reality. In: Bioscience Biotechnology Research Communications Special Issue, vol. 14(05), pp. 130–132 (2021). https://doi.org/10.21786/bbrc/14.5/25

32. Mora, D., Jain, S., Nalbach, O., Werth, D.: Holographic recommendations in brick-and-mortar stores. In: 2020 26th Americas Conference on Information Systems, AMCIS (2020)

33. Gupta, R., Nair, K.S.: Try-on with AR: impact on sensory brand experience and intention to use the mobile app. J. Manage. Inf. Decision Sci. **24**, 1–16 (2021)

34. Chandra, S., Kumar, K.N.: Exploring factors influencing organizational adoption of augmented reality in e-commerce: empirical analysis using technology-organization-environment model. J. Electron. Commer. Res. **19**(3), 237–265 (2018)

35. Yim, M.Y.C., Chu, S.C., Sauer, P.L.: Is augmented reality technology an effective tool for e-commerce? An interactivity and vividness perspective. J. Interact. Mark. **39**(1), 89–103 (2017). https://doi.org/10.1016/j.intmar.2017.04.001
36. Bodhani, A.: Getting a purchase on AR. Eng. Technol. **8**(4), 46–49 (2013)
37. Martínez-Navarro, J., Bigné, E., Guixeres, J., Alcañiz, M., Torrecilla, C.: The influence of virtual reality in e-commerce. J. Bus. Res. **100**, 475–482 (2019). https://doi.org/10.1016/j.jbusres.2018.10.054

Author Index

Printed in the United States
by Baker & Taylor Publisher Services